MW00862387

The Hemmings Book of

MERCURYS

ISBN 1-591150-02-7
Library of Congress Card Number: 2002100089

One of a series of Hemmings Motor News Collector-Car Books. Other books in the series include:
The Hemmings Book of Postwar American Independents; The Hemmings Book of Buicks; The Hemmings Motor News Book of Cadillacs; The Hemmings Book of Postwar Chevrolets; The Hemmings Motor News Book of Corvettes; The Hemmings Motor News Book of Chrysler Performance Cars; The Hemmings Book of Prewar Fords; The Hemmings Motor News Book of Postwar Fords; The Hemmings Book of Mustangs; The Hemmings Motor News Book of Hudsons; The Hemmings Book of Lincolns; The Hemmings Book of Plymouths; The Hemmings Book of Oldsmobiles; The Hemmings Motor News Book of Packards; The Hemmings Motor News Book of Pontiacs; The Hemmings Motor News Book of Studebakers.

Hemmings Motor News
Collector Car Publications and Marketplaces
1-800-CAR-HERE (227-4373)
www.hemmings.com

The Hemmings Book of
MERCURYS

Editor-In-Chief
Terry Ehrich

Editor
Richard A. Lentinello

Associate Editors
James Dietzler; Robert Gross

Designer
Nancy Bianco

Front cover: 1955 Mercury Montclair Sun Valley. Photo by Don Spiro
Back cover: 1946 Mercury Sportsman. Photo by Vince Manocchi

This book compiles driveReports which have appeared in *Hemmings Motor News*'s *Special Interest Autos* magazine (SIA) over the past 30 years. The editors at *Hemmings Motor News* express their gratitude to the following writers, photographers, and artists who made this book possible through their many fine contributions to *Special Interest Autos* magazine:

Dave Best	Robert Gross	Marc Madow
Linda Clark	Tim Howley	Vince Manocchi
Arch Brown	Bud Juneau	Alex Meredith
James Dietzler	John F. Katz	Roy Query
David Gooley	Michael Lamm	Russell von Sauers
E.T. (Bob) Gregorie	David L. Lewis	Vince Wright

We are also grateful to David Brownell, Michael Lamm, and Rich Taylor, the editors under whose guidance these driveReports were written and published. We thank Ford Archives, Henry Ford Museum; Edward A. Martin; Willys P. Wagner, and John H. Walter for graciously contributing photographs to *Special Interest Autos* magazine and this book.

CONTENTS

Special Interest Autos (SIA) magazine's back issues are referred to in this book by issue number. If in stock, copies may be purchased directly from Hemmings Motor News at 800-227-4373, ext. 550 or at www.hemmings.com/gifts.

The First Mercury
& How It Came To Be

By Michael Lamm and David L. Lewis

Clay from January 1938 shows Mercury's lines almost as they appeared. Bob Gregorie tried to talk Edsel Ford into making the Mercury more distinct from the Ford, but Edsel balked, and no body panels interchanged between the two cars. Most radically different body style was the sedan-coupe (below), which used convertible doors and very thin, chromed window surrounds.

Originally published in Special Interest Autos #23, Jul.-Aug. 1974

Nineteen men worked in Ford's design corner during Mercury's development (see chart, page 7). They styled 3 lines of cars plus Continental, trucks, and bus. Note 1940 Ford and Lincoln coupe under the bridges. Readings are taken off bridge grids and transferred to blueprints.

You'll recall that when SIA chronicled Henry Ford's two last great engineering achievements, the Model A and the 1932 V-8, we made use of what historians call oral reminiscences. These are the spoken memories, tape-recorded, of people close to actual events; in this case close to Ford events, and also in this case they were the memories of longtime Ford employees and retirees. Their words were put on tape during the early 1950s by members of the Ford Archives Oral History staff.

In past issues, we've used oral reminiscences to help trace the development of the first Model A ("The Birth of Ford's Interim Car," SIA #18) and the first Ford V-8 ("Henry Ford's Last Mechanical Triumph," SIA #21). We're now using the same technique to help recreate the development of the first Mercury. We feel that the actual words of people closest to the events can give not just an accurate history but can set the tone and capture the atmosphere of what took place.

The Ford Archives has again generously made transcriptions of its Reminiscences *available to SIA, and we've been lucky enough to supplement them with interviews we conducted ourselves. We telephoned all the Ford people we could find who were involved in the first Mercury's development. We're deeply grateful, as always, to the Ford Archives, Henry Ford Museum, Dearborn, and particularly to its director, Henry Edmunds, and his capable staff for their generous help.*

NO ONE KNOWS for sure, and we'll probably never know, just how much Henry Ford washed his hands of the Mercury. Henry apparently had almost nothing to do with the Mercury 5 development. It's generally agreed that the Mercury was Edsel Ford's idea from the start.

Somewhere along the line, though, Edsel had to talk his father into letting him go ahead with the Mercury. "Yes," says Ford Archives director Henry E. Edmunds, "but it could have been just as casual as walking across the street. You did not have the committee structure at that time, and you didn't have minutes of a meeting when they were walking across, say, the village green or something like that." It's a good point, because it shows how informally the company was run at that time.

It probably wasn't very hard for Edsel to get his father's consent, though, because the need for a medium-priced car was obvious. Here was a $500 hole between the Ford and the Lincoln Zephyr. When Ford customers got ready to trade up out of the low-price field, they had nowhere to go but to rival showrooms—Pontiac, Olds, Buick, Dodge, De Soto, Studebaker, Hudson, Nash, or Packard. Ford's sales people kept telling Henry that the company was grooming buyers for General Motors and Chrysler Corp.

and the various independents. The Lincoln Zephyr, which Edsel had championed against Henry's initial resistance, was selling ahead of its rivals during the months when the Mercury decision was made. And the V-8-60 appealed to buyers who put economy foremost. So the big gap—the one that shouted to be filled—stood in the medium price range, and it probably wasn't too hard for Edsel and Ford's sales people to convince Henry, conservative and stubborn as he was, of the need for a Mercury.

1939 Mercury Prices & Production

2-door sedan	$894	12,274
4-door sedan	934	33,140
sedan-coupe	934	7,664
sport convertible	994	7,102
chassis	N/A	34

Source: Ford Motor Co. and New York Times report. **Note:** Mercury prices changed throughout 1939, and toward the end of the year, they ranged from $920 to $1,180 f.o.b. Dearborn. All prices are given minus taxes and license. Production figures include 1938 production but are for the U.S. only.

Edsel named the car (after the Roman god of commerce and gain), and then followed it through to production. But unlike his father's T, A, and the first V-8, which had been *engineering* triumphs—engineering tours de force—the Mercury became a triumph of styling.

Ross Cousins, an illustrator/designer who would later render sumptuous ads for Cadillac and who joined Ford in 1938 as a young man not long out of Cass Tech, remembers, "We just had this one corner of the engineering lab. Henry didn't like us too well, but Edsel was our godfather and patron saint. They had the Zephyr on the bridge and the Mercury, too, when I got there [in 1938]. The Ford was taking on the Zephyr look, and this Mercury was supposed to be something entirely new. It was on a Ford chassis at that time, as I remember, slightly stretched. And then, of course, the Continental was just a bright idea that Gregorie had. He was ahead of his time as far as liking foreign cars was concerned. He drove…I think it was an SS Jag. That was pretty with-it for the time. So did Edsel [actually both Edsel and Gregorie drove a Jensen Ford], and he very much liked foreign cars as, I remember, Edsel did."

Ford's styling staff consisted of 19 people in 1938, of which seven were apprentices (see roster, p. 7). And they had their hands very full that year. Those 19 shared not only responsibility for: 1) designing the new Mercury, but were, simultaneously, busy 2) restyling the 1939-40 Fords, 3) facelifting the Zephyr, 4) creating the first Lincoln Continental as a personal car for Edsel Ford, 5) revamping the entire Ford truck line and, 6) just for good measure, had gotten an assignment to do a new Ford school bus. So they had six projects going all at the same time, three of them major.

When you look back today and see how well all the 1939-40 Ford Motor Co. cars and trucks turned out, you can't help but admire those 19 men. More than that, you begin to realize the importance of the 20th man—the one who *really* ran Ford's fledgling design department, Edsel Ford himself.

Photos on this page courtesy Ford Archives, Henry Ford Museum, and Edward A. Martin

Front end takes shape by June 1938, but grille still says "Ford-Mercury" and bumpers aren't grooved. Original prototypes were built on extended Ford frames. Earliest photo we have dates to November 1937 (right) and proposes much more Ford/Mercury sheet metal interchangeability.

Dozens of biographers have tackled Henry Ford's life, but no one has yet written a book about Edsel. Why not? Partly it's lack of material. Most of Edsel's records are in the hands of family lawyers, not in the Ford Archives. There's also the rumor that Henry Ford contributed to Edsel's death, not only by overshadowing and frustrating him but by his harsh, sometimes cruel treatment. We talked to at least two people who spontaneously stated that Henry had "killed Edsel."

It's true that Edsel developed stomach ulcers, and he died on May 26, 1943, of stomach cancer and undulant fever. The fever came from drinking unpasteurized milk from the Ford Farms cows (Henry didn't believe in pasteurization). It's a fact, too, that Edsel's mother, Clara, could hardly bring herself to speak to Henry for six weeks after Edsel's death. Henry was just as hard-hit. After a considerable period of grief, Henry asked his crony Harry Bennett: "Do you honestly think I was ever cruel to Edsel?"

Bennett hesitated. "Cruel, no, but unfair, yes. If that had been me, I'd have got mad."

Ford pounced on the statement. "That's what I wanted him to do—get mad." Henry Ford was never the same man after Edsel's death, physically or mentally.

The picture that's most often drawn of Henry shows him as hard, flinty, domineering, self assured, stubborn, cagey, opinionated, outspoken—the epitome of the successful common man. He was a hero to many Americans. He realized his own importance, but he didn't get carried away by it. Whether he was a mechanical genius remains debatable—he had more engineering integrity than engineering brilliance. His outlook on almost everything was basically conservative, and as he grew older he resisted change more and more stubbornly.

Henry Ford also contained a strange mixture of social conscience (the $5 day and the Peace Ship) and cruelty—a child-like, thoughtless streak. Henry was by no means always down on Edsel, but when he was, he didn't care who knew it. Henry insulted or snubbed Edsel in public, where others couldn't help but notice. Word got around that Henry always acted unkindly toward Edsel, which wasn't really so. More often than not, father and son got along fine, and there's ample reason to believe that they respected and loved each other deeply.

However, Edsel was quite another man, and very little like his father. He was essentially shy, quiet, almost introverted: he disliked publicity. He lent generous support to the Byrd Antarctic expedition, the Detroit Symphony, YMCA, Lincoln Highway, and the company effort in WW-II. He enjoyed art, and his hobbies included photography, speedboat racing, and automobile styling—he was definitely an auto enthusiast, perhaps even more than his father. But people outside the company knew Edsel primarily as "Henry Ford's son," not as a separate, distinct person.

Edsel Bryant Ford ("Edsel" means "from the wealthy man's hall" in Hebrew, but Henry didn't know that when he named him) was born on November 6, 1893, on Detroit's Bagley Avenue, in the same house where Henry built his first "Quadricycle." When Edsel was three, Henry took him for a Quadricycle ride; the son sat on his father's lap. They doted on each other, and Edsel emulated Henry's automotive interests. At age 10, Edsel supposedly helped his father build Old 999, the famous racing car.

In 1909, aged 16, Edsel designed and built a 6-cylinder speedster for himself. In the process he sliced off the tip of his left middle finger on the lathe and lost it. He did his best to keep up with his father's mechanical progress, but the company was growing so fast that the two of them began to drift apart.

Edsel discovered at some point in his teens that he wasn't so much interested in the mechanical aspects of cars as in their styling—the way they looked. There's a scrapbook in the Ford Archives that Edsel put together between about 1911 and 1925, and it shows the sorts of cars he admired most. In the beginning there are large, impressive European cars of the Edwardian era—the Daimlers, Rollses, Hissos, Minervas, Italas, etc. Around 1918, Edsel began to clip pictures of custom-bodied Model T's plus one-off American customs—the big, flashy ones. He would circle items that caught his eye: the curve of a Vauxhall fender, the rakish tilt of a V'd windshield, the sharp edge of a Ballot boattail,

Edsel went through high school in Detroit and then attended Detroit University School, a prep school, but he never went to college. He started working for his father in 1912 (at 19) and worked in various different departments in Highland Park. By 1915, he'd been made company secretary, and on December 31, 1918, Henry named him president. The title not only meant nothing, but it tended to isolate him.

As his father grew more conservative, Edsel seemed to grow more progressive, and he gathered about himself those few people in the organization who liked to think beyond the Model T. One was Ernest Kanzler, Edsel's brother-in-law, who got himself fired in 1926 by daring to suggest that the Model T might soon become obsolete. Another was Jack Davis, the imaginative sales manager that Henry Ford II brought back when he reorganized the company after WW-II. Only two men remained with Edsel for any length of time: John Crawford, his executive assistant and "shop master," a whiz at production; and Eugene Turrenne (Bob) Gregorie, Edsel's protege and the company's first styling director.

John Crawford recalls, "Bob Gregorie was the originator, a young man with ideas whom Edsel took under his wing and handled with kid gloves. I was the modifier. I had to figure out how or if the car could be built. Could we form a sheet of steel to the desired shape? Was chrome trim practical? And so on. But Edsel was the inspirer. Without him, none of those beautiful cars would have even existed."

Bob Gregorie continues in the same vein, "Mr. Ford [Edsel] had an instinctive liking for dignity in an automobile, but dignity that reflected its purpose. A dignified car could still look fast and active—sporting, exhilarating. The only people making such cars in our day were the small companies and the custom body builders, and they were all going out of business…. He [Edsel] always had the dream of combining the beauty of custom design with the low cost of production in quantity. In spite of serious difficulties—some personal but mainly the tradition that said it couldn't he done—he kept planting the seed and encouraging it to sprout.

"Mr. Ford had me set up the first true styling section the company ever had [in 1935], with three or four men at the start. He set up no rules. I had every chance to express myself. I didn't even keep regular hours. Sometimes I'd just take off for a long trip in a car to clear my brain. Mr. Ford respected imagination and talent—and such respect was rare, I can tell you, in the old automobile companies.

"When I started, we didn't even have body bridges to take off the dimensions accurately. The front end—grille, fenders, lamps, and so on—were treated as part of the chassis. Actually, no one ever got a chance to see what the car looked like until they'd hammered together a prototype. Edsel Ford alone seemed to appreci-

Edsel Ford stood behind Mercury despite Henry's lack of cooperation.

Marc Madow photos

FoMoCo's Design Staff, Circa 1938

The Mercury's cast of characters differs substantially from that which helped create the Model A and the 1932 V-8. Henry's aides were mostly engineers and production men, whereas those who worked with Edsel on the first Mercury were mostly stylists. To acquaint you with them, here's the complete Ford Motor Co. design staff as of 1938.

E.T. (Bob) Gregorie—chief designer
Edward A. Martin—drafting & planning
Martin Regitko—body surface development
John H. Walter—instrument panels
Walter Kruke—interior trim

Willys P. Wagner—bumpers, lights, ext. hardware
Bruno Kolt—grilles, sheet metal
James Lynch—shop foreman
Richard Beneicke—head clay modeler

Apprentices included G.E. (Bud) Adams, Ben Barbera, Frank Beyer, Frank Francis, John Najjar, Emmet O'Rear, and Robert Thomas. Working without title were Ross Cousins, Tucker Madawick, and Duncan McRae.

Source: John Najjar, Ford Design Staff, Dearborn

Merc was among faster cars of 1939, and 3.54 axle gave better gas mileage than Ford. This coupe belongs to Lee Roy Lienemann.

Mercury still used floorshift in '39. Clean panel includes trip odometer, battery meter, and clock. Steering spokes block gauges for short drivers.

This crisp roof is unique to Mercury. We asked designer E.T. Gregorie whether 1938 Cadillac 60-S influenced thin window channels. Mr. Gregorie said no. Continental adopted similar surrounds.

ate that this industry is a combination of vision, production, and sales. He had the vision [and] I did the work of translating his vision into workable designs."

Throughout the 1920s and '30s, Edsel owned a succession of unusual cars, both foreign and domestic. In the '20s, he favored custom-bodied Lincolns. Later, his tastes ran toward exotic speedsters like his custom 1932 boattail and the cut-down 1934 V-8 (see "Edsel Ford's Hot Rods," *SIA* #2). He also fancied fast, sporty European jobs. Gregorie shared this interest, and together, Edsel and he designed several one-offs.

William Laas writes in *Your Edsel Marketer* (1958): "In the styling department, Gregorie kept a number of old prototype cars for reference. They stood in a dark corner covered with dust sheets. At moments when business affairs grew too oppressive, Edsel Ford would appear in the studio, climb into one of the sheeted cars, and beckon to his lieutenant. 'There he would sit,' Gregorie recalls, 'in the cool dark, to meditate and to talk. Mr. Ford seemed to just relax. He would talk of anything that came into his head, such as boats, in which we had a common interest.'"

Edsel apparently had reason to he moody at times, because he could never escape company politics and intrigues. Gregorie refused, for instance, to work under Larry Sheldrick, but it was in Sheldrick's department that Gregorie had his studio. Sheldrick was Ford's untitled chief engineer. Willys P. Wagner, who worked for Gregorie and who designed the 1939 Mercury's lights, bumpers, and exterior hardware, remembers that, "…it's very interesting about Bob. He refused to knuckle under to Sheldrick. He refused to consider that he was in any way *under* Sheldrick. He worked only for Edsel Ford, nobody else. And he wouldn't punch a timecard when everybody else had to punch one. He wouldn't do a lot of things, and he got away with it. But you know, back in those days almost anything could happen. The boys up at the top—they were all jockeying for positions. Anybody who thought he could fire somebody and get away with it did it."

Ross Cousins amplifies: "There was so much

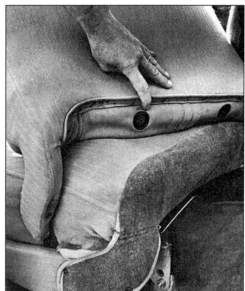

Key stands in steering-column web, with ignition directly above it. The seats tilt inward.

Vents in cushions help equalize pressure in- and outside seats. Carpet on backs wards off mud, prevents scuffing.

Mercury coupe has more rear leg room than most modern ones. Rear vision could be better—coupe has blind quarters.

At the same time Gregorie's tiny staff was designing Mercury and Continental. Henry tossed this bus at them.

John H. Walter

political crap going on that they used to drill holes in the partition to spy on him [Gregorie]. They had the watchman at the gate checking him in, checking him out, just so they might be able to get something on him so they could fire him. But they didn't. It was people like [Harry] Bennett and the top engineer, Sheldrick. They'd even come into our department and look in the toilet look under the doors and see if we were in there too long. We had to almost fight for our existence." Nor was smoking allowed—Henry even refused Edsel permission to smoke. So it was a rather heavy atmosphere in which the Mercury was born—a job complicated by politics as well as the pressures of other, concurrent jobs.

Larry Sheldrick doesn't mention company politics in his *Reminiscences*, but he sheds interesting light on the first Mercury's development. "In July of 1937," he says, "we got to talking about a larger car, another car between the Zephyr and the Ford. This was to become the Mercury, but it wasn't [called that] at the time. It was to be higher powered and have a larger displacement engine. We set the dimensions at 3-3/16 bore by 3-3/4 stroke, which came to 239 cubic inches. [The Mercury V-8 originally appeared in the 1938 Ford 81-T truck.]

"This [car] wasn't specifically aimed at a competitive price class. It was just aimed at the market in the big spread between the Ford and the Zephyr. All during 1937—from then on—we kicked back and forth the various ideas on just

how this thing was to be done. The Ford wheelbase at that time was 112 [inches], so we decided the Mercury was to be 116.

"The point was discussed whether that four inches would be put into the body or into the hood. It finally settled down to being the same body for both cars [*not so*], the additional four inches being put into the hood."

Sheldrick worked for Ford from 1922 until his leaving in 1943. He had major hands in helping develop the Fordson tractor, the Model A engine, and he later saw the 1932 V-8 through production engineering. Although Henry Ford had never officially handed him the title, Sheldrick acted as the company's chief engineer throughout the flathead V-8 era. His *Reminiscences* continue:

"I carried the responsibility for the entire chassis and mechanical end of the Mercury.... I contributed a lot of thoughts and arguments as to how the design would finally he worked out to have the greatest degree of interchangeability with the Ford car.

"I do recall this: The weight, not being much different—the Mercury wasn't very much heavier than the Ford—still had considerably more engine displacement, and we made up [for] the difference in rear-axle ratio. We provided a lower [numerical] ratio, thereby a slower turning engine, and we actually came out with as good economy, if not better, on the Mercury than we had in the Ford. That also created quite a little comment among buyers at that time—that they

were getting better economy out of this bigger car than they were the Ford.

"Consequently, later in this same year, 1937, [since] we knew the fact that you could get better economy out of this bigger car, there was serious consideration [given to] dropping the 3-1/16 bore and the 221 [-cubic-inch] engine out of the picture entirely and using the larger Mercury engine for both cars. However, that didn't materialize. I don't remember why that didn't come about. We didn't substitute it for the Ford engine. It was spoken of quite seriously during that year."

A further note about the new-for-1939 Mercury engine comes down to us from Eugene J. (Gene) Farkas, who worked under Sheldrick as head chassis engineer. In his *Reminiscences*, he tells us:

"The engine was practically the same as the V-8 for the Ford. What they did was, they had a sleeve about 1/16-inch thick in the Ford, and they took that sleeve out and put in a larger piston. That gave them 1/8 inch [more bore and] approximately 10 horsepower more. Instead of having 221-cubic-inch displacement, they had 239. That was the Mercury engine."

What Farkas doesn't mention is that the de-sleeved V-8 had originally been developed for truck and police duty. Fords were greatly favored by that day's constabulary as well as the Dillingers. They made good getaway cars. So to help catch crooks, Ford made a so-called "police" engine available—the de-sleeved

239—and that's what ended up powering the Mercury. Adds Farkas:

"The idea of the steel sleeve was very good, but there was a lot of trouble with it on account of overheating at the top. When steel is overheated, even if it is hard originally, it loses all its hardness, and trouble will develop. Of course, there is steel that doesn't lose its hardness, like chrome silicon steel, but we couldn't use that in the process of manufacturing. That all had to be drawn in a flat piece. They just used fender stock—soft steel. The only way they could harden that was cyanide hardening—put on a little case maybe .010 inch thick. They weren't very round either, but they got around that after they got pressed into the cylinder. The cylinder kept them round.

"As I said, the idea was excellent. Mr. Ford no doubt had in mind to increase the life of the Ford motor, but these little items like overheating the top end, getting warped, getting slightly out of round, and scoring, militated against the continuation of that. I think that was abandoned after a couple of years of trying." [1941 was the last year for sleeves.]

Bob Gregorie, who now lives in Daytona Beach and designs yachts, remembered this about the first Mercury. "The frame was lengthened out, but it was basically a Ford frame, with the same cross springs and axles. In fact, the whole underside was the same. That was one of the things that got [the Mercury] off to a rough start. The competition said, 'Just get down and look underneath it—it's all Ford.' The Ford understructure was so well known at that time that the car suffered....

"I think one of the most interesting things about the 1939 Mercury—the development of it—was the difficulty Mr. Edsel Ford seemed to have in grasping the idea of *what* this car was going to be. Oddly enough, he wasn't trying to step up far enough from the basic Ford. His whole concept was to tie it in with the Ford, and it was very difficult for me to get the point across—he was very touchy on the subject. In other words, to make this an effective [medium-priced] car, we thought that every effort should be made to dissuade the public that the Mercury was just a blown-up Ford which, of course, it really was. It suffered from that for a number of years.

"That went on during the development of the car, and Mr. Ford even insisted on the hubcaps being embossed with *Ford-Mercury*. He became very incensed when I tried to dissuade him from doing that, and as a matter of fact, he blew up one afternoon. He said, 'What's wrong with the name Ford? It's been good for 40 years, hasn't it?'

"We finally got that straightened out, but when the car was presented at the New York show, why the sales people all came after me and said, 'My gosh, we've got to get the name Ford off this car.' So I met Mr. Ford the next morning on the train back to Detroit, and he said 'Well, I'll look you up this afternoon. We've got to talk about some nameplate changes.' I didn't say anything, but anyway we made some very quick changes and got that part straightened out, too."

Asked whether the 1938 Cadillac 60-Special influenced the chrome channels around the 1939 Mercury coupe's windows, Mr. Gregorie replied, "No—that body shell was the convertible's. We used the same body shell for the convertible and the coupe. But the 60-Special didn't influence us so far as I remember. The Cadillac 60-Special at that time, while it became quite

103 Names Considered for Ford's Intermediate Car

Archer	Crest	Ford-Arrow	Hunter	Oxford	Swallow
Athenian	Crusader	Ford-Falcon	Kent	Panther	Trafford
Autocrat	Cyclops	Ford-Fleetwing	Key	Pathfinder	Trailblazer (The)
Beau Monde	Dart	Fordocrat	Leo	Patriot	Transford
Castle	Dearborn (The)	Ford-Olympic	Leopard	Pharoah 8	Triton
Charter	Diana	Forduke	Luxor	Phoenix	Trojan
Citadel	Drake	Ford-XL	Luxury 8	Plaza	Tower
Comet (The)	Eagle	Ford-Zephyr	Manor	Quicksilver (The)	Valiant
Constellation	Edison	Forerunner	Marathon	Rambler	Vanitie 8
Consul	Elford	Forlin	Mercar	Ranger	Vernon
Corinthian	Eros	Forzeli	Mercury	Regent	Victorine
Coronado	Europa	Gazelle (The)	Minerva	Rexford	Vista
Corsair	Exford	Groundflight (The)	Nassau	Sovereign	Warwick
Courageous	Explorer	Guilford	Normandy	Spartan	Washington
Courier	Falcon	Hercules	Olympia	Stylemaster	Winged Victory
Courser	Fleetford	Hermes	Olympic	Stylemeter	Zeon
Courtier	Fleetwing	Horizon	Olympus	Stylist	Zephord
					Zest

Source: Ford Archives, Henry Ford Museum, Dearborn, Michigan. **Note:** This list is assumed to be name suggestions for the 1939 Mercury, and its date indicates same, but the assumption has never been proven conclusively.

Some hubcap designs considered for the new "Ford-Mercury."

interesting later on, wasn't much talked about then. It was a very nice car, very handsome, but as I recall I don't believe it had a lot of influence. It became more popular later on and was then associated with this [Mercury] design, because they [General Motors] continued it for quite a while. And the Continental used those same light, airy window channels."

Willys P. Wagner adds, "I think the door—structurally at least—was a door that was in production, and this was a way of getting a new greenhouse, by putting a chrome frame just above it—what they're doing now with practically all the jobs. Back in those days, most doors were stamped in one piece from top to bottom, including the glass area. This was quite a departure, having everything above the beltline sort of an added-on structure of extruded parts. I think it was one of the first production cars to use that construction, which is so common now.

Mr. Wagner feels, too, that the Murray Corp. of America might have built the Mercury convertible and coupe bodies, and that they might have used the same supplier of extruded chrome

Tools fit into bin behind trunk, and spare takes up little room. Barrel lights have side markers.

Merc's 239 V-8 was Ford 221 without sleeves. This engine got its start in '38 trucks. Mercury used mostly modified Ford running gear.

Marc Madow photos

window channels that GM used for the 60-S. So it's possible that the Mercury did borrow some technology from Cadillac, albeit indirectly.

Another member of the first Mercury's styling staff was John H. Walter, whose basic responsibility was instrument panels. We asked him where the idea for the webbed steering column came from. "That came," he told us, "as a result of considerable pressure on the part of Gregorie and Edsel to make the interior look different, and I came up with the idea of the asymmetric design. I believe that was the first design, to my knowledge, that was not worked around a centerline. The web to the steering column—basically I would say we added that to clean it up. The bare column looked like hell, so it was pretty well aesthetic—to shroud it in and clean it up."

Several people we talked to referred to the 1939 Mercury as a "pumped-up Ford," and so it was. But so was the Pontiac a pumped-up Chevrolet, and Dodges, De Sotos, and Chryslers were pumped-up Plymouths. "Pumping up" was the most common, economical, and logical way to create a new car line.

Yet the 1939 (and 1940) Mercury differed much more from the Ford in sheet metal than the 1939 Pontiac from the Chevy or the '39 Chrysler from the Plymouth. While Mercury and Ford bodies look similar, *no* body panels interchange. It wasn't until 1941 that Ford/Mercury bodies became identical (except for trim). So the point Bob Gregorie makes about the Mercury being a distinctly different car is well made—it needn't have resembled the 1939 Ford at all except as an image consideration.

Comparing 1939 Ford and Mercury 4-door sedans, we find the Mercury body almost eight inches wider, about an inch lower from floor to roof, and 6.3 inches wider at the cowl. Doors are different lengths, with distinct curvatures, latches, and hinges. The Merc's windshield tilts back at a gentler angle, which might mean that both cars used essentially the same roof stamping, with minor changes in dies. It's even possible that the entire Mercury body (2- and 4-door sedans) used modified Ford dies, but that seems unlikely. No one has mentioned it, and no records exist to prove or refute the common-die theory.

Edsel reportedly considered more than 100 names before settling on *Mercury* (see chart, p. 109), but he'd had Mercury on his mind, at least lightly, since 1925. That year he asked company artist Irving Bacon to design a trophy for the winner of the National Air Reliability tour. Bacon's trophy showed Mercury, the Roman god, atop a globe, holding aloft an airplane. Edsel liked the design, and each year from 1925 through 1931, he presented the Mercury trophy to tour winners. (As an aside, there had been at least five previous automobiles named Mercury, three built in the U.S. and two in England. Mercury was also the name of a speedster body sold in kit form for the Model T during the 1920s.)

Development work on Edsel's Mercury began in July 1937, and exactly one year later—July 1938—the first two handbuilt running prototypes stood finished. One was a 2-door and the other a 4-door sedan. These cars were tested extensively on Ford's new test track in Dearborn and were later driven to those parts of the country with the severest weather conditions.

At that time, Edsel still favored the name *Ford-Mercury*, and early pilot-production models carried Ford-Mercury on their hoods and hubcaps. But as Bob Gregorie mentions, Edsel was later persuaded that the *Ford-* should be dropped, and by the car's press introduction on October 24, 1938, it was called simply the *Mercury 8.*

Pilot production began on September 21, 1938, at the Rouge assembly plant in Dearborn, and on September 29, the Ford-Mercury (still called that) was announced and shown to Ford dealers nationwide, either in the flesh or in photos. Then, on October 8, full production began in five U.S. Ford plants: Dearborn; Edgewater, New Jersey; Kansas City, Missouri; Louisville, Kentucky; and Richmond, California. That same month, Mercurys got rolling in Windsor, Ontario, and Chicago. By January, assembly had spread to Mexico, France, and Brazil. And later in the year, Mercurys were also assembled in Holland, Belgium. Denmark, and Rumania.

Public reaction to the Mercury's debut on November 4, 1938, isn't recorded. It didn't draw crowds like the Model A, the first V-8, or even the Zephyr. The press hailed the new Mercury as "half sister to the Lincoln Zephyr," and the *New York Times* added, "Modernly streamlined, the car has a family resemblance to the Lincoln-Zephyr." Actually, the resemblance favored *both* the Ford DeLuxe and the Zephyr, with successful borrowings from each.

Probably the Mercury's biggest send-off came at the 1939 New York Worlds Fair, at which the Ford Motor Co. had a 7-acre exhibit. There was keen competition between GM, Chrysler, and Ford to see who could bring off the most spectacular displays. Edsel took a great personal interest in the Ford exhibit, overseeing construction of an exhibit called "How Cars are Designed," and he made sure that the Mercury got a prominent spot. In April 1939, coinciding with the fair's opening, a stainless steel statue of the god Mercury was unveiled above the main entrance of the Ford exhibit. Passing underneath, visitors were invited to ride on the "Road of Tomorrow" in new Mercurys and other FoMoCo cars.

Edsel was so fascinated with daily goings-on at the Worlds Fair that he rented a house on nearby Manhasset Bay (where Walter Chrysler and GM board chairman Alfred P. Sloan also had homes) and became a frequent, delighted, camera-toting, incognito fairgoer himself. He often stopped by the design exhibit to chat with Ed Martin, who had charge of it. By August 1939, four months after the fair's opening, nearly five million people had visited the Ford pavilion.

John R. (Jack) Davis, Edsel's friend and Ford's astute sales manager, stressed the point that the Mercury shouldn't steal sales away from the DeLuxe Fords nor from stripped Zephyrs. The 1939 Mercury came in four body styles and sold at $894 to $994. The Ford's price range ran $540-920, and the Zephyr's began at $1,360, so there was very little overlap.

Davis set up the Mercury's merchandising plan to allow four different types of agencies: 1) those who could handle all Ford products—these were his strongest dealers; 2) those who could sell Lincolns and Mercurys only; 3) those who could sell Fords and Mercurys only; and 4) a final group who were allowed to sell Mercurys only if they sold enough Fords. The first three groups got a 25% dealer discount; the fourth a 20% discount.

Mercury sales were good from the beginning. That first year—1939—60,214 Mercurys were built in the U.S. and another 10,621 in foreign plants. Before WW-II interrupted all U.S. auto production, nearly a quarter million Mercs were already on the road.

We've always admired the clean lines of the 1939-40 Mercury sedan-coupe, and we were pleased to find a mint example in Oxnard, California. The car belongs to Lee Roy Lienemann, who bought it from its second owner in San Bernardino.

The 1939 Mercury impressed everyone who drove it as being one of the faster stock cars of its day, and no wonder, since it weighed only about 100 pounds more than the Ford. Not too many late-model stock car races were run in 1939 (we know of only two), but the 160-miler at Daytona Beach on March 19 was won by a

specifications

illustrations by Russell von Sauers, The Graphic Automobile Studio
© copyright 1974, Special Interest Autos

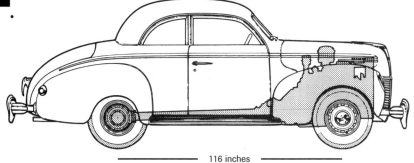
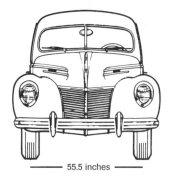

— 116 inches —

— 55.5 inches —

1939 Mercury 99-A Sedan Coupe

Price when new	$934 f.o.b. Dearborn (1939)
Options	None

ENGINE	
Type	L-head V-8, cast-iron block, water-cooled, 3 mains, pressure lubrication
Bore x stroke	3.187 inches x 3.75 inches
Displacement	239.4 cubic inches
Max. bhp @ rpm	95 @ 3,600
Torque @ rpm	170 @ 2,100
Compression ratio	6.15:1
Induction system	2-bbl. downdraft carburetor, mechanical fuel pump
Exhaust system	Cast-iron manifolds, crossover pipe, single muffler
Electrical system	6-volt battery/coil

TRANSMISSION	
Type	3-speed manual, floor lever, synchro 2-3
Ratios: 1st	2.82:1
2nd	1.60:1
3rd	1.00:1
Reverse	3.63:1

CLUTCH	
Type	Single dry plate
Diameter	10.0 inches
Actuation	Mechanical, foot pedal

DIFFERENTIAL	
Type	Spiral-bevel gears, torque tube drive
Ratio	3.54:1
Drive axles	3/4-floating

STEERING	
Type	Worm and roller
Ratio	18.2:1
Turns lock-to-lock	4.5
Turn Circle	40.0 feet

BRAKES	
Type	4-wheel hydraulic drums, internal expanding
Drum diameter	12.0 inches
Total lining area	162.0 square inches

CHASSIS & BODY	
Frame	Channel- and box-section steel, central X-member, double dropped
Body construction	All steel
Body style	2-door, 5-pass. coupe

SUSPENSION	
Front	I-beam axle, transverse leaf spring, lever hydraulic shock absorbers
Rear	Rigid axle, semi-elliptic springs
Shock absorbers	Solid axle, transverse leaf spring, lever hydraulic shock absorbers
Tires	6.00 x 16 inch 4-ply tube type
Wheels	Pressed steel, drop-center rims, lug-bolted to brake drums

WEIGHTS AND MEASURES	
Wheelbase	116 inches
Overall length	195.9 inches
Overall height	67.3 inches
Overall width	69.1 inches
Front track	55.5 inches
Rear track	58.3 inches
Ground clearance	8.4 inches
Curb weight	3,000 pounds

CAPACITIES	
Crankcase	5 quarts
Cooling system	22 quarts
Fuel tank	18 gallons

FUEL CONSUMPTION	
Best	17-21 mpg
Average	15-18 mpg

PERFORMANCE (from **The Motor**, 3/21/39 & **The Autocar** 4/19/39 resp.)	
0-30 mph	3.8 and 4.2 sec.
0-50 mph	9.2 and 9.7 sec.
0-60 mph	13.3 and 13.5 sec.
0-70 mph	19.1 and 19.6 sec.
Standing 1/4 mile	19.1 sec. and 70.0 mph
Top speed (av.)	90-95 mph

new Mercury. Johnny Rice averaged 70.34 mph on the combined road/beach course. Ford products dominated this race, with all 10 top money-winners being either Mercurys or Fords (Bill France finished third in a Ford).

Two British auto magazines tested new Mercurys that year, and here are some of their reactions. First, from *The Autocar*:

"Altogether remarkable performance is provided by the Mercury in both acceleration and maximum speed. ....Considering the all-out timed speed of nearly 95 mph, recorded during testing on Brooklands track, at its price the Mercury certainly affords the closest approach to 100 m.p.h. in a closed car."

Echoed *The Motor*: "A search through our road test figures for standard production cars has shown that [none] has gotten better performance figures than those obtained with the new Mercury Eight. Indeed, its lightning acceleration, combined with a high standard of comfort, good road holding and braking, make it one of the best £400-worth of motoring that is now offered on the market. ...Reference to the data...will show the excellence of its top-gear acceleration, its fleetness through the gears and its high maximum. The beauty of the Mercury, however, is that it does it all so quietly. From a standstill, it draws away sweetly, which smoothness is maintained up to a maxi-mum speed of just over 90 mph." *The Motor* also mentions one

quarter-mile acceleration run at 18.5, but its average of five runs came to 19.1 seconds.

Both magazines marveled at the Mercury's outstanding performance, and we've given both sets of acceleration figures in our own specification chart, p. 11. With the 3.54 axles, 60 mph draws only 2,550 rpm from the engine, so it's ticking over without strain and can hold 60 quietly. Even at 85, rpm is a relatively modest 3,570. There's that characteristic Ford drone on hard pressing—a moan from the carburetor—but the engine idles without a lope and in nearly total silence.

Driver controls are handy and flush with the instrument panel, as they were in all 1939 cars. The speedometer forms a rainbow within the steering rim. It's easy to see, but the two steering spokes block shorter drivers' view of the four auxiliary gauges. Also, we've never liked the so-called "battery condition" meter; we prefer a conventional ammeter so we can tell whether the generator is charging and not simply whether the battery is dead.

Light, quick steering (four turns lock to lock) makes the Mercury very maneuverable and pleasant to drive. As *The Autocar* says, "Some leaning over occurs on the more appreciable corners, but there seem to be definite limitations to this tendency, the body going so far and no further.... The Mercury takes the wide-radius curves of a modern road decidedly well at high speed. There is no

pitching tendency, and a regular passenger is apt to suggest that the back seat is as comfortable as the front."

Edsel Ford's convictions about auto design and the need for a medium-priced Ford line were vindicated with the Mercury. It soon became a solid success and has remained one. The Mercury plus the Continental—and to some extent the Zephyr—survive as testimonials to Edsel's personal vision. His importance to the company has, of course, been overshadowed by his father. Today, Edsel's memory is further distorted by the car that bore his name; so it might be a long time before he gets the credit and sympathetic understanding that's rightly his. ✎

The authors wish to thank Hank Edmunds, Dave Crippen, and Win Sears of the Ford Archives, Henry Ford Museum, Dearborn; Michael W.R. Davis, Owen Bombard, and Nick Bush of Ford Motor Co., Dearborn; John Najjar, Ford Design Staff; E.T. Gregorie, Daytona Beach, Florida; Willys P. Wagner, Tiburon, California; Al H. Esper, Dearborn; Edward A. Martin, Redondo Beach, California; John H. Walter, Grosse Pointe, Michigan; Ross Cousins, Bloomfield Hills, Michigan; Emil Zoerlein, Lake San Marcos, California; Gordon Chamberlin, Santa Monica, California; Ford Life Magazine, St. Helena, California; and Lee Roy Lienemann, Oxnard, California.

EDSEL'S BABY LINCOLN

1941 MERCURY CONVERTIBLE

by Arch Brown
photos by Bud Juneau

IT is highly probable that, left to his own devices, Henry Ford would have concentrated exclusively upon the production of low-priced automobiles. It was at the urging of his son, Edsel — and perhaps in part to embarrass his old nemesis, Henry Leland — that in 1921 Ford purchased the ailing Lincoln Motor Company. But the old man's attitude toward his newly acquired luxury car enterprise was probably best summarized in his pithy declaration that he had "no use for any car that has more spark plugs than a cow has teats."

All of which must surely have been an undisguised blessing for Edsel, for his father gave him virtually a free hand to run Lincoln as he saw fit. The result, of course, was some of the finest classic automobiles ever produced.

But by 1933, Lincoln was obviously dying. Production came to just 2,007 cars for the calendar year — less than a third of 1929's already limited output. The model year figure was even worse, totalling 1,647 units, and the company's books were awash in red ink. Charles Sorensen, Henry Ford's hard-bitten production chief, openly advocated writing off the entire Lincoln operation.

Originally published in Special Interest Autos #134, Mar.-Apr. 1993

Only the intercession of Edsel Ford kept Lincoln on the road. It must have taken a great deal of persuasion on his part to convince his father that Lincoln was really viable. And it was obvious to Edsel that just as Cadillac had a lower-priced "companion" car in the LaSalle, so Lincoln, in order to survive, would be forced to produce a medium-priced machine.

Meanwhile, officials of the Briggs Manufacturing Company were becoming increasingly concerned about the decreasing volume of their Ford Motor Company account. Moving aggressively, they hired Dutch-born, British-trained John Tjaarda away from General Motors, charging him with the development of a design that might become a smaller, lower-priced Lincoln (see *SIA* #10).

The result, as the reader will have deduced, was the 12-cylinder Lincoln Zephyr, introduced in November 1935 and priced just $95 higher than the LaSalle.

It was a wise move, and a profitable one. Production of the Zephyr, during its initial season, fell just six cars short of 15,000. Not a spectacular record, but an encouraging beginning. And a good thing, for sales of the firm's $4,200 Model K continued to fall.

But to Edsel Ford, a shrewd businessman and a much better analyst of market trends than his father, the Lincoln-Zephyr was only the first step. At $1,320, the new "baby Lincoln" cost more than twice as much as the Ford Deluxe Fordor sedan. Such a jump was beyond the means of the typical Ford buyer, and — as Edsel was well aware — the competition was capitalizing on the situation.

By 1937 automobile sales recovered substantially (if temporarily) from the effects of the Depression. Chevrolet's output was up 40 percent compared to 1934, Plymouth's by 46 percent, and Ford scored a 50 percent increase over the same three-year period. But it was in the lower-medium-priced field, a market in which the Ford Motor Company did not compete, that the really spectacular gains were being made:
- Oldsmobile, up 163 percent.
- Dodge, up 166 percent.
- Buick (paced by the price-leading Special series), up 188 percent.
- Pontiac, up 195 percent.
- Nash, up 200 percent.

Or to put it another way, during the worst of the Depression, more than 72 percent of the automobile market was held by the low-priced three: Chevrolet, Ford, and Plymouth. But by 1937 their share had fallen to 57 percent. Meaning, of course, that substantial numbers of upwardly mobile American motorists were abandoning the bottom end of the price scale and moving up a notch to Dodge, Pontiac, or any one of a number of other makes.

It was clear to Edsel that Ford would

Above: Merc abounds with neat details like the streamlined parking lamps. *Below:* Name appears on hood sides in stylish block letters. *Bottom:* Graceful winged hood ornament points the way.

have to develop an entry for this increasingly important market segment. His father, perhaps reluctantly, gave the green light to his son's proposal, and in July 1937 work commenced on the development of this new, as yet unnamed car. Edsel wanted it to be ready in time for the 1939 auto shows, scheduled for November 1938, just 16 months away.

According to the conventional wisdom it is (and was, even in those days) quite impossible to bring a new car from concept to showroom in just 16 months. In this instance, however, for Ford to have achieved this goal was something less than a miracle, for the newcomer was based almost entirely, apart from its body, on existing Ford components. In effect, the engineering work was already done.

The familiar Ford V-8 was bored for this application to 239 cubic inches, up from 221 as fitted to the Ford. Advertised horsepower was thus increased from 85 to 95, although there is reason to suspect that the Ford version may have deliberately been somewhat underrated. In any case, the new car's engine proved to be the nimblest powerplant in its field.

The wheelbase was stretched from 112 to 116 inches, and the brakes were suitably enlarged. But the buggy-type transverse springs, favored by Henry Ford since the days of the Model T and before, were retained, despite the fact that by that time virtually the entire industry, apart from Ford, had adopted independent front suspension.

We mentioned brakes. The story is told

that some time earlier at an executive luncheon, Edsel had had the temerity to suggest that the company would do well to adopt hydraulics. His father stood up, glared across the table and snapped, "Edsel, you shut up!" And with that, the old man left the meeting.

But by this time pressure from the sales force had prompted Henry Ford to capitulate. For 1939, hydraulics would be adopted throughout the entire Ford Motor Company line, with the sole exception of the limited-production, K-Series Lincolns.

No fewer than 101 titles were considered for the new car. Some, such as "The Groundflight," "The Winged Victory" and "Fordocart," seem almost silly now. Others, such as "Eros" and "Trojan," might be considered suggestive. Several — Comet, Falcon, Explorer and Courier come to mind — were used in later years to designate certain Ford and Mercury models, while still others, such as Rambler, Valiant, Dart, Eagle and Stylemaster, were picked up by the competition. But in the end Edsel Ford himself selected the name, borrowing it from the ancient Romans: Mercury.

The new car was a solid, if hardly a sensational success. Production for 1939, its first full year, came to 76,198 cars, enabling the Merc to slip past such

veterans as Chrysler, DeSoto and Nash to take over eleventh place in the industry.

Four body types were offered that first season: sedan (two-door), town sedan (four-door), sedan coupe and convertible. Very likely it was styling that did the most to attract attention to the new Mercury Eight, for in all four of its configurations it was a very attractive automobile.

The Merc was wider, roomier and more impressive in appearance than its stablemate. Lines were more curvaceous, some would say sexier, and the trim level was somewhat fancier than that of the Ford. Yet the family resemblance was strong. Not as strong, perhaps, as that of the Dodge to the Plymouth, but there was no mistaking the Mercury for anything but a Ford product.

Priced head-to-head with the Pontiac Deluxe Six and $25.00 higher (in sedan form) than the Dodge Deluxe Six, the Mercury represented excellent value for the money. And with a power-to-weight ratio that was 15 percent more favorable than that of the Dodge and 22 percent better than that of the Pontiac, it had a special appeal for the performance enthusiast. Even the Pontiac Eight, priced $48.00 higher than the Six, couldn't match the Mercury's speed and acceleration.

Only minor changes were made for 1940. A new, finer-textured grille was fitted and the gearshift lever was moved from the floor to the steering column. Sealed-beam headlamps were used, and a convertible sedan was added to the line. Production, on a calendar year basis, edged up to 82,770 units, though the Merc remained in eleventh place on the sales charts.

Ford advertisements for 1941 proclaimed "Size to Match its Power," and indeed the new Ford was larger and roomier than its predecessors. Large enough, in fact, that Mercury was able to employ the same body shell, stretched four inches ahead of the firewall in order to give it a longer, more impressive hood. The slow-selling convertible sedan was dropped, but three additional types were added to the line: business coupe, coupe with auxiliary seats, and station wagon.

Sales brochures proclaimed the new Mercury "The easiest-handling car you've ever driven." "No magic carpet ever rode so comfortably," the ads declared, but the big pitch had to do with fuel consumption. "The big car that stands alone in economy" was the slogan this time, for despite its outstanding power and performance, the Mercury delivered surprisingly good mileage. Owners routinely reported 20 miles to the gallon or better in highway travel.

Eight attractive colors were offered, initially, with additional hues added to the palette during the year. Buyers of the closed body types could choose between bedford cord or herringbone broadcloth interiors, while the club convertible and station wagon came with genuine hand-buffed leather upholstery in a choice of tan, blue or red. The electrically powered convertible top was supplied in either olive drab with matching edging, or black with vermilion edging.

Standard equipment on all models included an electric clock, locking glove compartment, snap-out cigarette lighter, lighted luggage compartment, stainless steel wheel trim rings and a dimming control for the instrument lights. Among the popular options were a "Roto-Selector" ratio with integral antenna, and a choice of two hot water heater/defrosters; and motorists who traveled long distances often specified the Columbia two-speed axle.

Driving Impressions

Martin Bogarian, a Fresno, California, realtor, has taken a special interest in 1941 Mercurys — especially the club convertible — ever since he was a teenager. In time he was able to acquire a '41 sedan, but as he explains, "the desire for a convertible was never fulfilled. Furthermore, it never diminished.

"In January of 1979, while going through *Hemmings Motor News*, I came across an ad and picture of a '41 Mercury convertible for sale in the Monte-

Facing page: Merc carries advanced front end styling for its time. **This page, above:** Radio antenna goes up and down à la Buick. **Below:** Built-in side mirrors add a custom touch.

Mercury vs. the Competition
1941 Lower-Medium-Priced Convertibles Compared

	Mercury Eight	Dodge Custom 6	Hudson Deluxe 6	Oldsmobile "76"	Pontiac Deluxe 8
Price, convertible	$1,070	$1,162	$1,070	$1,089	$1,048
Wheelbase	118 inches	119.5 inches	116 inches	119 inches	119 inches
Overall length	200.6 inches	202.8 inches	196.7 inches	204 inches	201.5 inches
Shipping weight	3,222 pounds	3,384 pounds	2,980 pounds	3,355 pounds	3,390 pounds
Engine	V-8	L-6	L-6	L-6	Straight 8
Bore	3³⁄₁₆ inches	3¼ inches	3 inches	3½ inches	3¼ inches
Stroke	3¾ inches	4⅜ inches	4⅛ inches	4⅛ inches	3¾ inches
C.I.D.	239.4	217.8	174.9	238.1	248.9
Compression ratio	6.15:1	6.50:1	7.25:1	6.10:1	6.50:1
Horsepower/rpm	95/3,600	91/3,800	92/4,000	100/3,400	103/3,500
Torque/rpm	176/2,100	170/1,200	138/1,400	190/1,400	190/2,200
Valve configuration	L-head	L-head	L-head	L-head	L-head
Main bearings	3	4	3	4	5
Clutch diameter	10 inches	10 inches	8¹¹⁄₁₆ inches	9¼ inches	9½ inches
Trans. ratios, 1/2	3.11/1.77	2.57/1.83	2.88/1.82	2.66/1.66	2.67/1.66
Axle ratio (std)	3.54:1	4.30:1	4.55:1	4.10:1	4.10:1
Steering ratio	18.2:1	18.2:1	18.2:1	19.0:1	19.0:1
Turning diameter	40 feet	40.2 feet	41.6 feet	37 feet	38.4 feet
Braking area	163.0	155.5	138.9	148.0	149.0
Drum diameter	12 inches	11 inches	10 inches	11 inches	11 inches
Calculated data:					
Horsepower/c.i.d.	.397	.418	.526	.420	.414
Weight (lb.)/hp	33.9	37.2	32.4	33.6	32.9
Weight/c.i.d.	13.5	15.5	17.0	14.1	13.6
Weight/sq. in. (brakes)	19.8	21.8	21.5	22.7	22.8
Stroke/bore ratio	1.11:1	1.35:1	1.38:1	1.18:1	1.15:1

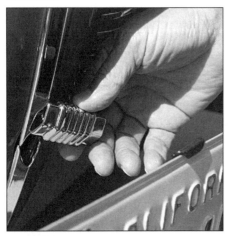

Above: Old-fashioned touch is provided by pinstriped wheels. Below left: Hand crank hole was still around in 1941. Below right: Horizontal taillamps preceded postwar Ford V-8 treatment.

bello area. I called my brother, who lives in Van Nuys, and asked him to look at it and call me from the nearest phone if it was a decent car. The next morning he called to say it was not a steal, but it was a straight, clean, unaltered convertible. That's all I needed to know! I bought it, and my brother stored it in his garage."

Martin's brother drove the car home to Van Nuys. It burned oil, the clutch slipped and the front end was loosey-goosey, but the car made the trip without incident. Six months later, Martin and his son picked the convertible up and trailered it to Fresno.

The dealer from whom Bogarian bought the Merc was unable, initially, to supply a clear title; so Martin contacted the previous owner, James Brucker, of Movie World Auto Sales and Rentals, located in Anaheim. Brucker asked if Martin knew the history of the car, to which Martin replied that he did not.

Brucker, it seems, bought the Mercury from United Artists, when the studio closed out its fleet and adopted the practice of renting vintage cars as needed. Reportedly, it had been Benson Ford's honeymoon car in 1941, and was later sold to the movie studio for $1.00, presumably for the publicity value that might accrue to the company from its use.

Brucker went on to say that he had been approached in 1965 by Ford Motor Company executives who wanted to purchase the car, restore it and present it to Benson and Edith Ford on the occasion of their 25th anniversary, in 1966. Brucker, perhaps to his later regret, held out for a higher price than the company was prepared to pay; so the convertible remained in his inventory for several more years.

In recent months, Martin Bogarian has been attempting — thus far without success — to confirm this account. It seems reasonably certain, however, that this is the Mercury ragtop that has appeared in a number of motion pictures, including 1943's *Crash Dive*, an early color feature starring Ann Baxter and Tyrone Power. Martin has purchased a video of that film, in which Power is seen at the wheel of a '41 Mercury ragtop finished in Florentine Blue, the original color of the Bogarian car.

Restoration of the Merc commenced in 1987, when Martin drove the car from Fresno to Pixley, California, and turned it over to Doyle Williams. "I had talked to Doyle about going through the drive train," Martin explains. "This is all I had intended to do, other than replace the top, as I wanted a driver, not a show car. But one thing led to another and I just continued removing parts."

With Martin's help, Doyle Williams and his family removed the body and went through every part of the car, "every screw, nut and washer," as Bogarian puts it. Don Cornell, of Clarksville, Georgia, did the woodgraining; seats were sent to LeBaron Bonney in Amesbury, Massachusetts, for reupholstering; Bob and Patti Logan of All-Weather Canvas, in Clovis, California, were responsible for the top. And Martin Bogarian himself stripped the body to the bare metal and repainted it in the original Florentine Blue, one of Mercury's mid-year 1941 colors. Every effort was made to retain the car's authenticity. Even the Fram oil filter carries the decal bearing the slogan "The Dipstick Tells the Story."

The standard axle ratio for a '41 Mercury is 3.54:1, but when the Columbia axle is fitted, as it is to this car, the lower ratio is 4.11:1, resulting in even

Mercury Production, 1939-42

	Model Year	Calendar Year	Rank in Industry
1939	59,071	76,198	11
1940	86,062	82,770	11
1941	98,293	80,085	12
1942	24,696	4,430	13

Dashboard is festooned with chrome trim, woodgraining and wonderful design touches like the radio controls and ashtray shape.

1941 Mercury
Table of Prices, Weights and Production

	Price	Weight	Production
Sedan (2-door)	$920	3,184	20,932
Town Sedan (4-door)	$960	3,221	42,984
Sedan Coupe	$950	3,118	18,263
Coupe w/auxiliary seats	$910	3,049	1,954
Coupe, 3-passenger	$885	3,008	3,313
Convertible Coupe	$1,070	3,222	8,556
Station Wagon, 8-pass.	$1,110	3,468	2,291

Note: The above production figures, which total 98,293 units, were taken from Dammann and Wagner's *The Cars of Lincoln-Mercury*. According to the same source, worldwide production for the season totalled 98,412 cars, suggesting that 119 cars must have been assembled in other countries.

specifications

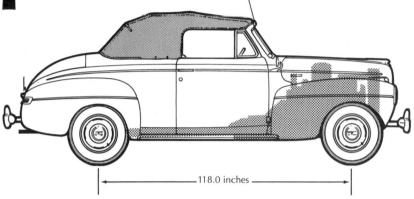

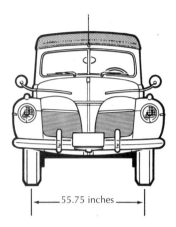

118.0 inches

55.75 inches

1941 Mercury Eight

Original price	$1,070 f.o.b. factory, with standard equipment
Standard equipment, this model	Snap-out type lighter, electric clock, glove compartment lock, twin horns, two sun visors, dual windshield wipers, dual stop and taillamps, wheel trim rings, illuminated luggage compartment, bumper guards
Options on dR car	Columbia 2-speed axle, radio, heater, white sidewall tires
Aftermarket access. on dR car	Twin outside mirrors, exhaust extension, turn signals, seat belts (front only)

ENGINE

Type	90-degree L-head V-8
Bore x stroke	3.19 inches x 3.75 inches
Displacement	239.4 cubic inches
Compression ratio	6.15:1
Horsepower @ rpm	95 @ 3,600
Torque @ rpm	176 @ 2,100
Taxable horsepower	32.5
Valve lifters	Mechanical
Main bearings	3
Lubrication system	Pressure to main, connecting rod and camshaft bearings
Cooling system	Centrifugal pump
Fuel system	Dual downdraft carburetor, camshaft pump
Exhaust system	Single
Electrical system	6-volt battery/coil

CLUTCH

Type	Single dry plate
Outside diameter	10 inches
Actuation	Mechanical, foot pedal

TRANSMISSION

Type	3-speed selective, synchronized 2nd and 3rd gears; column-mounted lever
Ratios: 1st	3.11:1
2nd	1.77:1
3rd	1.00:1
Reverse	4.00:1

DIFFERENTIAL

Type	Columbia 2-speed (Spiral bevel)
Ratios	4.11:1 and 2.94:1
Drive axles	3/4 floating
Torque medium	Torque tube

STEERING

Type	Gemmer worm-and-roller
Ratio	18.2:1
Turning diameter	40 feet
Turns, lock to lock	4.5

BRAKES

Type	4-wheel hydraulic; steel drums with cast-iron braking surfaces
Drum diameter	12 inches
Total swept area	163 square inches

CONSTRUCTION

Type	Body-on-frame
Frame	Reinforced X-type with rigid box sections
Body	All steel
Body type	Club convertible

SUSPENSION

Front	Solid axle, 44.5-inch x 2-inch transverse semi-elliptic spring; torsional stabilizer
Rear	Rigid axle, 40-inch x 2.25-inch transverse semi-elliptic spring
Shock absorbers	Double-acting hydraulic
Wheels	Steel disc with 5-inch rims
Tires	6.50/16 4-ply

WEIGHTS AND MEASURES

Wheelbase	118 inches
Springbase	129.38 inches
Overall length	200.61 inches
Overall width	74 inches
Overall height	66 inches
Front track	55.75 inches
Rear track	58.25 inches
Min. road clearance	8.4 inches
Shipping weight	3,222 pounds

CAPACITIES

Crankcase	5 quarts
Cooling system	23.75 quarts
Fuel tank	17 gallons
Transmission	2.75 pints
Rear axle	2.5 pints

CALCULATED DATA

Horsepower per c.i.d.	.397
Weight per hp	33.9 pounds
Weight per c.i.d.	13.5 pounds
P.S.I. (brakes)	19.8
Color	Florentine Blue

This page: Instrument cluster design theme is decidedly horizontal. *Facing page:* Ford-derived flathead V-8 has a bit more displacement and horses.

faster acceleration than usual for this model. Then at highway speeds, the axle is shifted (with a bit of a "thud") to high range, and the ratio drops to 2.94:1. The engine, already smooth and quiet, becomes almost inaudible at this point.

The front seat is roomy and comfortable, though — typically, for this body style — quarters are a bit cramped in the rear. Trunk space is ample, despite some intrusion by the spare tire. The broad expanse of canvas behind the doors, coupled with the small backlight, creates a blind spot that is downright dangerous, although it was typical of most convertibles in 1941.

Ford products of this vintage often have chattery clutches. Not so this car; clutch action is smooth, and pedal pressure is moderate. The transmission shifts easily, the steering column control operates smoothly, and the synchronizers are highly effective. Steering is pleasantly light, except of course in parallel parking. The brakes, we found, are excellent; evidently when Ford finally got around to adopting hydraulics, they did the job right.

Corners are taken without excessive leaning, and although we experienced a moderate degree of choppiness, the ride is more comfortable than one might expect, given the nature of the Mercury's suspension system. The car is lively and responsive, really a delight to drive. And despite its outstanding record at the recent concours, its owner

still views it as a driver. At last reports he was getting ready for a tour down the Pacific Coast to San Louis Obispo and Cambria.

It will be a great car for a trip like that. ॐ

Acknowledgements and Bibliography
Automotive Industries, *October 15, 1940, and March 1, 1941; Dammann, George H. and James K. Wagner,* The Cars of Lincoln-Mercury; *Editors of* Automobile Quarterly, *"The American Car Since 1775"; Kimes, Beverly Rae and Henry Austin Clark, Jr. (editors),* Standard Catalog of American Cars, 1805-1942; *Langworth, Richard M.,* Encyclopedia of American Cars, 1940-1970; *Mercury Division factory literature; Nevins, Allan,* Ford: Decline and Rebirth, 1933-1962.

Our thanks to Doloris Carruth, Fresno, California; John Cavagnaro, Stockton, California; Ben Gostanian, Fresno, California. Special thanks to Martin Bogarian, Fresno, California.

1941

If we look back over the history of our nation, there have been certain years that must be considered pivotal. Surely 1941 was such a time. World War II was raging in Europe, and without question America's sentiments were almost universally on the side of Britain as it fought bravely on, following the fall of France. And yet, while we felt a rising sense of urgency and alarm, isolationist sentiment was still very strong in the United States.

I was a junior at the University of California, Berkeley, when the year opened. The first peacetime draft in our country's history had gone into effect the previous October, and we watched as some of our classmates received that dreaded letter that opened, ironically, with "Greeting." Others of us, myself included, dropped out of school to take advantage of the high wages being paid by defense industries.

In those days there was a rathskeller in San Francisco that had become a favorite spot with the college crowd — an ideal place to take a girl for an inexpensive date. It was a happy place, at least on the surface. The food was cheap and the beer was plentiful; there was a fine German band and a good dance floor; and the cover charge, as I recall, was only 50 cents a couple. But then one day the place was padlocked, and we were told that our favorite nightspot had been headquarters for the German-American Bund.

In Washington that May, President Franklin D. Roosevelt signed the Lend-Lease Act, granting desperately needed aid to Great Britain and — ultimately — Russia. Two months later the president declared "an unlimited state of national emergency," and on June 14 the assets of Germany and Italy in the United States were frozen and their vessels were seized in American ports. German consulates were closed, and although I don't recall specifically, I presume this must have been the time when the rathskeller was put out of business.

That July, the United States Marines established a base in Iceland, at the request of that nation's government. In August President Roosevelt and Prime Minister Churchill met at a secret rendezvous in the North Atlantic, where they drafted the eight principles of the historic Atlantic Charter. The outlook, for anyone honest and courageous enough to face it, was grim.

And yet, while these fateful events were taking place, life in the United States was deceptively normal, at least on the face of it. Theater audiences were titillated by comedies such as *Arsenic and Old Lace* and *Claudia*, as well as Noel Coward's *Blithe Spirit*. At the movies we saw *Citizen Kane*, Orson Welles's thinly disguised and unflattering biography of publisher William Randolph Hearst. Other films that year included *The Man Who Came to Din-*

ner, starring Monte Wooley and Bette Davis; *Suspicion*, with Cary Grant and Joan Fontaine; and *Kings Row*, featuring an all-star cast that included Ronald Reagan.

The Swing Era was at its height. Among the top bands were those of Benny Goodman, Tommy Dorsey, Harry James and Duke Ellington, but unquestionably the most popular of the lot was the Glenn Miller organization, whose recordings that year included the catchy "Chattanooga Choo Choo," from the film *Sun Valley Serenade*. Other hit songs of the season ranged from "Deep in the Heart of Texas" to Johnny Mercer's "Blues in the Night" to "I Don't Want to Walk Without You," popularized by the Harry James band with Helen Forrest doing the vocal. Teenage girls were swooning over young Frank Sinatra's rendition of "This Love of Mine," and people with close ties to England got misty-eyed over "The White Cliffs of Dover."

Call it "escapism" if you will, but in most respects 1941 was a great time to be young.

That is, until December 7, when the Japanese attacked Pearl Harbor and we found ourselves fighting, literally, for our nation's life. It was, in Franklin Roosevelt's ringing phrase, "a date that will live in infamy."

Suddenly, the party was over; war had become a grim reality for all of us.

1946 MERCURY SPORTSMAN

Top left: Taillamps and fenders are carried over from stock '41 Ford units. Above left: Woodwork exhibits admirable hand craftsman-ship throughout. Above: Front end styling is much more baroque than its Ford cousins. Below: That's a fact.

by Tim Howley
photos by David Gooley

WHILE attending the 1995 Wave-crest woody meet in Carlsbad, California, this writer had the shock of his life. There, standing in one of the front rows, in superbly restored condition, was what had to be the only 1946 Mercury Sportsman left. It had to be the Don Narus car, which he mentioned in his 1977 book, *Great American Wagons and Woodies.*

Now, 1946-48 Ford Sportsmen are pretty unusual. Krause's *Standard Catalog of American Cars* reports that

3,025 were built, and it is possible that close to 200 have survived. They do turn up at shows. There were two of them at Wavecrest. *SIA* carried a very definitive driveReport on a 1947 Ford Sportsman in its tenth issue, April-May 1972. The

Mercury Sportsman is far rarer. It was offered for 1946 only, and only for eight months. For reasons unknown, it is believed that only one authentic example has survived, although there are reportedly three replicas out there, probably utilizing Ford Sportsman bodies which were identical.

A plaque accompanying the car at Wavecrest read: "You are looking at the rarest of the rare, the last remaining factory-built 1946 Mercury Sportsman that exists in the world today. There are

Only 205 Were Built. Only One Is Left.

three other known privately constructed Sportsmen that were created from 1946-48 Mercury convertible coupes. The workmanship on these hand-crafted models is excellent, and it is difficult to determine which is a factory model and which are copies. Only knowledgeable Sportsman buffs such as Don Narus, Ollie Smith, Barrett McGregor and Dan Krehbiel, to name a few, know the ancestry of these cars and can tell the subtle differences.

"There is no mystery about the history or authenticity of this car. The body number is 382 and the serial number is 1140582. The car is mentioned on Page 88 of the Don Narus book . . . Don started restoration of the car, but ultimately Don Newby of Bondurant, Iowa, finished it. Don did a superb, lengthy frame up restoration of the car, completed in 1983.

"The first Mercury Sportsman rolled off the line in April 1946, and the last unit was completed in November 1946. The retail price was $2,209. Disappointing sales were probably the reason

the line was not offered in 1947. This particular car has several distinguishing features. It has the rare Ford accessory windshield washers, also the unique factory installed self canceling turn signal indicator that is built into the steering mast housing."

The present owner, Curt Heaton, of Corona Del Mar, California, was nowhere to be found. A phone call later disclosed that he was on a fishing trip in Alaska. When Mr. Heaton returned in October, he graciously consented to a driveReport on this rarest and most endangered of all Ford species from the forties. It's hard to say why so few were built, and for such a short period. Very likely, Ford production people decided to simplify things by only offering the Ford version at a time when there were far more urgent priorities at Ford.

Consider the tenor of the times. Edsel Ford died in May 1943. A senile Henry Ford returned to the helm. Problems at Ford were so out of hand at the height of World War II that President Franklin D. Roosevelt allowed young Henry Ford II

to be released from the Navy to assist his grandfather. The old man was furious that a young whippersnapper would dare try to take over. But when Henry Ford's wife, Clara, and daughter-in-law, Eleanor, brought considerable pressure to bear on the old autocrat, Henry I reluctantly turned over the presidency of the world's second largest car manufacturer to Henry II in September 1945. From that point on it was a race against time to get the all-new 1949 Ford into production and put the company back in the black.

Few realize today how close the Ford Motor Company came to going under in the dark 1945-48 period. There was no priority like the '49 Ford. The Lincoln and Mercury really hardly mattered. From a historic perspective, ask not why Ford took the Mercury Sportsman out of production; better to ask why they ever bothered producing it at all!

The Ford and Mercury Sportsmen were the first and only new models Ford put into production right after the War. Mercury production resumed on No-

1946 MERCURY

vember 1, 1945, three months later than Ford. Mercury dropped the business coupe and, as in years past, offered only one series, not a Deluxe or Super Deluxe as was the case with Ford. Nor did Mercury offer Ford's six-cylinder engine. Like the Ford, the 1946 Mercury was a facelifted version of the '42. The byzantine new grille had an upper section of vertical bars with a sheet metal frame painted the body color; a lower painted catwalk section housed horizontal chrome and stainless bars. The lower section was an integral part of the front fenders.

Models offered were a two-door sedan coupe or club coupe, two-door sedan, four-door sedan, station wagon, two-door convertible, and of course, the Sportsman. Prices averaged $188 more, model for model, than those of the Super Deluxe Ford V-8. In all, 86,603 Mercurys were produced for the 1946 model year. Despite the Mercury's more upscale trim, the Mercury and Ford are otherwise identical, except for the Mercury's four-inch-longer wheelbase.

1946 Ford and Mercury engines each develop 100 bhp at 3,800 rpm. Engine improvements for 1946 in both makes included four-ringed aluminum pistons, new tri-alloy bearings, high-pressure radiator caps that increased water pressure for higher temperature operation, and increased brake lining area.

The probable reason why Henry Ford II offered the Sportsman in both makes was that he wanted something new and appealing to put on showroom floors, and he wanted it put into production quickly. The 1946 Lincoln Continental would not be introduced until the early summer of 1946. In 1945 he had E.T. "Bob" Gregorie build him a Sportsman forerunner, utilizing a 1931 Model A Ford chassis. Ford was already building station wagon bodies at their plant in Iron Mountain, Michigan. Why not simply build a convertible version of the wagon? At first, only one was built, a Ford for Henry II's personal use. Ultimately it was sold to actress Ella Raines, who took delivery in Hollywood on Christmas Day, 1945. Henry II was quite the ladies man, and reportedly he was having an affair with Ella Raines at the time. Raines sold the car approximately two years later, and nobody seems to know what happened to that original Sportsman.

General production of the Ford Sportsman did not get under way until July 1946, and it ceased in November 1947; thus all 1948 Ford Sportsmen are actually 1947 models. In all probability, production of the Sportsman was slated to come much earlier, but problems, especially with suppliers, delayed it until mid-year.

In preparing the original *SIA* Sportsman article in 1972, Mike Lamm interviewed John Bennett, a manufacturing

Getting Ford Back on the Road

When the 1946 Fords began rolling off the assembly line at the Rouge on July 3, 1945, they were the first post World War II cars to get back in production. On August 29, Henry Ford II personally delivered the first one, an off-white Super Deluxe two-door sedan, to President Harry S. Truman, in one of the neatest publicity stunts of the year. Many other notables and celebrities were seen with the first 1946 Fords, and also the first 1946 Mercurys, which began production on November 1, 1945. But unless you were among the rich and famous, you probably couldn't get your hands on a 1946 Ford until mid-1946. The Mercurys, being a little more expensive, did not have quite as long a waiting list.

Getting 1946 Fords and Mercurys into production was relatively easy compared to producing them in any significant numbers. Many of the problems stemmed from prices which were set by the Office of Price Administration. At the prices that were set, many suppliers refused to provide the manufacturers with parts. Then there were strikes, more with the suppliers than with the automobile manufacturers. This postponed the introduction of the 1946 Ford to the public until late October 1945. By the end of calendar 1945 Ford had produced only 34,439 automobiles.

We do not know how many movie stars owned 1946 Fords and Mercurys. We do know that both Bob Hope and Jack Benny had 1946 Lincoln Continentals. Ronald Reagan was pictured with a 1946 Lincoln Continental, but never actually owned one. His first Lincoln was a 1949 model.

Ford production went up dramatically during 1946 and even more so in 1947. Still, there were never quite enough Fords to fill the pent-up wartime demand until some time after the introduction of the 1949 models. During all of these years, it was easier to get a Mercury than a Ford, but until mid-1949, if you wanted either make you probably had to slip the dealer a few hundred "sweetener" dollars under the table or take a well-loaded model for the same sort of money.

Left: Rubber stone shields are also Ford-derived. **Center:** Factory spotlight adds flash to Merc. **Top right:** Script was also shared with Ford. **Above right:** Front is well protected with factory accessory grille guard and bumper ends.

engineer at the time who said, "The Sportsman was to be strictly wooden panels over a regular convertible body. They had taken the metal skins off the doors, the rear quarters, and the decklid, and replaced them with wood. The wooden panels at the start, of course, were tailor-made—made to fit the car—because there were no blueprint drawings or anything of that nature to start with, only a perspective styling drawing. All the development was done in our Iron Mountain plant.

"The wood was built right along with the station wagon. There was a separate line to put the panels onto the car. The body was built up completely at Iron Mountain — just the body, though. It was trimmed . . . hydraulic window lifts, instrument panel, top, everything back to the cowl put in . . . then shipped to Dearborn where it was put onto the chassis."

In the early seventies, Dr. Tom Garrett researched the Sportsman quite extensively.

He discovered that there were three different wood types used in the cars, which he called A, B and C, although B and C were practically identical. The main difference was that the A style had horizontal pieces running full length across the doors and quarters. In the B and C styles, the full-length members ran vertically from top to bottom. All 1946 Sportsmen used the A panels, whereas '47s were divided between all three. The Sportsman also used 1941 Ford taillamps and rear fenders from the sedan delivery, as did the station wagon. These fenders did not wrap

around as in other body styles. Otherwise, all other sheet metal was standard Super Deluxe Ford or Mercury convertible. Garrett also discovered that only the Sportsman had hydraulic, power window lifts, same as the 1946 Lincoln convertible. Ford and Mercury convertibles could not be so equipped. On the Sportsman, the color of the plastic on the control buttons was maroon, not white as on the Lincoln.

Dr. Garrett concluded that the total number of Sportsmen built was 3,392, quite a bit higher than the Krause Publications figure. We would presume that this figure included the Mercurys, but Garrett noted that not even the Ford Archives knew how many Mercury

The Phantom '46 Ford

It still obsesses me in my dreams, 42 years after I last saw it. Not a week goes by that I don't dream of my dad's gun-metal gray 1946 Ford club coupe. It glides along Central Avenue and Stinson Boulevard in Minneapolis, where I grew up with that car. It visits every one of Minnesota's 10,000 lakes. It haunts ghost towns in Nevada and Arizona. I try to forget it by reading books about the *Titanic.* Then I dream we are all standing on the deck of the *Queen Mary* and the Ford is stored below ready for a holiday in England or Ireland.

That car really did exist. My dad took delivery on a sunny day in July 1946, from C.E. Johnson Motor Sales on North Broadway, in Minneapolis. But it might have been a '46 Mercury. That's what he wanted; Mom didn't want to pay the price. Dad never had a new car in the thirties. Nobody had a new car after World War II broke out. The first thing Dad did when the new cars were announced in 1945 was visit the Lincoln-Mercury dealer in downtown Minneapolis. I was with him on the day he specified a maroon '46 Mercury club coupe. But he soon found that not only did the car list for $188 more than a Ford Super Deluxe, he would have had to take a package of options that brought the total price up to about $1,800. But he

could have had almost immediate delivery. Appalled at the slickness of the Lincoln-Mercury dealer, he went across the street to the crowded Ford showroom where he got pretty much the same line for a few hundred dollars less, and no promises at all on delivery date. Eventually he made his way out to C.E. Johnson in the blue-collar part of town, where delivery was promised in about three months and he could have a maroon Ford Super Deluxe club coupe with no options for the list price of $1,295. Delivery actually took nine months, but the price of $1,295 remained. It is because of this experience in my childhood that every detail of Fords and Mercurys of 1946-48 sticks in my mind like it was only yesterday.

I personally think that the '46 Ford Super Deluxe was a more stylish looking car for a bit less money. The Mercury's trim was a bit overdone. The ride of both cars is identical. Tom McCahill commented in 1946 on how completely gadgetless the '46 Mercury was. For example, he noted that the choke was still manually operated. He could have said the same about the Ford. Wonderful cars from a halcyon time that still tugs at the strings of my subconscious.

specifications

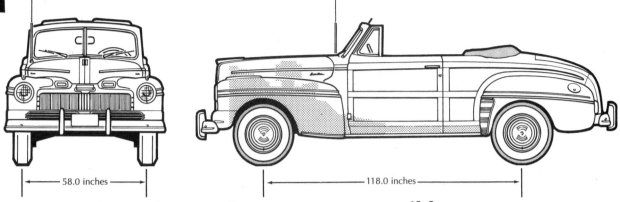

← 58.0 inches →   ← 118.0 inches →

1946 Mercury Sportsman convertible coupe

Price when new	$2,209 f.o.b. Dearborn
Options on this car	Radio, heater, twin rear-view mirrors, turn signals, windshield washers, white sidewall tires, Columbia overdrive

ENGINE

Type	L-head V-8, cast en bloc, water-cooled, 3 mains, full pressure lubrication
Bore x stroke	3.1875 inches x 3.75 inches
Displacement	239.4 cubic inches
Compression ratio	6.75:1
Max. bhp @ rpm	100 @ 3,800
Max. torque @ rpm	180 @ 2,000
Induction system	2-bbl Holley downdraft carburetor, mechanical fuel pump
Exhaust system	Cast-iron manifolds, crossover pipe, single muffler
Electrical system	6-volt battery/coil

TRANSMISSION

Type	3-speed manual, 2-3 synchro, column lever
Ratios: 1st	3.11:1
2nd	1.77:1
3rd	1.00:1
Reverse	4.00:1

CLUTCH

Type	Single dry plate, woven asbestos lining
Diameter	10 inches
Actuation	Mechanical, foot pedal

DIFFERENTIAL

Type	Hypoid, spiral bevel gears
Ratio	3.54:1 (2.70:1 with Columbia overdrive engaged)
Drive axles	3/4 floating

STEERING

Type	Gemmer worm and roller
Turns lock-to-lock	4.5
Ratios	18.2:1
Turning circle	40 feet

BRAKES

Type	4-wheel hydraulic drums, internal expanding
Drum diameter	12 inches
Total lining area	169.92 square inches

CHASSIS & BODY

Frame	Channel-section steel, central X-member
Body construction	Wood-paneled steel
Body style	5-passenger convertible coupe, hydraulic top and windows

SUSPENSION

Front	I-beam axle, transverse leaf spring, tubular hydraulic shock absorbers
Rear	Solid axle, transverse leaf spring, tubular hydraulic shock absorbers
Tires	6.50 x 15, 4-ply tube type
Wheels	Pressed steel, drop-center rims, lug-bolted to brake drum

WEIGHTS AND MEASURES

Wheelbase	118 inches
Overall length	201.8 inches
Overall width	74 inches
Overall height	62 inches at top of windshield
Front track	58 inches
Rear track	60 inches
Ground clearance	8.5 inches
Curb weight	3,407 pounds

CAPACITIES

Crankcase	5 quarts
Cooling system	22 quarts
Fuel tank	17 gallons
Rear axle	3 pints

FUEL CONSUMPTION

Best	22 mpg (with overdrive)
Average	16 mpg

PERFORMANCE

Top speed	85 mph
Acceleration: 0-30 mph	7.9 seconds
0-50 mph	15.1 seconds
0-60 mph	19.4 seconds
0-70 mph	27.3 seconds

Source: *Mechanix Illustrated*, 1946

Right: Hydraulic window lifts were standard in both Merc and Ford Sportsman. Facing page: Transverse leaf spring may have been technically archaic, but it does outstanding job of roadholding under all conditions.

1946 MERCURY

Sportsmen were built. We do not know where the figure of 205 comes from. It is the one cited in all catalogs and books. A more recent figure quoted in some publications is 3,730 for all Sportsmen, and there may be an explanation for this: 723 Fords were produced for the 1946 model year, 2,274 for 1947, and 28 were sold as 1946 models. The actual 1947 figure may have been 2,774. Curt Heaton also owns the last Ford Sportsman built and the number of that one is 3,725.

The wood for all Sportsmen and wagons was solid maple framing with mahogany panels. There was no bending or laminating of the body panels as in 1949-51 Ford wagons. The trunk plywood panel was originally molded in a compound curve using a special machine. Duplicating the original Sportsman body is no job for the amateur. Even skilled, professional cabinetmakers have trouble fabricating these bodies. The cost of building a Sportsman body today can easily run $10,000 or more.

Some special notes on this sole original Mercury Sportsman: Don Narus purchased this car from Franklin Ledru Moody of Orwell, Ohio, in 1973. Moody was the second owner. He had bought the car from Bartholomew Motor, Inc. of Warren, Ohio, in 1949. They had sold it new to a steel executive whose name seems to have fallen into the sands of

time. Narus kept the car for a few years and then sold it to the aforementioned Dr. Tom Garrett. When Narus acquired the car it was pretty rough, having been in a dirt-floor barn in Northeastern Ohio for many years. Evidently Narus became discouraged with the restoration. We do not know how many hands it went through before the restoration was completed. Don Newby purchased the car from one Bruce Feight. The car arrived in boxes, completely disassembled. Most of the restoration work was done while Newby owned the car. Newby sold it to Bob Dixon of Rockford, Illinois, and somehow it got into the hands of the late Wisconsin classic-car dealer, Bob Adams. Adams sold it to a Tom Dero,

and eventually it was passed on to Curt Heaton in California.

Driving Impressions

The first two cars that Tom McCahill ever tested for *Mechanix Illustrated* were the 1946 Ford and Buick for the February 1946 issue. He loved the Ford, hated the Buick. In the July 1946 issue he tested the Mercury, commenting: "I selected Southern California and the tough Hollywood hills for giving the Mercury a real workout. I knew how the engine would perform, for I had just driven one of these new engines from coast to coast and purposely abused it whenever the going got tough. With a

1948 Mercury Wins the 1951 Mexican Road Race

During the early fifties, the Mexican Road Race or Carrera PanAmericana, became one of the great automotive contests of the world. Today, over 40 years later, the races are being run again, although on a less grand scale.

In the 1951 race, a 1948 Mercury club coupe gained headlines in the racing car world by placing fourth overall. Driver Troy Ruttman and co-pilot Clay Smith bought the Merc on a used car lot in the Los Angeles area for $1,000. Smith, perhaps the finest race-car mechanic of the day, went through the car, had all critical parts magnafluxed, bored out the block one-eighth inch, presumably had the engine balanced, added Edelbrock heads, Edmunds two-carb manifold, split exhaust headers, increased the oil

capacity and installed a larger radiator core and sway bar. He installed a Kong distributor, reworked the springs, added four more shock absorbers, and put vents in the backing plates of the brakes. Total investment: $2,500. Top speed: 115 mph.

The second Mexican Road Race was run in November 1951 from Tuxtla Gutierrez, 244 miles north of the Guatemalan border, to Ciudad Juarez, on the Rio Grande, across from El Paso, Texas. The first and second place cars were Ferraris; third place went to a Kiekhaifer Chrysler. Against such odds it's amazing that the Mercury placed at all, let alone finished fourth. Those were the days when anything could happen in racing, and usually did.

*This page: Sportsman's appearance combines a unique look of fun and tradition. Front seating is generous. **Facing page, top:** Flathead V-8's rated at 100 bhp. **Center left:** Rare accessory tire pump in driveReport car. **Center right:** Dash is full of chrome and woodgrain. Complete tool kit's also a rarity. **Bottom:** Lettering on glove box is pure 1940s.*

1946 MERCURY

fully loaded car, I never once took it out of high while crossing some of the toughest passes in the Rockies and later the High Sierras. At times my speed had been reduced from 70 to as little as 15 mph, but it was still in high and kept going without a buck. Across Texas and through Arizona I had driven this new engine as much as 650 miles in a day, several times covering as much as 70 miles in a single hour; so I can say with assurance that if there is an engine around that will top the Mercury for high-speed cruising, and I mean an engine that does it without strain or heating up, then I don't know about it." (He never mentioned that it was the same identical engine as the Ford.)

McCahill went on to say, "When I took

the new Mercury from the Ford Long Beach Plant, I was interested in finding out if the rest of the car was as good as the engine. To test the riding qualities, I slammed it over bumps and road holes which it took in its stride with indifferent ease. For hill climbing, I tried it in the Hollywood hills. On one of the severest tests I give cars, that of slowing down to around 10 mph in high and then giving it full throttle just as I reach a steep grade, the Mercury took hold and gathered speed. Even though it is definitely not a mountain goat, it's doubtful if you will ever have to shift, and it will, in its own sweet time, take any grade that comes along."

If you've ever driven a '42 or '47 Ford or Mercury, you will wonder if the '46 models have lost some of their punch. This is because the 1946 models have a 3.54:1 rear-end ratio, as opposed to 3.78:1. This means that a lot of other makes will take them up to 40 mph, but

over this figure they really come into their own. Interestingly enough, the Ford has a higher top speed than the Mercury because it has 16-inch wheels as opposed to the Mercury's 15-inch. For this same reason the Mercury has better pickup than the Ford. But you can cruise effortlessly in either make all day at 70 mph.

Roadability is outstanding, even by standards of modern cars. Whoever said that old Henry Ford's transverse springing was antiquated obviously preferred Buick's marshmallow ride. No other car of the period hangs into the corners like a 1946-48 Ford or Mercury and still gives excellent high speed ride and control. This author wouldn't argue a bit with McCahill when he wrote that the '46 Mercury "cannot be surpassed and is rarely equaled by the most expensive cars made."

This particular car is equipped with Columbia overdrive. This gives an "overdrive" ratio of 2.70:1, which is considerably lower than the 3.54:1 ratio that McCahill commented upon. Postwar Columbia overdrive had an automatic electric control. To shift into overdrive you merely press a toggle switch lever and then push out the clutch pedal. The car remains in overdrive until it is brought to a complete stop. With the Columbia engaged at highway speeds, revolutions per minute are cut from about 2,450 to 1,820, for a significant increase in fuel economy and engine life.

Granted, the open Mercury, especially with the wooden body, does not have the quiet of the enclosed car. The 100-plus pounds of extra weight over the sedan does take away from performance, but not a lot. This fully restored body is remarkably free of squeaks, as we suspect any Mercury or Ford Sportsman was in 1946. Overall, it's a superb automobile, and a fine example of everything

a flathead Ford should be. In driving any Ford or Mercury of this period, we have to wonder how much automobile technology has really progressed in 50 years. 👓

Acknowledgments and Bibliography

"1946 Ford road test," Mechanix Illustrated, *February 1946;* "1946 Mercury road test," Mechanix Illustrated, *July 1946;* "1947 Ford and Mercury road test," Mechanix Illustrated, *August 1947;* "1947 Ford Sportsman drive-Report," Special Interest Autos #10, *April-May 1972;* "Sportsman Expert, Dr. Tom Garrett," Ford Life, *November-December 1970;* Standard Catalog of Ford, 1903-1990, *Krause Publications.*

Special thanks to Curt W. Heaton, Corona Del Mar, California, for furnishing our driveReport car and providing historical data.

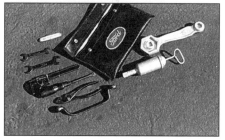

Canadian Conversion

Ford of Canada's rendition of a restyled Mercury: the 1947 Monarch Convertible

By Tim Howley
Photography by David Gooley

Compared to most cars of the day, the 1947 Monarch is a breath of fresh air to drive. The car has all the driving characteristics of a 1947 Mercury or Ford, cars that were considered antiquated in their day by all but hot rodders. In 1947, Ford's Model T transverse springing was regarded by the competition as a joke. But it provides for a remarkably agile car more than a half century after it was built, a car that is surprisingly well suited to today's driving conditions. In fact, if you were to pick an old car to use as a daily driver it would be hard to make a better choice than any 1946-48 Ford or Mercury, including this 1947 Canadian Monarch.

Ford built cars in Canada since 1904, when one Gordon McGregor secured a franchise from Henry Ford to assemble in Canada. And right up until World War II, Ford of Canada had 40 to 50 percent of the Canadian market. But General Motors embarked on major expansion in Canada right after the war. Ford of Canada answered with its own expansion plans. Up until this time a single network of dealers handled all Canadian-built Ford and Mercury cars and the Lincolns imported from the United States. When Lincoln became a separate division in 1946, a second dealer group was given an exclusive franchise for Mercury and Lincoln. This hurt the Ford dealers even more than GM. Furthermore, Mercury offered Canadian Mercurys on both 114- and 118-inch wheelbases. A 221-cu.in. flathead V-8 was exclusive to the 114-inch wheelbase model, while the 118-inch wheelbase models carried Ford and Mercury's larger, 239.4-cu.in. flathead. Only the 118-inch-wheelbase Mercury was built in the U.S. The purpose here was to better compete with GM, but the result was more competition with Canadian Ford dealers.

Canadian Ford dealers, left without a medium-priced line, quickly came out with a slightly restyled Mercury of sorts, on a 118-inch wheelbase, and called it the Monarch. It was offered at one trim level and in five body types for 1946 and 1947: sedan coupe, Tudor sedan, Fordor Town sedan, convertible, and wooden-bodied station wagon.

For 1949 the Monarch was continued on the Mercury body, and the smaller Mercury, utilizing a 1949 Ford body, was renamed the Meteor. Both Monarch and Meteor continued through 1961. The Monarch name was revived on the 1975 Mercury version of the Granada, while the Meteor name returned in 1961 as a series of the full-sized Mercury, then became the compact Mercury introduced for 1962.

The Fords and Mercurys from the 1946-48 era have weathered the years amazingly well. When I last owned one in 1972 they were coming on strong as collector cars, yet still served well as daily drivers. Now, nearly three decades later, they are more popular than ever with collectors and seem to have a timeless ability to keep up with modern traffic. The reasons why these cars are still

Originally published in Special Interest Autos #183, May-June 2001

"hanging in there" in all respects are threefold—ageless styling, engineering that has adapted itself to 21st century driving conditions, and a cottage industry of parts unequaled by any other marque of the period.

Our driveReport Monarch is a fascinating combination of Ford and Mercury, with a different badge and built under a different flag. The frame is a 118-inch Mercury, four inches longer than a Ford. The extra four inches are located up front, which accommodates a 100hp, 239.4-cu.in. flathead V-8, same as Ford and Mercury. The grille shell is based on the 1947 Mercury and had Mercury's unique lower catwalk area, which means front fenders are not the same as Ford. But the trim is not Mercury. Both inside and outside it whispers 1946 Ford, but it's "not exactly" a Ford either.

The 1947-48 models are especially adaptable to modern driving, due to their 3.78:1 rear axle ratio. This Monarch has a 4.11:1 rear gear (when the overdrive is not engaged). This makes the car a star performer in climbing the many hills we encountered in the suburbs just east of San Diego. The Monarch took to all but the steepest grades like a greased arrow, and in high gear. As a 1947 Ford-Mercury, it is the best American hill climber of its day. Obviously it's not a mountain goat like most modern cars, but it is certainly no slug in the hills, like its 1947 competitors.

At any speed above 15 mph, the car handles nearly as well as a modern mid-sized car. I experienced very little lean in the turns and hardly knew I was driving a vehicle without power steering. This was mostly due to the transverse springing, which many considered obsolete in 1947. After more than 50 years, Henry Ford has had the last laugh from the grave. No other car of the period corners as well as Fords and Mercurys from the Forties, and few from their era could out-accelerate them. Admittedly, the car's ride is pretty stiff, but I did not find the stiffness objectionable.

However, there are some downsides to driving this 1947 Monarch. The 12-inch drum brakes were barely adequate in their day, and their shortcomings are even more obvious now. While the Monarch charged up the hills effortlessly, it took all the foot pressure on the brake pedal I could muster coming down, and I found myself constantly shifting into second gear to keep from going off the road on those steep downhill corners.

It was hard to judge this car from the point of quietness and ride because it's a convertible. Closed Fords and Mercurys from the Forties were quite tight and rattle free, every bit as quiet on the inside as Chevrolets and Pontiacs, although not nearly as comfortable. You sit high in the front seat, with an excellent view except in the rear quarters when the top is up. The body of this convertible was solid as Plymouth Rock, and there was a total absence of rattles and squeaks.

While the seating is comfortable enough when the road is straight, I found myself constantly sliding on the slippery cowhide in the turns. The seats provide no side or shoulder support whatsoever. Coming out of my 1992 Lincoln Town Car, which I drive daily, I had a hard time getting used to the "hard bench" driver's seat in the Monarch. But in the interests of keeping the car pure, you just wouldn't put bucket seats in your Monarch

Mercury front end sports a Ford-like grille.

because that's not the way Ford addressed driver comfort way back then.

All of the instruments are well placed and easy to read; the controls are simple and straightforward. I praise the car's handling in the turns. Where I miss the power steering is when parking at curbside, or even turning into a driveway. That big Ford steering wheel requires all the muscle of an old-time bus driver at any speed below about 15 mph. Conversely, out on the highway the Monarch is a pleasure to drive, especially when the Columbia overdrive is engaged. The car will keep up with modern traffic all the way to 70 mph, and lack of seat support is only a minor objection when you are going in a straight line. The 100hp flathead Ford V-8 was superb in its day, and still is. It is quiet, powerful, and extremely long-lived, using today's detergent oils. You can drive a car like this all day long on the Interstate without getting tired. Little wonder that in the late Forties Ford and Mercury were the first choice of salesmen. It was the bad roads that fatigued the drivers, not the Fords.

At higher speeds the Ford or Mercury could outdistance all price rivals; they were among the best high-speed cruisers ever built in the country, prior to 1949. But even with the same gear ratio in the two cars, the Ford had a slightly higher top speed than the Mercury due to its larger-diameter, 16-inch wheels, against Mercury's 15-inch. The smaller wheels were an advantage off the line, which is why the Mercury accelerated slightly faster. It is gratifying that so many of these cars are still being driven cross-country to car meets, especially to the Early Ford V-8 Club's meets. While owners of other makes brag about their modern trailers, early Ford V-8 people brag about how they travel 2,000 miles in less than four days!

Of course, any old car today is only as good as its parts sources. There are so many parts suppliers around today for all early V-8 Fords, 1932 through 1953, that you would literally have to be driving across the Sahara Desert or Siberia to be more than a 100 miles from one or more parts sources. Or, to put it another way, the parts supply for your 1946-48 Ford-built car is every bit as good as

Everything on the woodgrained dash, including the big speedo and clock, are well placed.

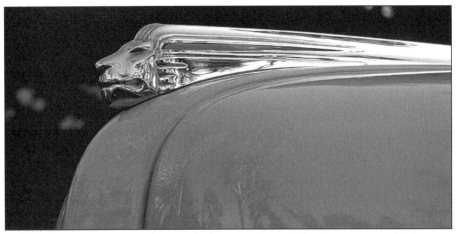
Unique to the Monarch is the lion symbol that's used on the hood ornament and hubcaps.

Emblem with scripted logo very elegant.

Adorned taillamps now sport blue dots.

PARTS PRICES

Rebuilt carburetor $195
Complete brake rebuild kit $170
Clutch/pressure plate $155
Starter..$90
Centerlink $85
Engine gasket set..$82
Universal joint..$45
Fuel pump $44
Door mirror...$38
Taillight assembly...$30
Distributor cap and rotor $21

WHAT TO PAY

Low	Average	High
$10,000	$17,000	$24,000

CLUB SCENE

International Mercury Owners Association
6445 West Grand Ave.
Chicago, IL. 60707-3410
773-622-6445
Dues: $35/year; Membership: 1,000

Early Ford V-8 Club of America
P.O. Box 2122
San Leandro, CA 94577
925-606-1925
Dues: $30/year; Membership: 10,000

that car lovers the world over won't still be driving 1946-48 Fords and Mercurys 100 years from now if parts can still be found and if the price of gas hasn't risen to $100 per gallon. Expect to get 12 to 15 mpg average and close to 20 with overdrive engaged.

When owner Bob Sobrito set out looking for a Forties Ford convertible, he had no idea he would luck into one of the rarest of them all. Sold by Canadian Ford dealers as part of an upscale car line, only 40 Monarch convertibles were built for 1947, 52 for 1946, and none for 1948. This makes it even rarer in its day than the 1947 Mercury Sportsman we tested in *SIA* #152, March/April, 1996 (205 produced, only one survivor). Since finding this car, fully restored, in Huntsville, Alabama, in 1996, Bob has never seen another but has heard there may be one in Florida.

The authentic Ford Maize Yellow paint was on the car when he bought it, but he had to repaint the hood and trunk lid due to body damage. Bob had to go through the entire brake system and take out the transmission for repair. While the transmission was being rebuilt, he installed a Columbia two-speed rear.

At the time Bob bought the car it had a radio with foot and push-bar control, Ford spotlight, blue dot taillights, beauty rings, bumper wings, and Ford dealer twin rear-view mirrors. He has since added backup lights and a dealer accessory light under the hood. The fog light switch has a light which lets you know when the fog lights are on. He also has found the correct Ford glove-box light and foot lights that go up under the instrument panel and go on when you open the doors. Most of these items came from watching ads in *Hemmings Motor News*.

for a late-model Dodge, Saturn or Toyota!

While styling is always subjective, Ford styling from about 1938 through 1948 has never gone out of style. As a matter of fact, this high art-deco styling may be more appealing now than it was 50 or 60 years ago. To many, modern aerodynamics is just old Bob Gregorie and Edsel Ford basics warmed over. These were clean designs when new, and they remain clean as ever as we enter the 21st century. Who's to say

Addition of a Columbia overdrive makes cruising at highway speeds very pleasurable.

Other performance alterations Bob made to the car were the installation of Fenton headers and a dual exhaust system for some extra power, exchanging the generator for an alternator, and installing an electronic ignition within the old distributor. He has also installed an electric fuel pump and has two sets of tires. The original bias-ply tires and rims are strictly for car shows, while a set of steel-belted radials are for driving. While this car is restored to show condition, Bob is primarily interested in driveability and reliability, not trophies. He enters local shows and cruise nights, but he has never entered it in Early Ford V-8 Club of America competition, where it would only be accepted in a new class for custom-modified cars, definitely not in the Touring Division, Rouge, or Dearborn Divisions. Even though this car is as stock as Murphy's pig on the outside, there are considerable concessions to today's driving conditions underneath.

Bob hasn't had any difficulty finding parts, and even most of the Monarch trim parts can be bought off Canadian Ford parts cars. There may be no convertible parts cars available, however the trim can be sourced from the several thousand closed Monarchs built in Canada in those years. Bob has seen all of the Monarch trim parts advertised except for the Monarch lion hubcaps, which he believes may be impossible to find.

Overall, the 1946 Fords and Mercurys are considered works of art by many Ford enthusiasts. But for the 1947-48 models, Ford nickled and dimed these cars to death by putting cheap touches everywhere, such as the elimination of the wind-wing cranks on the Ford models, and cheapening the instruments, upholstery, and trim on both makes.

Firm three-on-the-tree shifting very precise.

Hidden ash tray atop dash slides open.

Hard to find hubcaps feature lion emblem.

FoMoCo heater ideal for southern climates.

PARTS SUPPLIERS

American Parts
3075 Lexington Rd.
Dept. SIA-183
Richmond, KY 40475
859-624-1942
Quality used body and trim parts

Antique Ford V-8 Parts
658 Buckley Hwy.
Dept. SIA-183
Union, CT 06076
860-684-3853
Mechanical and electrical parts, shock absorber rebuilding

Baxter Ford Parts
131 Arkansas Street
Dept. SIA-183
Lawrence, KS 66044
785-842-9256
NOS, rebuilt and used mechanical, electrical and trim parts

Bob Drake Reproductions
1819 N.W. Washington Blvd.
Dept. SIA-183
Grants Pass, OR 97526
800-221-FORD (3673)
www.bobdrake.com
Reproduction body, trim and interior parts

C & G Early Ford Parts
1941 Commercial St.
Dept. SIA-183
Escondido, CA 92029
760-740-2400
www.cgfordparts.com
Chrome trim, emblems, weatherstripping and wiring

Dennis Carpenter Reproductions
4140 Concord Parkway
Dept. SIA-183
South Concord, NC 28027
800-476-9653
www.dennis-carpenter.com
Plastic, rubber, chrome and mechanical components

Early Ford Parts
2948 Summer St.
Dept. SIA-183
Memphis, TN 38112
901-323-2179
Interior and body trim

Early Ford V-8 Sales
Bldg. 37 Curtis Industrial Park
831 Rt. 67
Dept. SIA-183
Balston Spa, NY 12020
518-884-2825
www.earlyford.com
New and used parts

Engineering & Manufacturing Services
P.O. Box 24362
Dept. SIA-183
Cleveland, OH 44124
216-541-4585
Reproduction sheetmetal and weatherstripping

Garton's Auto
401 North 5th St.
Dept. SIA-183
Millville, NJ 08332-3129
609-825-3618
Fenders, grilles, bumpers and radiators

Joblot Automotive
98-11 21 211th St.
Dept. SIA-183
Queens Village, NY 11429
718- 468-8585
Mechanical and electrical parts

Kanter Auto Products
76 Monroe St.
Dept. SIA-183
Boonton, NJ 07005
800-526-1096
Engine, brake and suspension parts

LeBaron Bonney
P.O. Box 6
6 Chestnut St.
Dept. SIA-183
Amesbury, MA 01913
800-221-5408
Reproduction interiors and tops

Little Dearborn Parts, Inc.
2424 University Ave. SE
Dept. SIA-183
Minneapolis, MN 55414
888-282-2066
Upholstery, carpeting and panel sets

Mac's Antique Auto Parts
1051 Lincoln Ave.
Dept. SIA-183
Lockport, NY 14094
800-777-0948
www.macsautoparts.com
Repro weatherstripping, interior and trim

Obsolete Ford Parts
8701 South I-35
Dept. SIA-183
Oklahoma City, OK 73149
405-631-3933
Mechanical, electrical, and trim parts

Old Ford Parts
35 4th Avenue N.
Dept. SIA-183
Algona, WA 98001
253-833-8494
New mechanical and trim parts

Patrick's Antique Cars and Trucks
P.O. Box 10648
Dept. SIA-183
Casa Grande, AZ 85239
520-836-1117
Pistons, cylinder heads and engine rebuild kits

PMX Custom Alternators
8420 SE Hinckley
Dept. SIA-183
Portland, OR 97266
503-777-7172
Alternator kits for flathead V-8s

illustrations by Russell von Sauers, The Graphic Automobile Studio

© copyright 2001, Special Interest Autos

specifications

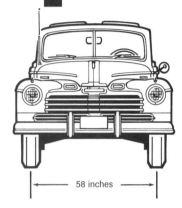

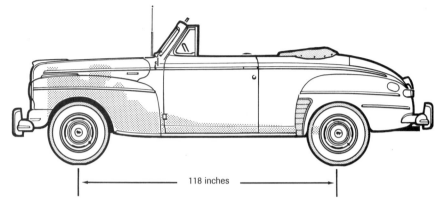

← 58 inches →

← 118 inches →

1947 Monarch convertible

ENGINE

Type	L-head V-8, cast-iron block, water-cooled, pressure lubrication
Bore x stroke	3.1875 inches x 3.75 inches
Displacement	239.4 cubic inches
Max. bhp @ rpm	100 @ 3,800
Max. torque @ rpm	180 @ 2,000
Compression ratio	6.75:1
Main bearings	3
Induction system	Holley 2-bbl downdraft carburetor, mechanical fuel pump
Exhaust system	Cast-iron manifolds, crossover pipe (now modified with headers and dual exhaust)
Electrical system	Generator (now modified w/ alternator and electronic ignition)

TRANSMISSION

Type	3-speed selective manual, column-mounted control; synchronized second and third gears

CLUTCH

Type	Single dry disc
Outside diameter	10.0 inches
Actuation	Mechanical, foot pedal

Differential

Type	Spiral bevel gears, torque tube drive
Ratio	4.11:1 (2.70:1 with Columbia overdrive engaged)
Drive axles	3/4-floating

STEERING

Type	Worm and roller
Turns lock-to-lock	4.5
Ratio	18.2:1
Turn circle	40 feet

BRAKES

Type	4-wheel hydraulic drums, internal expanding
Drum diameter	12 inches
Total swept area	162 square inches

CHASSIS & BODY

Frame	Channel and box section steel, central X member, double dropped
Body construction	Rigid all steel bolted to frame
Body style	5-passenger, 2-door convertible

SUSPENSION

Front	I-beam axle, transverse leaf spring, stabilizer bar, lever shock absorbers
Rear	Solid axle, transverse leaf spring, lever shock absorbers

Tires	6.00 x 15 inch 4-ply tube type
Wheels	Pressed steel discs, drop-center rims, lug-bolted to brake drums

WEIGHTS AND MEASURES

Wheelbase	118 inches
Overall length	201.75 inches
Overall height	69.0625 inches (sedan)
Overall width	73.5 inches
Front track	58 inches
Rear track	60 inches
Ground clearance	6.82 inches
Shipping weight	3,368 pounds

CAPACITIES

Crankcase	5 quarts
Cooling system	22 quarts
Fuel tank	17 gallons

FUEL CONSUMPTION

Average	12-15 mpg

Monarch's speaker grille and stainless trim around the gauges were unique to the Mercury.

For 1947 Mercury eliminated the trip odometer, but it was still used in the Monarch, which changed very little from 1946. And the heater-defroster, which was standard equipment on the Monarch, was not standard on U.S.-built Fords and Mercurys at the time.

All told, there were 3,851 Monarchs built for the 1946 model year, 6,670 for 1947, and 723 for 1948. Then production rose to 11,317 with the new 1949 model. Still, this is nothing compared to Ford and Mercury production for these years, making any Monarch of the period quite rare. Monarch grilles in 1946 are slightly different than the '47 grilles, and there are other very minor trim changes between the two years.

On the exterior, most of the trim is neither Ford nor Mercury but is unique to the car, including side and rear stainless, Monarch Lion hood ornament, insignias, and Monarch Lion hubcaps. Some of the side stainless may be the same as on the 1947 Mercury; we are not quite sure. The parking lights are 1946-48 Mercury, while the taillamps are 1946-48 Ford. The interior trim is more 1946 Ford than anything. The instrument panel on the 1947 Mercury was much different than the 1947 Ford. The Mercury instrument panel plastic encircled the speedometer and clock but did not extend over the gauges and glove box as on the Ford. The radio speaker grille and stainless steel trim around the gauges and on the glove box were unique to the Mercury. So were all the instrument faces.

The Monarch, meanwhile, has the 1946 Ford instrument panel plastic, only it's a greenish gray as opposed to the Ford's light pearlescent gray. There's a similar plastic piece repeated on the glove box, and plastic as opposed to stainless steel surrounds the gauges; this is all unique to the Monarch. The radio grille is 1946 Ford design with three stainless stripes instead of one and the 1947 Monarch insignia added to the grille. The speedometer and clock are 1946 Ford design, but whereas these Ford items have red numerals on a black background, the Monarch has white numerals on a silver background. The speedometer has a trip meter. (The 1946 Ford never had this item, and Mercury eliminated it in 1947.) The steering wheel is a greenish gray, mottled-composition material, colored to match the instrument panel plastic. The horn ring carries the Monarch Lion and is a unique design to the Monarch. The instrument panel woodgraining is very dark as opposed to the Mercury's, which is very light.

In all probability, the Monarch trim was developed in the Ford design studio in Dearborn. Clay mockups from the period indicate that the grille was an offshoot of wartime designs. Unfortunately, books on Ford design of the period say nothing about the Canadian cousins, relatives that any car collector would be proud to have in the family.

🔊

Transverse springing, albeit stiff, provides flatter cornering than its competitors of the era.

Big wheel needed to combat heavy steering.

Flathead V-8 makes 100hp and 180-lbs.ft.

Added seatbelts increase backseat safety.

Spare tire uses lots of room in deep trunk.

From the Driver's Seat

During my high school years in the 1950s, I fell in love with the style and beauty of the 1940s-era Fords. I owned two Ford Tudor sedans during that time and have always dreamed of owning a convertible. Some forty years later, I found myself in a position where I could afford both the time and upkeep to indulge my teenage fantasy.

The feeling of driving the Mercury gives ultimate satisfaction. Acceleration is brisk, and the ride is fairly smooth. An aftermarket Columbia two-speed differential and modern radial tires allow highway speeds in excess of 60 mph. Steering is light at speed, but parallel parking, even with the large steering wheel, requires lots of shoulder muscles. Although the suspension consists of front and rear single transverse-leaf springs, the rear torsion bar permits surprisingly nice handling. Thanks to modern DOT 5 silicon brake fluid, the brakes give exceptional stopping power for an early postwar car.

With plenty of cushion, you really sink into the front seats, and starting the car is a sequence of events. First, turn the key to unlock the wheel, then activate the ignition by flipping a toggle switch. Next, pull out the choke and push in the starter button. Sit a few minutes for the engine to warm up and, little by little, push in the choke.

The Mercury is fun to drive with the top down, though with the top up and windows closed, wind

noise is fairly noticeable. Front passengers have good protection from the wind, but the rear passengers really get blasted at speed. Rear- and driver's side-view mirrors give good visibility, but the passenger's side mirror doesn't have enough adjustment to be useful.

My wife Agnes and I enjoy cruising around the San Diego area and are amazed at the number of people who appreciate the Monarch's style and beauty. We get a lot of horn toots and thumbs-up, and it's gratifying to see people's faces light up with a smile of recognition.

By Bob Sobrito

By Arch Brown
Photos by Vince Manocchi

IT WAS 1949, a year of transition from the familiar world of prewar times to the excitement — and yes, the anxiety — of a new, technologically sophisticated age.

Twenty-four years earlier, in 1925, Americans had excitedly tuned in on their crystal sets and heard the first broadcast of an inauguration. It was for President Calvin Coolidge.

1949 MERCURY STATION WAGON

The Senator's Campaign Companion

This time it was Harry S. Truman who was taking the oath, and we could actually see the inauguration, on television. A B-47 bomber made a 2,269-mile, transcontinental flight in a record-shattering 3 hours, 46 minutes. The jet age had arrived, though few of us comprehended, yet, the changes it would bring to our lives.

When a series of blizzards isolated two million cattle and sheep in snow-bound areas of the western states, five tons of hay were dropped by C-82 "Flying Boxcars" to save the stranded animals from starvation. They called it "Operation Haylift."

Meanwhile, a similar mission was under way in Europe, as the "Berlin Airlift" continued to bring food and other supplies to that blockaded city. Only this time it wasn't livestock whose lives were at stake, it was people.

And Detroit found itself facing a buyer's market for the first time in eight years.

The Motor City was ready. Most of the independents had already introduced their newly designed models, stealing a march on their larger competitors. But by early 1949 all the manufacturers (and there were a lot more of them then than now!) had new, really new cars in their showrooms.

Unequivocally, no other manufacturer was displaying automobiles that were as new — that is to say, as completely changed — as the cars from the Ford Motor Company. Ford, Mercury and Lincoln all differed radically from their immediate predecessors.

It had taken something of an industrial miracle to bring about this rapid and drastic changeover. For at war's end, Ford's far-flung domain had been in almost total disarray, its very survival in doubt.

But a new leadership team was in place. Henry Ford II, in many respects infinitely more farsighted than his famous grandfather. had persuaded Ernest R. Breech (see sidebar, page 39) to leave the comfort and security of the presidency of Bendix and take his chances with the rapidly sinking Ford enterprise. And Breech, in turn, had brought aboard a talented group of executives, most of them recruited from General Motors' various divisions. Breech knew all about "crash" programs of product development: he had experienced little else in four years with Bendix. Now, drawing upon that experience, he did the same thing at Ford.

Fortunately, some good developmental work had already been under way, under the direction of E.T. "Bob" Gregorie. Two new Fords had been planned, one of them a "compact" — though George Romney had not yet coined the term — and the other a considerably larger automobile than any previous Ford.

They wouldn't do. On the one hand, Americans were in an extravagant mood; the time was clearly not right for a small, austere economy car. So the little machine was shipped off to Ford of France, where it became the highly successful Vedette.

That left the proposed "big" Ford. Too big. It's a safe bet that Ernie Breech was privy to what was being planned at General Motors. The Chevy, he knew, was already 115 pounds lighter than its counterpart from Ford, and the '49 model was projected to be lighter yet. And here was Ford with a proposal that would substantially increase both the heft and the price of its new car. In the hotly competitive postwar market that Breech correctly foresaw, Ford could hardly afford to be so seriously out of step.

And so, as recounted in *SIA* #5, a

Originally published in Special Interest Autos #81, May-June 1984

design competition was held for the development of a new Ford of more modest size and weight. Ford Motor Company's own head of design, "Bob" Gregorie, submitted a proposal. So did free-lancer George Walker. The Walker design was selected, and five days later Gregorie resigned.

But apart from its size and projected cost, there really wasn't anything the matter with that original Gregorie design. It was a handsome, impressive car. Clearly it didn't belong in the low-priced field, but moved up a notch it should do very well.

And indeed it did, for Gregorie's "big Ford" became the 1949 Mercury.

The '49 Lincoln, introduced on April 22, 1948, was the first of the true postwar cars to come from one of America's "Big Three" manufacturers. The new Mercury followed a week later, with the Ford making its appearance in June. Together they represented a radical departure from Ford tradition; not since the Model A replaced old Henry's ubiquitous T, more than two decades earlier, had Ford so drastically changed its product line,

Gone, for example, were the archaic transverse springs to which the elder Ford had stubbornly clung. Instead, these cars featured a thoroughly modern suspension system: independent coil springs at the front, longitudinal semi-elliptics at the rear.

Gone, too, was the stodgy styling theme, held over from 1941—and virtually indistinguishable between Mercury and Ford. This time the Merc actually shared the body shell of the base Lincoln. Compared to the 1948 model it was 5 inches longer, over 3.5 inches wider, nearly 4.5 inches lower and—nevitably, 132 pounds heavier. No more could the Mercury be thought of as a "glorified Ford." Rather, it had become "Everyman's Lincoln,"

The contrast between the 1949 Mercury and Ford serves to illustrate why Ernie Breech had sent his people back to the drawing boards. Wheelbases remained unchanged—118 inches for the Merc, 114 for the Ford. But while the 1949 Ford was shedding 216 pounds, the Mercury was gaining (in sedan form) an extra 88. The smaller car varied little in length, and its overall width was an inch and a half narrower than before—while the Merc grew in every dimension save height.

It's not that this sleek new Mercury was totally new—nor was the Ford, for that matter. Under the hoods of both cars resided the familiar flathead V-8, its stroke lengthened by a quarter of an inch in the Mercury application in order to compensate for the additional weight it had to carry. For the same reason, there was a numerical increase in the axle ratio. The Mercury valued its reputation for sparkling acceleration!

Facing page: Up front, Mercury's styling gives it a somewhat chubby-cheeked appearance. **This page, above:** Along with body styling, ultra-modern hood ornament was new for '49. **Below:** In the tradition of woodie wagons, spare tire rides on outside of tailgate.

Probably the engine was the least advanced and the least desirable part of the car. For although the hoary V-8 was fast, smooth and tough, it continued to be plagued by the twin problems of overheating and vapor lock. Even an over-size cooling system, with a capacity nearly double that of the Buick Super, failed to correct the situation.

But there was nothing to be done about that. Neither time nor available funding permitted the development of a new powerplant—yet. That part would simply have to wait.

Never mind; the engine was adequate for the present, and the styling was sensational. And the car was a bargain!

Substantially larger in every dimension than Oldsmobile's new 88 series, the Merc undersold the Olds by $234—a price differential of ten percent!

Not a single body panel interchanged between the new Mercury and the Ford. That had been true in 1939-40, too, but in those days the two cars had looked very much alike. The 1949 models, however, having sprung from different design studios, bore little resemblance to each other. With one exception: the station wagon.

Ford, of course, had been primarily responsible for popularizing the woodie, and throughout the thirties and forties had dominated the market. Four-door

jobs they had been, with bodies crafted of fine hardwoods.

For 1949, however, Ford developed a totally different body, evidently in the hope of inaugurating two new design trends, For starts, the structure was partially of steel, with wood used liberally for trim, as well as for certain structural parts. It was probably safer, certainly more durable than the previous type; a substantial improvement. It didn't take rival manufacturers long to follow suit—and indeed to go Ford one better with the introduction of all steel bodies.

The other big switch was to a two-door configuration. This one isn't quite so easy to understand, for access to the third seat in a two-door wagon is difficult, and its cargo area can't be loaded from the sides—an important plus for the four-door style, as any wagon owner can attest. And although the two-door arrangement was popular for a number of years in such utility vehicles as Plymouth's Suburban (see *SIA* #72), it failed to make the grade with upscale vehicles like the Mercury. When the 1949-51 styling cycle had run its course, Merc wagons were once again accessible through four doors.

Meanwhile, however, the two-door styling and part-steel construction probably gave Mercury (and Ford) a little price advantage compared to the four-door, wooden-bodied competition. It's interesting to note that, while the Dodge Coronet sedan was $104 cheaper than the Merc, in station wagon form the Dodge was the costlier of the two by a margin of $167.

In one sense especially, however, that station wagon body was a very clever piece of work. It was adaptable to either the Ford or Mercury chassis—pulled in a little at the front doors, in the former case, in order to match up with the narrower front sheet metal of the smaller car.

It was, like all wagon bodies — especially in those days—heavy, out-weighing the sedan, in the case of the Mercury, by 240 pounds. (The differential was 530 pounds as applied to the Ford, suggesting that this may have been basically a Mercury body adapted for use on the Ford, rather than the other way about.)

Driving Impressions

It seems to us that the '49 Mercury wagon would make an excellent traveling companion for just about anyone. It's roomy, comfortable, and plenty fast enough for anybody with any sense at all! Evidently our feeling was shared by Arizona Senator Barry Goldwater, because for the first 21 years of its life our driveReport car was owned by the senator, carrying him through many a political campaign—including, of course, his ill-fated try for the presidency in 1964. One can readily visualize a huge set of loudspeakers fitted to the Mercury's heavy-duty roof rack, and can't you almost hear Barry Goldwater's gravelly voice making a pitch for the conservative cause he has always espoused?

Today, the Merc belongs to Tom and Donna McArdle, of Granada Hills, California, and they were kind enough to permit us to take it for a romp as this driveReport was being prepared.

The first impression of the car is one if ample space. Head room, for instance: A man could wear a top hat in this Mercury! Seats are wide, the front one especially, and if leg room is a little tight in the second and third seats, it's more than sufficient up front. The third seat is perched high—Tom and Donna's kids love it—and Tom tells us it can be reversed, if anyone wants an "observation car" view. The cargo area would be

Mercury Versus The Competition

From 1933 until the close of the decade of the thirties, Dodge had been the sales leader of the lower-medium price field, with Pontiac hard on its heels. In 1940-41 their positions were reversed, but when World War II drew to a close, Dodge moved into the lead once more—if only briefly.

But in the meantime a newcomer had entered this hotly competitive field: Mercury. With a production total of just over 76,000 cars in its first year, the Merc's position was a distant third to its two major competitors, yet it had managed to upstage such established marques as De Soto and Nash. It was a promising start.

Over the next two years, until war intervened and put a stop to civilian automobile production, Mercury's output remained almost level while Pontiac, in particular, was taking off in spectacular fashion. There must have been anxiety in Dearborn, for the Mercury was failing to fulfill its early promise.

In the immediate postwar years, demand was such that every automobile manufacturer could sell all the cars its factories could build; production was limited only by the availability of materials. Mercury, during those years, managed to increase its market penetration, despite the fact that its 1946-1948 models differed little from the division's 1941 car.

But with the introduction of the 1949 model, Mercury began to score. By 1950 it had elbowed Dodge out of second place in its price class; and although it bobbled a bit in 1951-52, Ford's newest automobile had found its place in the sun—and in the American motorist's heart.

CALENDAR YEAR PRODUCTION, 1939-1954

Year	Mercury	Dodge	Pontiac
1939	76,198	186,474	170,726
1940	82,770	225,595	249,303
1941	80,085	215,575	282,087
1946	70,955	156,080	131,538
1947	124,612	232,216	222,991
1948	154,702	232,390	253,472
1949	203,339	298,399	336,466
1950	334,081	332,782	469,813
1951	238,854	325,694	345,617
1952	195,261	259,519	278,140
1953	320,369	293,714	415,335
1954	256,730	151,766	370,887

(War years, 1942-1945 are omitted.)

Source: Heasley, Jerry, The Production Figure Book for U.S. Cars.

Right: Wagon holds nine adults, even more kids. *Far right:* Second seat also folds for access to rear. *Below:* Wheel cover design is plain and simple. *Bottom:* Distinctive slotted grille was carried over to 1950 models.

generous with the rear and center seats removed.

We found the driving position to be very comfortable, the seat pleasantly supportive. It's not a car that would break your back on a long drive. It's easy to understand the senator's choice of this one for his campaign tours.

The wagon is nicely finished. Door panels are mahogany, and of course the exterior hardwood is birch with mahogany inserts, a nice complement to the maroon paint. With one exception, the body construction appears to be very solid and sturdy. That one drawback is the doors. Tom reports that in time they tend to sag. This car, having recently been expertly restored, shows no evidence of any such problem.

The Merc's performance is just what we expected it to be: responsive and fairly lively. The clutch engages smoothly; shifts are easy. Steering, though quite slow, is light and reasonably precise. There's plenty of acceleration, and power to spare when it comes to passing. At 65 miles an hour, the wagon settles into a comfortable cruising speed. The engine is busy, but not straining. The Borg-Warner overdrive, a Mercury option in 1949, would have been a good investment. Even without it, though, the McArdles report a highway average of 16 miles to the gallon.

The Merc does not take kindly to lugging at low speeds. Not even in second gear. The V-8 engine needs to wind up a bit before it's ready to flex its muscles! Here again, the overdrive would be helpful, especially in view of the station wagon's weight, since it was used in combination with (numerically) higher differential gears.

Old Henry Ford's stubborn resistance to hydraulic brakes had been overcome a decade before this Mercury was built,

Roof rack gives Merc the illusion of being taller than it actually is.

Ernest R. Breech: The Man Who Saved Ford

There are people who simply cannot resist a challenge. And seemingly, the more formidable the odds, the more appealing the venture!

Such a man was Ernie Breech.

Only in his mid-thirties when he undertook to put the struggling North American Aviation Corporation on its feet, he went on to become a prime trouble-shooter for General Motors before accepting the presidency of Bendix Aviation in 1942. Shortly thereafter he became chairman of the Central Aircraft Council, charged with the responsibility of organizing the aircraft industry in such a manner that—in the interest of furthering America's war effort—information, production methods and even tooling would be freely exchanged among rival manufacturers.

At Bendix, meanwhile, life consisted of one "crash" program after another: a solid fuel injection system, for instance, designed to prevent the engine fires that had plagued the B-29 bomber. And a gyroscopic compass, impervious to the magnetic pull that had created severe problems for planes flying near the north pole. These developments were round-the-clock efforts, compressing into a few short months work that would ordinarily have taken years to complete.

Within a year of Breech's election to its presidency, Bendix production had trebled.

In the meantime, following the death of Edsel Ford in May 1943, the Ford Motor Company was floundering. Henry Ford was no longer fully competent, and the highly centralized Ford organization found itself functioning virtually without a head. So serious was the situation that President Franklin D. Roosevelt actually considered the possibility of a government seizure of the company, lest its vast facilities be lost to the country's war production program.

Instead, the president called for the release from active duty with the Navy of Henry Ford II, the old man's grandson, evidently in the hope that the young man would be able to hold the company together and sustain its output.

Somehow, it worked. Young Henry proved to be both shrewd and tough. By 1944 Ford was making nearly half of all the B-24 "Liberator" bombers then being produced. A

year later that figure had risen to 70 percent. Other military hardware being turned out by Ford included aircraft engines, gliders, tanks and tank engines, jeeps and military trucks.

But then the war ended, and young Ford—who took over the presidency of the company from his rapidly failing grandfather on September 25, 1945—was faced with the critical task of reconversion to peacetime production, as well as that of developing, posthaste, a completely revamped product line.

Henry Ford II was a very bright young man—bright enough, certainly, to recognize the limitations imposed by his own inexperience. It was apparent to him that the Ford Motor Company would have to be completely reorganized—decentralized, in the interest of accountability, and modernized throughout. He chose the General Motors organization as his model, but he needed just the right man to spearhead his reorganization effort.

It was evidently Ernest Kanzler, Henry's uncle by marriage and a close friend of his late father, who first suggested Ernest R. Breech as the man best qualified to revamp the Ford Motor Company. Young Henry, familiar with Breech's reputation, was quick to agree. Selling Breech on the idea proved to be more difficult, but in the end he came aboard, on July 1, 1946. In explaining his decision to his wife, Breech observed, "Here is a young man only one year older than our oldest son. He needs help. It's a great challenge, and if I don't accept it I shall always regret it."

A great challenge indeed! Even the optimistic, self-confident Ernie Breech described it as "almost overwhelming." As he later observed, "[We] faced the postwar market with run-down plants, obsolete products, almost nonexistent financial control, an inadequate engineering staff, and just sufficient cash to meet daily operating requirements. As we looked forward to the future, we saw that we would be unable to last when the competitive market returned, unless we remade ourselves completely into a strong, modern, going concern."

Breech might have added that Ford's labor relations, and indeed employee morale even

in the upper echelons, still suffered from the years of intimidation experienced at the hands of the malevolent Harry Bennett.

And worst of all, Ford was losing money at the rate of nearly $10 million a month!

Quickly, Breech put together a new management team. Some of its members came from within the Ford organization, but most of his "top hands" were men with whom he had worked at General Motors:

• Lewis D. Crusoe, formerly assistant treasurer at GM, became Ford's chief fiscal officer. A precise man with rather a sharp tongue, he was not universally beloved, but he got the job done.

• Harold T. Youngren, chief engineer at Borg-Warner and an alumnus of GM's Oldsmobile Division, undertook to reorganize Ford's engineering department.

• Delmar S. Harder, who had formerly supervised production at General Motors, assumed the same responsibilities at Ford.

Then, drawing upon his wartime contacts, Breech brought aboard Albert J. Browning, formerly merchandising manager for Montgomery Ward and more recently the director of purchasing for the War Department. He undertook a similar assignment at Ford.

The new team took hold promptly and functioned smoothly from the start. By 1947 the losses which had so dangerously bled the Ford Motor Company had been turned around; a profit of over $66 million was shown for the year!

Ernie Breech remained with Ford until 1967—first as executive vice president, then (in 1955) as the company's first chairman of the board, and finally, after his retirement from active management in 1960, as a member of the board of directors.

One might expect that Breech would have had enough of trouble-shooting. But in the 1960's, responding once again to an appeal for help, he became board chairman of Trans World Airlines, and under his guidance that troubled organization became, within four years, the second most profitable airline in the world!

In June 1978, Ernest Robert Breech, then 81 years of age, suffered a massive heart attack. A few days later, on July 3rd, he died.

But what a legacy he left!

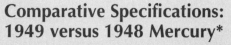

Comparative Specifications: 1949 versus 1948 Mercury*

	1949	1948
Shipping weight	3,430 pounds	3,298 pounds
Engine displacement	255.4 cubic inches	239.4 cubic inches
Horsepower @ rpm	110/3,600	100/3,800
Torque @ rpm	200/2,000	180/2,000
Compression ratio	6.80:1	6.75:1
Horsepower per c.i.d.	.431	.418
Weight per horsepower	31.18	32.98
Weight per c.i.d.	13.43	13.78
Choke	automatic	manual
Drive	Hotchkiss	Torque tube
Rear axle	Hypoid	Bevel gear
Final drive ratio	3.91:1	3.78:1
Brake lining area	179.0 square inches	162.0 square inches
Lbs. per sq. in. (lining)	19.2	20.4
Front springs	Individual coil	Transverse leaf
Rear springs	Semi-elliptic/long.	Transverse leaf
Tire size	7.10 x 15	6.50 x 15
Front tread	58.5 inches	58 inches
Rear tread	60 inches	60 inches
Wheelbase	118 inches	118 inches
Overall length	206.8 inches	201.75 inches
Overall width	76.9 inches	73.25 inches
Overall height (no load)	64.8 inches	69.063 inches

*Figures refer to 4-door sedans

and we found the binders to be very good. With relatively moderate pedal pressure they bring the heavy wagon to a halt quickly, smoothly and in a straight line.

This is a low-mileage automobile. The clock registered 73,080 when we picked it up for this report, and the reading is documented as original. Evidently Senator Goldwater used the car very little, except for campaign purposes. Nor was it given heavy use by its second owner, a Utah furniture dealer who acquired it in 1970. The third owner, a Los Angeles collector named Rich Farr, overhauled the engine, and finally the cosmetic restoration was done for the present owners by Ernie Kay.

Come to think of it, you may have seen this Mercury before, on your television screen. Just recently it played a part in a commercial for Charlie perfume.

And that figures. It's a nice automobile. ◌

illustrations by Russell von Sauers, The Graphic Automobile Studio

© copyright 1984, Special Interest Autos

specifications

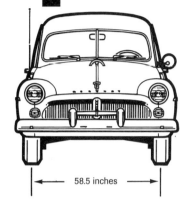

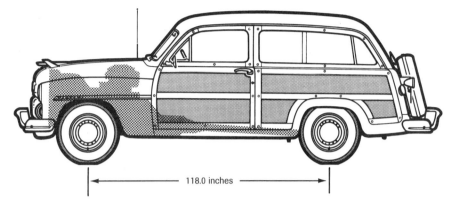

58.5 inches

118.0 inches

1949 Mercury

Price $2,716 f.o.b. factory, with standard equipment (as of 5/7/49). Federal excise tax and handling charges included

ENGINE
Type	L-head V-8
Bore x stroke	3.3125 inches x 4 inches
Displacement	255.4 cubic inches
Compression ratio	6.8:1
Max. bhp @ rpm	110 @ 3,600
Max. torque @ rpm	200 @ 2,000
Induction system	Holley downdraft dual concentric carburetor, mechanical fuel pump
Lubrication system	Full pressure
Electrical system	6-volt

TRANSMISSION
Type	3-speed selective, synchronized 2nd and 3rd gears
Ratios: 1st	2.8:1
2nd	1.60:1
3rd	Direct
Reverse	3.62:1

CLUTCH
Type	Single dry disc
Outside diameter	10 inches
Actuation	Mechanical, foot pedal

DIFFERENTIAL
Type	Hypoid
Drive	Hotchkiss
Ratio	3.91:1
Drive axles	Semi-floating

STEERING
Type	Gemmer worm and roller
Ratio	18.2:1
Turns lock-to-lock	4.75
Turning radius	21' 10"

BRAKES
Type	4-wheel hydraulic, drum type
Drum diameter	11 inches
Total braking area	179 square inches

CHASSIS & BODY
Construction	X-type
Body construction	Steel with wood overlay
Body style	2-door station wagon, 8 passenger

SUSPENSION
Front	Independent, coil springs
Rear	Semi-elliptical longitudinal leaf springs
Tires	7.10 x 15
Wheels	Pressed steel

WEIGHTS AND MEASURES
Wheelbase	118 inches
Overall length	206.8 inches
Overall width	76.9 inches
Overall height	64.8 inches
Front track	58.5 inches
Rear track	60.0 inches
Ground clearance	7.8 inches
Shipping weight	3,626 pounds

PERFORMANCE
Weight per hp	33.0 pounds
Weight per c.i.d.	14.2 pounds
Hp. per c.i.d.	431
Top speed	80 plus mph (est.)

Facing page, top left: Merc's sturdy flathead V-8 developed 110 bhp. *Below left:* With third seat out and tailgate down, there's room for lots of cargo and six passengers. *Top right:* With third seat in, it's a handy observation deck for younger passengers. *Middle right:* Up front, driving position is roomy and comfortable. *Bottom right:* Although the Mercury was all-new in 1949, the split rear window is a throwback to earlier days of station wagon design. *This page, left:* Wagon weighs nearly 200 pounds more than its sedan counterpart, so it's not exactly a ball of fire through the gears. As a highway cruiser, however, it's more than satisfactory.

1950 Mercury vs.
1950 Oldsmobile 88

By Tim Howley
Photos by the author

SINCE much has already been written here on the 1949-50 Mercury (see *SIA* #12 and #81) and Olds 88 (see *SIA* #1), we will only highlight their histories as we compare the two in detail. The Mercury was the car that should have been the '49 Ford but got bumped up a notch when Henry Ford II's new management in 1946 decided to build the '49 Ford from a clean sheet of paper. The Mercury was designed during World War II as a Ford, and did not change a great deal except for grille treatment. It stood on a 118-inch wheelbase, measured 206.8 inches overall, and in the 1950 club coupe version weighed 3,430 pounds and listed for $1,980. Mercury only built a club coupe, not a two-door sedan, but the rear seat space was somewhat greater than that of the Olds two-door, and was much greater than that of the Olds club coupe. The Mercury body was shared, not with Ford, but with the junior Lincoln. The frame was shared with the Lincoln, which had a three-inch-longer wheelbase. The flathead V-8 engine is nearly identical to the Ford's, except for one quarter inch more stroke, which gave it 255.4 c.i.d., compared to the Ford's 239.4, which meant a 10-horse-power increase to 110 at the same 3,600 rpm.

It is significant to note that the 1949-51 Mercurys were engineered under Harold T. Youngren, who came over from Olds about the time that the Rocket V-8 engine was put into development.

The 1949-50 Olds had its own frame and suspension, shared with no other make in the GM camp. The 88 series stood on a 119½-inch wheelbase, measured 202 inches overall, and in the 1950 Deluxe two-door-sedan version weighed 3,490 pounds and listed for $1,982. HydraMatic was a power option in Oldsmobile, not available on the Mercury, but available on the junior Lincoln. While the Olds frame and suspension were unique, the 88's A body was shared with Chevrolet and Pontiac. What made the Olds 88 50 special was the 303-c.i.d., ohv V-8, developing 135 horsepower at 3,600 rpm. The engine was derived from the Olds 98 and was put in the 76 series early in the 1949 model year, creating not only the 88 but the dawn of the high-performance era.

With all of this in mind, we know that the Olds 88 is going to win our comparison on a pure performance basis. But what about the other qualities? Suspension, handling, ride, economy, comparative quality of the two vehicles? We vent into this comparison believing that the Olds would win on just about every count. Some of the answers we got, however, came as quite a surprise. Even a bit of a shock.

Styling

While styling is highly subjective, in

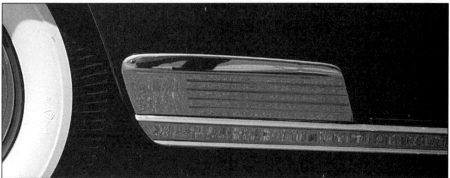

Above: *Olds and Merc stylists had very different approaches to design of gravel shields.* ***Below:*** *Same goes for sidelamps, with Olds's unique vent-style treatment vs. Merc's rather ordinary solution.*

retrospect we found that the Merc definitely has the edge. Like "Miss Daisy's" 1948 Hudson, it had great forties styling that has gone full circle and is now back with us again in the latest international aerodynamic creations. We feel that the 1949-50 Merc is as contemporary looking today as it was four decades ago. Like *Rebel Without A Cause*, the James Dean Mercury is timeless. The Oldsmobile's '49 Chevrolet body, on the other hand, appears to us as just more dated. It's shorter than the Mercury by nearly five inches, despite a slightly longer wheelbase. Even though the Olds and Mercury are nearly the same height, the Mercury appears lower, due to its design. The Mercury is 1.7 inches wider than the Olds on the outside, but appears to be much wider. While the Olds is far better trimmed and detailed than the Chevrolet, its low-priced body heritage still shows.

Interiors

Both makes have high-quality, comfortable interiors. Instrumentation on both is excellent, with full sets of gauges and excellent instrument visibility. The Mercury dash is patterned after the Lincoln, the Olds after the Cadillac. But the Mercury dash is just a bit better detailed, as is the entire Mercury interior. For example, the Mercury has decorations on the window sills and rear-seat ash trays, plus cord handles on the front seat backs and large, thick arm rests in the rear. The Mercury seat material and design also appears to be of better quality, although we were comparing an original Mercury interior with an extremely well done but replacement interior on the Oldsmobile.

The Mercury clearly has the advantage on interior dimensions. It is six inches wider at the center cowl to afford a four-inch-wider front seat and wider, deeper rear seats. The Mercury has considerably more leg and foot room front and rear. Three inches less head room in the Mercury is not really a disadvantage because the seats are slightly lower than in the Olds. In short, the Mercury is a big, roomy car in the Lincoln tradi-

Above: Hood emblems use a stylized coat of arms for Mercury, a stylized globe to tie in with Olds's "rocket" theme. *Below:* Olds taillamp treatment grew backup lamps in 1950; Mercury carried over '49 taillamps.

tion. And even though it is a club coupe, it still has more rear seat room than the Olds two-door sedan. This is not to say that you feel cramped in the Olds. The body is simply limited to Chevrolet/Pontiac interior dimensions. We further noted that the fancy horn ring on the Olds is an extra, standard on the Mercury, and the Mercury steering wheel is somewhat better positioned than on the Olds. Small items, you might say, but we think important.

However, one interior area where the Olds is far superior is visibility. The Olds has a nice big, curved, one-piece windshield. By contrast, the Merc has a squatty, flat, two-piece windshield. The Olds side windows are one inch higher. The Mercury has many more blind spots, especially in the rear. The rear blind spot was corrected in 1951 with a much larger rear window. The Olds visibility is so good it is associated with much later cars. We can only describe the Mercury visibility as no better than that of 48 Packards and Hudsons. Obviously we are dealing with a design of the past as opposed to a design of the future.

Body Construction

Here, again, we're dealing with a fairly subjective subject. But we couldn't help note that the Mercury doors had a solid, heavy, big-car sound and feel when we closed them. To a lesser degree, this was true in closing the hood and trunk. We're not criticizing the Olds body construction, we're just pointing out its Chevrolet derivation, compared to a

Mercury and Oldsmobile in the Mobilgas Economy Runs

While it might easily be argued that the Mobilgas Economy Runs proved considerably less about economy than the Mexican Road Races proved about performance, nobody would deny Mercury's inherent good gas mileage in its last flathead years.

Mercury came into the spotlight when a 1950 four-door sedan driven by Bill Stroppe and co-piloted by Clay Smith took the sweepstakes award at 61.27 ton-mpg and 26.52 mpg. This is the same Bill Stroppe who co-piloted the Mantz Lincoln in the first Mexican Road Race.

Could anybody else receive such amazing results? Probably not. While the car was admittedly stock, Stroppe and Smith removed the engine and all its components at their Long Beach speed shop. Everything was carefully checked and rebuilt if there were any doubts. The engine was balanced and super-tuned with the most sophisticated equipment available at the time. Remember, beginning in 1952,

Stroppe and Smith's specially prepared Lincolns came to absolutely dominate the Mexican Road Races with this kind of treatment

In the 1950 Mobilgas Run, the cars were driven from Los Angeles to the South Rim of the Grand Canyon, a distance of 751.3 miles. They went from downtown Los Angeles traffic and smog to below sea level in Death Valley to snow covered mountain peaks. The average speed was 40.6 mph and the average fuel economy was 22.074 mpg for 31 cars. In addition to winning the Sweepstakes award, here's how Olds stacked up in its class, Class D, which included the Olds 88:

	MPG.	TON MPG
Mercury	26.52	61.27
Nash Ambassador	26.42	58.46
Studebaker Commander	23.79	52.65
Hudson Pacemaker	22.60	52.25
Oldsmobile 88	20.19	47.60
De Soto Custom	18.78	43.43

The 1951 course was essentially the same route, extended to 840 miles. The winning car was a baby Lincoln four-door sedan entered by Bob Estes Lincoln-Mercury, Inglewood, California, prepared by Stroppe and Smith and driven by Les Viland. Like the Mercury of the previous year, it had a stick shift and overdrive, even though HydraMatic was available on Lincoln at the time. The Lincoln averaged 25.448 mpg and 66.484 ton mpg.

Mercury won again in 1952. This time Stroppe was driving again in another Bob Estes entry. It was a Monterey four-door sedan with a mpg figure of 25.4 and a ton mpg figure of 59.7118. This year the run was 1,415 miles going from Los Angeles to Sun Valley, Idaho.

In 1953 Les Viland won the Sweepstakes with a Ford six. Mercury was never a serious contender again.

Mercury body derived from a Lincoln.

Frames and Suspension

The Mercury frame is the X member type with K reinforcement. Independent A-arm front suspension replaced the earlier I-beam axle. Coil springs, tubular hydraulic shocks and a stabilizer bar were employed. Longitudinal leaf springs at the rear replaced the old Ford transverse springs, which had been used on all Fords (front and rear) since before the Model T. Hotchkiss drive replaced the old torque tube, and hypoid gears were used instead of the spiral bevel type. Three-quarter floating rear axles of previous days were replaced with hypoid semi-floating axles. While all of this was new to Ford, none of it was new to the industry.

While the Olds's frame and front suspension were quite similar to the Mercury's, the Olds has additional coils at the rear wheels and sway bars both front and rear to dampen sideway better than the Mercury. Like the Mercury, there were tubular shocks at all four wheels. Drivetrain and rear axles were the same as the Mercury's. The difference was that Olds had employed this type of drivetrain and rear end for years.

Engines

The Mercury 255.4 flathead might best be described as an excellent, time-proven power plant which had reached the limit of its performance potential. It had its origins in the old Leland L-head V-8 of the twenties and the Ford flathead V-8, introduced in 1932. In 1950 Ford was still the world's largest producer of this type of engine. The engine reeked of reliability and simple straightforward design that had been refined to the ultimate degree over the years. But its days were numbered, and the 6.8:1 compression ratio was about as high as Ford flathead compression was going to get. By 1953, the last year of Ford flathead production, the engine was a dinosaur living in a contemporary body. The Olds Rocket 88 engine, on the other hand, was only at the beginning of its performance potential. Olds began developing its own ohv V-8 powerplant in 1946, the same year as Ford. Only, with a decade of Cadillac development experience behind them, they were able to get the new engine into production in three years. Ford's first ohv V-8 did not appear until 1952 in the Lincoln and 1954 in the Ford and Mercury. Even then it left something to be desired in the latter versions. The Ford ohv V-8s were developed as a corporate family of engines. The Olds ohv V-8 was developed quite independently of Cadillac from 1946 on. While it is similar in concept to the Cadillac engine, the two share no interchangeable parts, and their carburetor setups were quite different. (This is also mostly true of the

Top: Rocket ornament says it's an Olds, but what does the Merc ornament represent? *Above:* Both cars have a good-looking rear trim/bumper guard appearance. *Below:* Merc has a bit of the "aero" look of today. Olds looks more like typical 1950 design.

three Ford engines.) Knowing that L-head-design engines had a compression ratio limit of about 8:1, Olds engineers came up with an engine that could accommodate compression ratios up to 12.5:1. In the original form, the Rocket 88's compression ratio was 7.25:1, and it never did get much beyond 10:1. The engine was designed for economy and to take advantage of the new, high-octane fuels coming on the market. Competition was never in the minds of Olds engineers, evidenced by the Division's halfhearted support for stock-car racing and unwillingness to carry performance parts on the shelf until much later.

The Oldsmobile Division in the late

forties was about as liberal as William F. Buckley, Jr. But when, for experimental purposes, they dropped their new Rocket V-8 in a Series 76 Olds (the one with the Chevrolet body), they immediately saw the potential. With reluctant corporate approval, the Olds 88 was born, and made its showroom debut in February 1949, nearly three months after the 1949 Olds Rocket 98 came on the market. The stock car fraternity took to the new car instantly. Olds 88s dominated the first Grand National seasons in 1949 and 1950; won the Daytona Beach Speed Week in 1950; and an Olds also won the first Mexican Road Race in 1950. The winning Olds,

Above: Leaf springs at rear hold Merc flatter through corners than Olds's all-coil layout. *Below:* Both cars use high quality materials inside.

SIA comparisonReport

piloted by young Hershel McGriff, was a two-door sedan, much like our driveReport car but not equipped with HydraMatic.

Transmissions

The only transmission available on a 1950 Mercury was a three-speed manual, 3.91:1 rear-end ratio in the standard version, 4,27:1 with overdrive. Ford did not offer Merc-O-Matic until 1951. The Olds HydraMatic had been around since 1940. The rear axle ratio was 3.64:1 with the three-speed manual transmission or with HydraMatic. Even though HydraMatic was an extra cost option on the 88, it was not easy to find one

equipped with the three-speed for this only year it was offered. The three-speed was a short-tailshaft version of the memorable Cadillac/LaSalle side shifter of the late thirties. Unfortunately, Olds did not offer an overdrive.

Driving Impressions

Our two test cars were about as evenly matched as you are going to get in 41-year-old automobiles, from the standpoint of comparable condition. The Olds 88 two-door sedan is a frame-up, high quality restoration with just under 40,000 miles since the restoration was completed about six years ago. The car is owned by Larry Volk, Rialto, California, a lifelong hot rod and custom car enthusiast; thus his early Olds 88 interest. The Olds is as stock as they came, save the "fuzzy dice" on the rearview mirror. Larry drives the car regularly on

car tours in the Riverside area, and keeps it in top performing condition.

The Mercury club coupe is a bona fide 38,500-original-mile car that was originally from Pasadena, California, and once was in Harrah's Automobile Collection. Harrah's sold it to a private collector in the early seventies, when they obtained the original James Dean 1949 Mercury club coupe used in the 1954 motion picture *Rebel Without A Cause.* The present owner is Ed Rouhe, DDS, of Riverside. He is the second owner since Harrah's. Dr. Rouhe has a large collection of Mercurys and assorted other makes, and has a particular penchant for fine, original, low-mileage cars. Like Volk, he keeps the Mercury in top performing condition, but does not drive it regularly.

The Olds has HydraMatic, the Mercury has overdrive. That's just what we wanted for our comparison. We were especially fortunate to find two owners living close by and perfectly willing to put their fine cars through all the paces, letting the chips fall where they may, and in this case they really did.

The '50 Olds 88 still has the performance edge after all these years. Only we expected we would feel the difference in driving the two cars. We didn't. *Motor Trend* tested them both in 1950. The Merc stayed with the Olds up to 30 mph. But the Olds's 0-60 time was nearly four seconds faster. The Mercury continues to fall behind after 60. In actually driving the cars, we found the HydraMatic had an annoying jerk when it shifted. It is a slightly rough transmission by today's standards, and the slippage was quite evident. This was not the fault of the transmission rebuild. This was how those earlier HydraMatics behaved when they were new. Conversely, the standard Mercury transmission shifted like butter and was as smooth as anything we've ever experienced in the era. With the overdrive disengaged, the Mercury lacks little in performance by 1950 standards, until the Olds confidently moves out in front at around 35 mph. By the time the Merc gets up to 70, the Olds is far down the road. That's when you realize you're driving a car whose years were numbered in 1950. *Motor Trend*'s 1950 test figures showed it this way:

1950 Mercury

0-30 mph	. . . . .4.55 sec.
0-40 mph	. . . . .7.80 sec.
0-50 mph	. . . . .11.00 sec.
0-60 mph	. . . . .15.98 sec.
0-70 mph	. . . . .21.40 sec.
Standing 1/4 mi.	.20.88 sec., 69 mph
Top speed	. . . . .83.75 mph

1950 Olds 88

0-30 mph	. . . . . . .4.60 (Dr), 3.99 (Lo)
0-60 mph	. . .12.44 (Dr), 12.22 (Lo-Dr)
10-60 mph in high	. . . . . . .11.91 (Dr)
30-60 mph in high	. . . . . .11.96 (4th), 8.45 (3rd)

Standing 1/4- mi . . . . . . .20.47 (Dr),
19.86 . . . .(Lo-Dr)
Top speed . . . . .92.11 mph

Tom McCahill was fortunate enough to obtain a 1950 Olds 88 two-door with a standard transmission and tested it for *Mechanix Illustrated*, July 1950. He reported the following results, which were predictably even better than with the four-speed HydraMatic. Wrote Uncle Tom:

"The fastest time I've ever recorded for an Olds 88 HydraMatic is 0 to 60 in 13.4 seconds, and I've tested quite a few. In the Olds 88 conventional (rough shift and all) I did 0-60 in 12 seconds flat, which is a new American stock car record for this run. Zero to 30 mph, average 4.4 seconds; zero to 60 mph, 12 seconds flat average; 0-70 went 16.8 and zero to 80 took 21.9 seconds. After 85 mph, the Olds's terrific acceleration starts to flatten out considerably. Best top speeds over a measured mile in almost a dead calm, on east and west runs, were 96.4 and 96.9 mph. One half mile from a standing start, through the gears, took 30 seconds flat.

("Note: Best time we have recorded for the Olds HydraMatic for a half-mile from a standing start was 31.5 seconds.)

"This means that at a half-mile from a standing start and all other regular *MT* acceleration or pickup tests for a 50-mile spread (40 to 90 mph), the Oldsmobile with conventional transmission is America's top performing car. However, it can be beaten top and bottom. The Ford 6 will outjump it up to 30 mph on getaway, and several cars will take it for top speed, including Cadillac and Lincoln."

Dash layouts on both cars have complete gauges, but Olds's, above, is a bit easier to read at a glance.

Specifications: 1950 Mercury and Olds 88

	Mercury	Oldsmobile
Price (f.o. b. factory)	$1,980	$1,982
Model tested	Club coupe	Two-door sedan
Optional equipment	Radio, whitewall tires overdrive, heater/defroster turn signals.	HydraMatic, radio, deluxe steering wheel, whitewall tires, rear fender skirts turn signals.
ENGINE	90-degree flathead V-8	Ohv V-8
Bore & stroke	3 3/16" x 4"	3 3/4" x 3.4375"
Displacement	255.4 cubic inches	303.7 cubic inches
Max bhp. @ rpm.	110 @ 3,600	135 @ 3,600
Max torque @ rpm.	200 @ 2,000	263 @ 1,800
Compression ratio	6.8:1	7.25:1
Valve configuration	L-head	Overhead
Valve lifters	Mechanical	Hydraulic
Main bearings	3	5
Induction system	Dual downdraft carburetor, camshaft pump	2 bbl. downdraft carburetor, automatic choke.
Exhaust system	Single	Single
Electrical system	6-volt	6-volt
TRANSMISSION	3-speed selective manual with overdrive	HydraMatic 4-speed automatic with fluid torque converter, 2 planetary gears
Ratios	1st: 2.82:1	1st: 3.82:1
	2nd: 1.60:1	2nd: 2.63:1
	3rd: 1:1	3rd: 1.45:1
	Overdrive: 0.72:1	4th: 1:1
	Reverse: 3.62:1	Reverse: 4.31:1
DIFFERENTIAL	Hypoid	Hypoid
Ratio	4.27:1 (3.91:1 std.)	3.64:1
Drive axles	Semi floating	Semi floating
STEERING	Gemmer worm & roller	Saginaw worm & roller
Turns lock-to-lock	5.25	4.5
Ratio	18.2:1	19:1
Turn circle	43 ft.	40 ft.
BRAKES	4-wheel hydraulic drums, internal expanding	4-wheel hydraulic drums, internal expanding
Drum diameter	11 inches	11 inches
Total swept area	159.1 sq. in.	191.7 sq. in.
CHASSIS & BODY		
Frame	Channel-section steel, X and front K members.	Channel-section steel, X-member double dropped.
Body construction	All steel	All steel
Body style	2-door six pass. coupe	2-door six pass. sedan
SUSPENSION		
Front	Independent A-arms, coil springs, tubular hydraulic shocks, linked stabilizer bar	Unequal A-arms, coil springs, double-acting lever shocks, anti-roll bar.
Rear	Solid axle, longitudinal semi-elliptic leaf springs, tubular hydraulic shocks	Solid axle, coil springs, lever shocks, control arms, anti-roll bar
TIRES & WHEELS		
Tires	7.10 x 15 tube type, 4-ply	7.60 x 15 tube type, 4-ply
Wheels	Pressed steel, drop center rims, lug bolted to brake drums	Pressed steel, drop center rims, lug bolted to brake drums
WEIGHTS & MEASURES		
Wheelbase	118 inches	119.5 inches
Overall length	206.8 inches	202 inches
Overall height	65 inches	64 inches
Overall width	76.9 inches	75.2 inches
Front tread	58.5 inches	57 inches
Rear tread	60 inches	59 inches
around clearance	7.1 inches	8 inches
Curb weight	3,430 pounds	3,490 pounds
CAPACITIES		
Crankcase	5 quarts	5 quarts
Cooling system	22.25 quarts	21.5 quarts.
Fuel tank	19.5 gallons	18 gallons
FUEL CONSUMPTION		
Best	19-21 mpg	17-19 mpg
Average.	16-18 mpg	14-16 mpg

Above: Steering wheel designs on both cars are quite futuristic. *Below:* Olds's interior is more understated than the Mercury's.

SIA comparisonReport

It surprised us to discover that the Mercury handled and cornered better than the Olds at all speeds. Even though the Mercury steering is slightly slower than the Olds's, it is much lighter and effortless even at very low speeds. Moreover, the Olds plows into the turns. We wanted to turn; the 88 wanted to keep going straight ahead. We could hear the front tires squealing in agony.

While the Mercury naturally does not handle like a modern car, its handling, especially in the turns, is not at all bad by 1950 standards. The Mercury steering won't lead you into the turns, but it won't fight you either. At no time during the tests did the front tires squeal, either. Somebody commented that the handling of both cars would have been better with radial tires. Yeah, but then we wouldn't have a fair 1950 test. We rather suspect that the handling problems with the Olds were a combination of the soft coil springs at the rear and the big Olds Rocket engine carried in a

body and frame that were simply never designed for high-performance engines. Remember how Olds was always breaking wheel spindles and having other front-end failures during those early NASCAR races? And if the rear coil springs were so wonderful, then why did Olds go back to leaf springs in the rear in 1952?

Some minor observations: We mentioned earlier that the Mercury steering wheel has a better position, relative to the driver. This becomes more apparent the longer you drive each make. The Mercury engine is definitely quieter, which is not to say that the Rocket is noisy. But by the late forties and early fifties, Ford flatheads had achieved a level of quiet and balance that remains the envy of the international industry to this day. Some things get so good they just never can be improved upon. We did learn that Olds Rockets were quite hard starting until they went to the 12-volt system. And the lifters were slow to pump up in the early days. But we did not experience those problems with this particular car.

Braking on the Olds is very good, even without vacuum assist. There's little nosedive in panic stops, and very little brake fade, even after several panic stops. While the Mercury is not prone to nosediving, its brakes will tend to fade after two or three panics. This is probably because of total swept area—191.7 square inches in the Olds, compared to 159.1 square inches in the Mercury. Both makes have 11-inch brake drums. We doubt that vacuum assist, not available for either make in 1950, would have done much to help the Mercury's inherently insufficient total swept area.

A footnote on nosediving. While this

Lincoln and Olds in the First Mexican Road Race, 1950

Sixteen Lincolns, 11 Mercurys and 12 Oldsmobiles were among the 132 cars entered in the first Carrera Panamericana, May 1950. The race was run from north to south, a distance of 2,135 miles, from Ciudad Juarez to El Ocotal on the Guatemalan border. The two most remembered cars in the race were the winning 1950 Olds 88 and the 1949 Lincoln club coupe which placed ninth.

The Lincoln was much like a Mercury in that it had the same body, frame and suspension, although the wheelbase was lengthened to 121 inches. The engine was Lincoln's 336.7-c.i.d. flathead V-8, combined with a standard transmission. This was car #38, entered by Bob Estes Lincoln-Mercury, Inglewood, California, and driven by Johnny Mantz with Bill Stroppe as his co-pilot. The car was prepared by Stroppe and Les Viland in Stroppe's Long Beach, California, speed shop.

The Olds was an 88 two-door sedan with standard transmission. It was car #52, entered by Ray Sundstrom,

Portland, Oregon, and driven by 22-year-old Hershel McGriff.

The McGriff Olds went hardly noticed, as Mantz moved up to first place overall on the fourth and fifth legs. Then, on the sixth leg Mantz began falling back, and came into Mexico City feeling ill. Coming out of Mexico City the next day, bad luck prevailed. Mantz was now running a fever and had dysentery. The weather turned sour and his brakes gave out. He finished the leg in 69th place, and fell back to ninth place overall. By the eighth leg, steady but unspectacular McGriff moved into second place overall, hot on the heels of the first-place car, a 1950 Cadillac driven by Tom Deal, El Paso, Texas.

Mantz held his ninth-place position right to the end. The last 171 miles, from Tuxtla Gutierrez to El Ocotal were gravel/unpaved. The road cost Mantz all of his remaining tires. He slid across the finish line on his rims.

McGriff aided by calm veteran driver and co-pilot/Ray Elliot, had remained in

fourth place overall for the first six legs, and even by Mexico City nobody seriously thought he could continue to hold on. When Mantz fell back, McGriff moved up to third and quickly to second, coming into the lead only on the final leg. The gods were in his favor. He avoided Mexican food and water and did not suffer a single mishap or mechanical failure until the very end. McGriff simply hung in there while others fell by the wayside. His victory was as much a tribute to the reliability of the Olds 88 as to his driving. But just before the finish line a rock punctured a hole in the oil pan. McGriff couldn't have lasted another mile.

Fewer than 60 cars finished the race. Three Oldsmobiles finished in the top 10. There were seven Oldsmobiles in the top 20. Only one Lincoln, the Mantz car, finished in the top 10. Four Lincolns were in the top 20. If one considers the first Mexican Road Race to be a valid test of performance then the Olds 88 has to be the winner hands down. It even fared better than the ohv V-8 Cadillac.

Continued on page 57

Color Gallery

Photograph by Marc Madow

1939 99-A Coupe Sedan
Created to fill the void between the low-cost Fords and high-priced Lincoln Zephyrs, 60,214 examples of the 1939 Mercury were built across four body styles, including 34 that were sold as bare chassis. Power came from the 239.4-cu.in L-head V-8 of 95hp; suspension was the basic Ford system on a longer frame. The depicted Coupe Sedan was priced at $934, and 7,664 were built.

Photograph by David Gooley

1940 9A Convertible Sedan
Styling had changed little for Mercury's second year aside from minor grille, bumper and lighting revisions, but there were many engineering improvements. The gearshift was now on the column, a torsion bar stabilizer smoothed its ride, and an Art Deco interior, better ventilation and more leg room greeted passengers. Only 979 4-door Convertible Sedans were built, priced at $1,212.

Photograph by Bud Juneau

1941 19A Convertible Club Coupe

The make's biggest year yet saw Mercurys looking more like parent Ford than before, and the bodies were shared between the two divisions for the first time. Of the 98,293 built, 8,556 were the 2-door convertible, priced at $1,100. Now, both styling and engineering saw extensive work, with a box-section frame replacing the previous X-type. Power still came from the de-sleeved, 95hp, 239.4-cu.in. Ford V-8.

Photograph by David Gooley

1946 Sportsman

Still considered to be little more than a glorified Ford, the '46 Mercury used the prewar body shell with a new fine vertical bar grille treatment that resembled the head of an electric razor. Its 239.4-cu.in. V-8 produced 100 horsepower and was linked to a 3-speed manual. Despite demand, total production was down slightly from the prewar high of 1941, with 86,597 built. Of these, the $2,209 2-door Sportsman convertible was the rarest of the lot, with only 206 built.

Photograph by David Gooley

1947 Monarch convertible

When Mercury grilles looked to have been inspired by a company named Remington or Norelco, buyers in Canada, where Ford was in hot competition with GM, were treated to this Fordish hybrid. Built on the 118-in. wheelbase Mercury, it had Ford-derived trim and the 10hp, 239.4-cu.in. V-8 for power. Considered a Mercury Monarch, though there aren't any Mercury badges on it, it filled a mid-level gap for Ford dealers. Sales were not staggering; sedans, coupes and wagons did well, but only 40 Monarch convertibles were built in '47.

Photograph by Vince Manocchi

1949 9CM Station Wagon

Featuring a largely steel body structure, the new wagon did away with the four-door configuration until the 1952 models appeared. Once again, Ford and Mercury sheet metal was unique to each brand. Though heavier than its four-door predecessor, the longer stroke, 110hp, 255.4-cu.in. V-8 made enough power to offset the difference in weight. A popular wagon among woody collectors, 8,044 of the $2,716 woodies were made.

1950 Monterey

What can be viewed as the first of the "named" Mercury models appeared as the Monterey 2-door coupe. Launched to compete with the Chrysler and GM 2-door hardtops, it was the most expensive Mercury save for the convertible and station wagon. Based on the 181-inch wheelbase chassis, it featured a leather interior and was distinguishable from the rest of the coupes by its padded vinyl top. It is estimated that between 800 and 5,000 of these $2,146 coupes were built.

1950 OCM Coupe

In the year the millionth Mercury was built, the three 2-door-coupe styles outsold the lone 4-door by a small margin. Popular with customizers, the '49-51s can be difficult to find in original condition despite the 151,489 2-doors built. Prices ranged from $1,875 for this Coupe to $2,146 for the new Monterey. Exterior styling changed little; the 110hp, 255.4-cu.in. V-8 was still standard, but the interior was extensively reworked.

Photograph by Dr. G. Napoliello

1951 1CM Convertible

The 1951 Mercurys would be the last of the line with the heavy-pillared, two-piece flat windshield design. Changes, as in the previous year, were minimal; the most noticeable were the turn signal lights fully integrated into the wrap-around grille assembly, a trim panel on the lower quarter matching the rear bumper line, vertical taillights and another 2hp — now totaling 112hp — from the 255.4-cu.in flathead V-8. Only 6,759 of these $2,380 soft-tops were built.

Photograph by Darryl Norenberg

1952 Monterey

For 1952, Mercurys were back in the Ford camp; that is, the drivetrain, chassis and quite a bit of sheet metal were shared with Ford. A clean profile with attractive, somewhat conservative styling was visible in all three of the FoMoCo lines. The first hardtop Mercury was found in the $2,225 Monterey 2-door coupe and 24,453 were built. Though the new Y-block V-8 had been considered, the 125hp, 255.4-cu.in. flathead V-8 was used.

Photograph by Bud Juneau

Photograph by Tim Howley

1954 Monterey and 1950 Convertible

In 1950, the millionth Mercury was built. Exterior styling changed little; the 110hp, 255.4-cu.in. V-8 was still standard, but the interior was extensively reworked. Priced at $3,412, 8,341 1950 convertibles (right) were built. The sweeping look of the '49-51 models was replaced in 1952 with a more stately design. Power brakes and steering bowed in during the '53 model year. The new Y-block V-8, bored to 256-cu.in., produced 162hp. Only 7,293 of the $2,610 1954 Monterey (left) soft-tops were built.

1954 Sun Valley

The overall styling of the '54 models was little different than that seen on the '52-53 Mercurys. They were given an extensive facelift before the newly styled '55 models debuted. After being tested for two years in the Lincolns, the 256-cu.in Y-block V-8 and MacPherson-strut ball-joint front suspension made it into the Mercury and Ford lines. The Sun Valley with its namesake green plexiglass roof section was found in the Monterey model line; costing $2,582, 9,761 were built.

Photograph by Vince Wright

1956 Montclair

Despite the introduction of the low-cost Medalist series that differed mainly in trim and quality of interior appointments, the top-of-the-line Montclair series was where one could find the best selling Merc. This was also the year the "Big M" received its own body shell. The top-of-the-line Montclair series offered a 2-door sedan, hardtop and convertible, the latter of which found 7,762 buyers at $2,900 a pop. All series used the 312-cu.in. Y-block V-8, rated at 210hp.

Photograph by Robert Gross

1958 Montclair Turnpike Cruiser

One of the most gadget-laden cars of the '50s, the Turnpike Cruiser bowed in for the '57 model year as its own series in 2- and 4-door hardtop and convertible styles. For 1958, it was relegated to the Montclair line and the convertible was dropped. Two-doors were priced at $3,284; only 2,864 were built. The 330hp, 383-cu.in Marauder V-8 was standard; the 360hp, 430-cu.in. Lincoln-based V-8 was optional.

1964 Montclair Marauder

The Marauder nameplate was used for the pillarless fastback hardtop body style in both 2- and 4-door form in the Monterey and Montclair lines. The 390-cu.in. FE engine of 250hp was the standard powerplant, and next to the convertible, the 2-door Marauder was the most expensive of the Montclair line. Priced at $2,957, only 4,143 were built.

1964 Comet Cyclone

Introduced as a mid-year contender to the Pontiac GTO, the Cyclone in standard guise fell a bit short of its muscle car mission, for its standard 289-cu.in. small-block was only rated at 210hp. However, a "Super Cyclone High-Performance Option" version of the 289 offered a more respectable 271hp. Priced at $2,655, only 7,454 of the 189,936 Comets built in 1964 were of the top-level Cyclone.

Continued from page 48

Above and below: *The old and the new. Merc's flathead V-8 has its origins in '32 Ford L head. Olds's ohv high-compression V-8 was the very latest engine technology from GM in 1950.* **Below center:** *Trunk space appears to be just about equal.* **Bottom:** *Merc's rounded shape made it a favorite with customers for years. Olds looks better when left stock.*

1950 Olds didn't, we were told that most of them did, due to the four coils. The coils also made them bob down the road like a jackrabbit, especially as the springs got older.

What we liked best about the Mercury was the smooth application of power and solid comfort all the way up to 70 mph and higher. The '50 Mercury is a solid, quiet road car that literally floats along the freeway in utter confidence, and even travels over dips and bumps almost like it's floating on air. Perhaps the outstanding road feel is more psychological than real, but we couldn't help commenting on it. The '50 Olds 88 is not a bad road car at all, but it is good by Chevrolet/Pontiac standards. The Mercury reaches the level of roadability of the 1950 Lincoln. The unvarnished truth is that the Mercury has more in common with the Lincoln than the Olds 88 has with the Cadillac.

Gas economy is an area of special comparison where Merc wins again. In the 1950 Mobilgas Economy Run, the Sweepstakes award went to a 1950 Mercury with overdrive, which achieved 26.52 mpg and 61.27 ton mpg. Second and third place respectively were a Cadillac 60 Special and a Cadillac 62. The Olds 88 averaged only 20.19 mpg, to be beaten out by Kaiser, Frazer, Studebaker, Ford 6 and V-8 and several others.

Yes, we went into this test with a degree of prejudice—in favor of the Olds 88, mainly because my dad once had one. But we came away convinced that all around the Mercury was the better buy for the money. It listed for $2 less in the versions tested. We found the Mercury had the edge in just about every respect, except straightaway performance. Even there, the Olds was not ahead by the great margin we were previously led to believe. In summation, they were both great cars in their day and remain so as special interest vehicles today. If we had to pick just one to collect, it would be a tough decision. We guess the best answer would be to build a double garage and have one of each.

1950 Mercury

The 1949 Mercury was, actually, originally intended to become the 1948 Ford. And therein lies a tale.

No sooner had Edsel Ford passed away in May 1943 when the Old Man, Henry, then 80, became almost too senile to run the company. The great Ford empire began to crumble, and as Henry slipped into his dotage, Harry Bennett made plans to take control. Thomas L. Hibbard, previously of Hibbard & Darrin and LeBaron, worked at Ford from 1941 through 1948, and he wrote me recently that, "That era of postwar happenings at Ford was one of unbelievable confusion, and many things that took place seem irrational today."

Even before the end of the war, some of Ford's ablest men were irrationally forced out of their jobs. The political maneuvering and back stabbing took on Shakespearean unreality. Cast-iron Charlie Sorensen, the man who laid out Ford's first assembly lines, was apparently maneuvered into picking a fight with chief engineer Larry Sheldrick. After Sorensen had gotten Sheldrick mad enough to quit, he found himself forced into a similar corner, and he, too, left. The man believed to be behind most of this skulduggery was ex-boxer Harry Bennett, Ford's security chief.

When the Old Man began to lose his grip and his key men, the federal government got increasingly worried. Washington wasn't anxious to lose the wartime production facilities at Willow Run and the Rouge. After watching the company stumble along without an effective head, President Roosevelt considered letting the federal government take over. Instead, though, FDR asked Navy Secretary Knox to

release Henry Ford II from active duty—this in the rather idealistic hope that the Old Man's 25-year-old grandson could keep the company grinding out war materiel. Miraculously, HF-II and Ford did.

Larry Sheldrick, several years after he'd left his engineering post at Ford, talked about company goings-on during wartime—about his attitudes and proposals for postwar cars. Sheldrick made some interesting points, among them that: 1) the elder Henry Ford was only vaguely aware of Edsel Ford's, Sheldrick's, and E.T. Gregorie's thoughts on and prototypes for postwar cars; 2) that Edsel had moved toward making postwar changes, but the old Man hadn't; and 3) that the senior Henry Ford would have no part of new-fangled ideas like independent front suspension, although Sheldrick recalls, "...we were doing quite a little exploring as to types of independent suspension that could become a part of a more modern postwar product. there were several complete layouts made both in the Ford and Mercury class. Also, they were doing quite a little work at the Lincoln plant on torsion-bar suspension.

When HF-II came in in December 1943, he naturally tried to learn as much about the business as possible in the shortest time possible. Poking around and asking questions, he had Gregorie show him some of his postwar clays and drawings. Then HF-II asked Sheldrick to demonstrate some of his new engineering ideas. When Sorensen heard about this, he reportedly got hopping mad. "What's the big idea of you filling the young man's head with all these crazy modern ideas of yours of postwar cars? Sorensen barked at Shel-

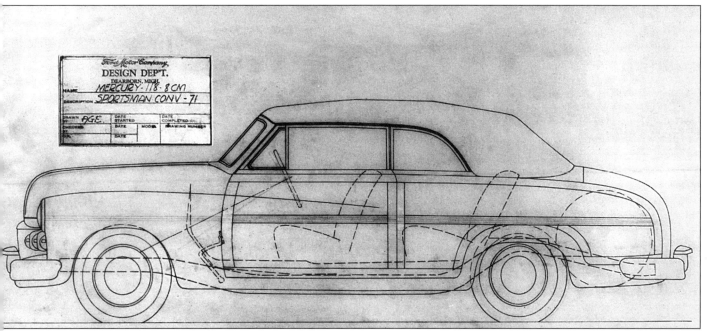

Wood-bodied Sportsman was proposed for 1949 Merc, also for Lincoln and Ford. Just how seriously these were considered isn't known. The '49 Mercury began as Gregorie's postwar Ford, but Breech deemed it too expensive, so Ford became Merc, crash program began for '49 Ford.

Power windows, top use same hydraulic system.

Rear window lift, dome light switch look alike.

Wraparound taillights act as rear side markers.

drick. Sheldrick theorized later that Sorensen was trying to keep the Old Man's power absolute—to make sure postwar decisions would be Old Henry's, not Young Henry's.

But they would have to be Young Henry's, because the Old Man wasn't capable of making decisions anymore. By September 1945, HF-II found himself president of a dying company. His recovery program had to be based on what he had at hand—initially on the little work Sheldrick and Gregorie had done semi-secretly during the war.

One thing they'd done in the open, successfully, was to facelift the 1946 Ford, Mercury, and Lincoln. These had been Tom Hibbard's designs. FoMoCo's 1946 models went into production on July 3, 1945. Ford was given a government-set quota of 39,910 units. The company could build that many cars during that calendar year. Theoretically. Fighting strikes, work stoppages, steel and material shortages, and OPA ceiling prices, Ford produced 34,439 cars during 1945, and lost an estimated $300 on each one. Why the loss? Because prices were fixed, based on 1942 levels, and with Ford at nothing like volume production, manufacturing costs went about $300 per car over income. For awhile there, Ford was losing $10 million a month.

Meanwhile, HF-II knew he had to go ahead with plans for radical product changes—grossly updated postwar models. Kaisers and Frazers were all new for 1946, Studebaker was well along with its back-to-front 1947s, Hudson would introduce its Step-Downs for 1948, Cad and Olds and Packard were completely restyled that year, and by 1949 the dam would break.

HF-II, with help from Ernest Kanzler and Mrs. Edsel Ford, had the foresight to surround himself with good, capable, eager new men just after the war: Ernie Breech; Tex Thornton, leader of the so-called Whiz Kids; ex-Olds engineer Harold Youngren; Lewis Crusoe; Del Harder, plus a dozen others. *SIA* detailed these men and their backgrounds in the 1949 Ford driveReport (*SIA* #5, pp. 16-21), so I won't repeat them here. Suffice it to say that Ernie Breech became HF-II's right-hand man and played a very important role in developing all 1949 FoMoCo car lines.

Breech and the younger Ford set a target date of February 1948 for the company's postwar model debut. Plans went ahead throughout 1945, 1946, and early 1947—a general plan that encompassed the entire FoMo-Co line-up. This general plan was based largely on designs that Sheldrick and Gregorie had worked out during the war. It's interesting to look back now at the full lineup proposed at that time, because it's very unlike what reached production as the 1949 Ford, Mercury, and Lincoln.

During 1945, 1946, and the first quarter of 1947, there were to be four separate, distinct car lines: 1) a small, inexpensive, compact Ford; 2) a standard-sized Ford; 3) a Mercury on two different wheelbases, and 4) Lincolns on three different wheelbases. To detail these more fully:

1) Ford called its compact the light car, and in April 1946 established a specific Light Car Division. Ford had been toying with a compact since the early 1930s. But just before and during WW-II, GM seemed poised to bring out a compact, so Ford got serious with one, too. The Ford light car's specs varied from proposal to proposal, wheelbase ranging from 97

to 105 inches. Power considered for it included in-line, L-head 4-, 5-, and 6-cylinder engines. "The 5," recalls E.T. Gregorie, who drove one occasionally, "felt like a 6 with one cylinder chopped off—very rough." Four-cylinder prototypes were built, tested, and the car was almost put into production here in the U.S. But when GM dropped its plans for a compact, late in 1947, Ford did, too. Ford shipped its light car to France, where it became the French Ford Vedette.

2) The master plan's standard-sized Ford was to span a 118-inch wheelbase. Styling looked almost exactly like what the 1949 Mercury turned out to be. Eight body styles were projected, including 2- and 4-door fastback and notchback sedans, a 3-passenger business coupe, a woody wagon, plus a wood-bodied convertible sport wagon.

3) Mercurys were to be made in normal (120-inch) and Custom (123-inch) wheelbases in all the body styles mentioned above, plus a wood-bodied Sportsman convertible.

4) Finally came the Lincoln, whose standard wheelbase was to be 125 inches. A Custom (Cosmopolitan) series ran to a 128-inch span, and the projected, completely changed Continental and Lincoln limousines were stretched to 132.

Specifications for all these proposals got shuffled and reshuffled from time to time, but the general plan held through August 1946. In July 1946, though, when Ernie Breech first drove the initial Gregorie prototype, proposed as the new 1948 ("") Ford, he decided it was too heavy and thus would be too expensive to produce as a standard-sized Ford. Breech continued to hold this view for a full month but couldn't make up his mind what to do about it. Meanwhile, some die models and tooling for "1948 Ford" body panels on the 118-inch wheelbase were already being prepared.

Breech agonized over what to do, because he really wasn't happy with Gregorie's proposed Ford. Finally, on August 23, 1946, Breech spoke up at a meeting of the Ford policy committee and strongly suggested that the Gregorie Ford be made the Mercury and that the Gregorie Mercury become the new Lincoln. The committee voted and decided to go along with Breech's suggestions.

What, then, would be the radically new and different Ford?

Breech said the company would have to start a new Ford from scratch—institute a crash program like those of WW-II. Designers and engineers would start fresh, and it was just before this time that ex-Olds engineer Youngren arrived. Meanwhile, Breech had hired George W. Walker as a styling consultant, and he (Breech) suggested that both Walker and Gregorie submit new design proposals for the 1949 Ford. Youngren drew up a "package" on a 114-inch wheelbase. All hope of making a February 1948 deadline for any introduction had vanished by now.

Walker and Gregorie did indeed submit designs, and the policy committee voted on them. Both clays looked very much alike, because Youngren's package pretty thoroughly spelled out dimensions, seating, etc. The committee's vote favored Walker's proposal, and on December 15, 1946, Gregorie turned in his resignation. He left the company on friendly terms and returned to his first love, designing yachts. As mentioned in previous articles, Gregorie had been trained as a naval architect, and even today he maintains his own studio in Florida, where he designs trawler yachts.

While the 1949 Ford sedan ended up weighing 216 pounds less than its 1948 counterpart, the 1949 Merc weighed 132 pounds more. Youngren had arrived too late to greatly influence paring weight off the Mercury/Lincoln frames, which were still the old-style X-member type instead of Ford's new ladder type.

But so far as engineering went, the new Ford and Mercury turned out to be basically the same. Both got Hotchkiss drive and almost identical front and rear suspension systems—conventional but modern, for a change. Again, we've described most of the Merc's engineering features in our 1949 Ford driveReport, so there's no need to repeat them here.

Even the Ford and Mercury engines were nearly identical, principal difference being 1/4-inch more stroke for the Merc. This gave it 255.4 c.i.d. against Ford's 239.4, and it also meant 110 bhp to Ford's 100. Mercury's extra weight, though, more than overwhelmed the extra 10 bhp. The Mercury crankshaft interchanged with all Fords' and Mercurys' back to 1939, as we've mentioned in "Hot Roddable Engine," pp. 36-39 of SIA #12, and it became a very popular hop-up item. Otherwise, Youngren updated and revamped what had essentially been the old-style Ford/Mercury flat-bead V-8—he made it burn less oil, less gas, and improved cooling and exhaust flow.

With 10 more bhp than the 1949 Ford, 400 more pounds, and a Standard 3.91 rear axle to Ford's 3.73, the Merc and Ford were pretty evenly matched

in acceleration. Yet Mercury seemed to lack some of the old Ford snap—in fact, it lacked some of the old Merc snap. Floyd Clymer wrote that the 1949 Mercury would do over 100 mph, but that's strictly the speedometer's over-optimism. Motor Trend's figures showed a top speed of 83.76 mph.

Where the Merc surprised everyone, though, was in fuel economy. In the 1950 Mobilgas Grand Canyon Sweepstakes, a 1950 Mercury won its class hands down with a 26.52-mpg showing. This was only .03 mpg less than the overall winner. Part of the credit has to go to the Borg-Warner overdrive, which became a Mercury option for the first time in 1949. And part has to go to the Holley carb, with its sidedraft inlet and miserly jetting. The Ford V-8 used an entirely different Ford-built carburetor.

The 1949 Mercury's dashboard is unique to that year model, and it developed from one of Bob Gregorie's wartime designs. It housed all gauges in five round dials in front of the driver, the dials set into something like a projecting metal box. For 1950, while exterior sheet metal and running gear remained virtually unchanged, the dashboard was completely redone, this time very much resembling the 1949 Cadillac's instrument panel.

Top offering for 1950 was the Monterey sport coupe, with its padded vinyl top. It arrived at about the same time and in the same vein as the Ford Crestliner. Both were Ford's answers to GM's hardtops, because Ford couldn't get a hardtop into production until 1951, and GM's hardtops were selling like crazy.

For 1951, the Mercury got a slightly different grille treatment, extended rear fenders, and the Merc-O-Matic transmission. Throughout these three years—1949-51—Mercury shared body panels, doors, roofs, and glass with Lincolns but not with the Cosmopolitan (Cosmos being on 125-inch wheelbases as against the standard Lincoln's 121).

Mercury offered some interesting options during that era. Among them

THE 1949-51 MERC
WAS BOB GREGORIE'S BABY

SIA asked E.T. (Bob) Gregorie to give us his remembrances of designing the car that became the 1949 Mercury.

"You will recall that the postwar Ford was originally to be produced in two lines—one of about 98-inch wheelbase and the larger line to give dealers a broader sales spread. Both Jack Davis, then sales manager, with whom I worked very closely, and I (as well as Management) agreed that this was logical, good, long-range vision (as today's scheme of things seems to bear out).

"About mid-summer 1946, Ernie Breech entered the Ford picture. He lost little time selling Mr. Henry Ford II on a GM-type management setup. In line with this, he brought in a selection of previous associates from GM. Incidentally, I well recall a bit of conversation with Mr. Ford II regarding the necessity of weeding out some of the 'old dead-wood' and bringing in some new energy. I don't know if I'm the only one who made this suggestion—at any rate, he took this seriously. This, of course, created a period of confusion at a time when production plans were pretty well established. Engineering and tooling was already in progress on what was to become the new 1948 (not 1949) Fords, Lincoln, and Mercury.

"But then the decision was suddenly made to fit the larger Ford into the Merc slot alongside the Lincoln Cosmopolitan in the then-new Lincoln-Mercury sales setup. As I mentioned previously, the smaller Ford project was shipped off to Europe.

"About this time, the new 1946-47 'double-ended' Studebaker suddenly created quite a stir within Ford. It seemed a logical pattern in size and weight for a new Ford layout. From this evolved a fixed formula, dictated largely by engineering and production considerations, specifying wheelbase, tread, basic overall body dimensions, etc. This, of course, pretty well bracketed and controlled the styling of the Ford-to-be.

"Breech's next move was to bring George Walker, a longtime acquaintance, into the picture as a consultant. General opinion was that this was Breech's device to bring future styling activity more or less under his direct control. In previous years, I had managed this department directly under Mr. Edsel Ford and then under Mr. HF-II. As time went on, it became obvious that this was an annoyance to Mr. Breech and his revised management strategy. He was not a particularly agreeable man to deal with, nor was he well versed in styling matters.

"Late in 1946, before completion of my styling department model and the Walker version of the new-formula Ford, it was obvious that this had to be Breech's show all the way. I considered it best not to be involved in possible future differences with Mr. Breech, and I conveyed this decision to Mr. Ford.

"Incidentally, the two proposals for the 1949 Ford—Walker's and mine—turned out to be very similar except for minor details. This is no doubt the result of the controlled outline, etc. Management voted, chose Walker's Ford, and my designs made previously became the Mercury and Lincoln.

"Aside from the above, Mr. Breech, of course, is credited with doing a spectacular job with Ford, and the styling situation was perhaps only minor in the overall course of events at the time.

"My able assistant, Tom Hibbard, took over styling management for a time after my departure, and as I recall, there were several succeeding people who ran the department, including George Walker."

—E.T. Gregorie

Modified starter motor powers top. Rear roof bow houses dome light, which could accidently be left on with top down, become fire hazard.

Touches that distinguish 1950 from '49 Merc include different decklid ornament, unlettered hubcaps, pushbuttons instead of pull door handles.

Meet the New Ford

Convertible Sport Wagon

THE FORD MOTOR DESIGN DEPARTMENT

Ross Cousins, an artist in Bob Gregorie's styling department, drew up sketches to sell FoMoCo management on convertible station wagon. Dated 1944, the drawings show lines adopted by Merc.

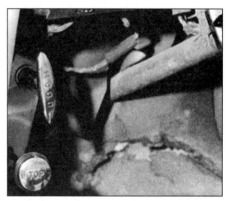

Hood release and top push-pull knob stand too close together. We kept grabbing the wrong one.

Decklid ornament hides lock and serves as lift. This 1950 version replaces '49's large casting.

Seems like 1950 Merc borrowed several items from 1949 Cad, such as parking lamp design.

Seems like 1950 Merc borrowed several items from 1949 Cad, such as parking lamp design.

Hood insignia looks very Lincoln-ish. In 1950, Mercury convertible paced Indianapolis 500.

Another page from Cadillac's book: 1950 Merc dash is amazingly like 1949 Cad's. It's a good layout—handsome, with all gauges easy to read.

Low hood necessitates sidedraft carb inlet, offset aircleaner. 110-bhp flathead gives good mileage, adequate though not sparkling performance.

were three different sets of matched luggage specifically tailored for the Merc's trunk. Also available was a rear window wiper, monogram initial plates, a "spare air" extension that let the spare tire's pressure be checked under the gas filler door, an engine compartment lamp with mercury (!) switch, a detachable rear-seat speaker, and that huge sunvisor that came to symbolize old-maid-ism in the early 1950s.

Moviegoers and insomniacs have been catching quite a lot of 1949-51 Mercs on the screen recently—in everything from *The Last Picture Show* to re-runs of James Dean in *Rebel Without a Cause*. You might have noticed yet another Mercury in a recent nostalgia-attuned 7-Up commercial. The 7-Up Merc has flames painted on the hood, which is a good touch, because no sooner did a teenager get hold of one of these Bathtub Mercurys than off came all the chrome. It was a very customizable car, and you rarely saw a stock one after about 1954. The vogue was to set the body so low that you couldn't slip a cigarette paper between it and the street. These Mercs never were too fast, but kids just loved to doll them up.

Our driveReport 1950 Mercury convertible belongs to Tony Nieto, a truck driver from South San Francisco. Tony bought the car in 1970 and immediately set about de-customizing it. "The kid who'd owned it," says Tony, "was in the process of making a hot rod out of it, and it had been customized a couple of times before that. So my first job was to take out or off all the non-stock stuff and put it all back original."

This included taking the body off the frame and then taking apart every component that would come apart. Tony overhauled the engine and went through all the running gear, including the overdrive. Luckily such items as the power windows and top mechanism were still there, although most of the hydraulic cylinders needed reworking.

The car now has over 100,000 miles on it, yet it feels as tight and solid as new. The starter has that familiar Ford ring after the engine grabs, and there's a slight ching as you drop into low. The clutch is extremely smooth.

As expected, acceleration isn't neck-snapping, but it's surely adequate, and you never feel you're pressing the V-8 to keep up with traffic. Overdrive makes open highway cruising a breeze. Even at 70 with the top down, you can hold a normal-volume conversation in the front seat, but not in the back. Rear riders have a tough time even catching their breath—the wind hits them in the face with hurricane force.

The Merc's ride feels soft but not mushy—quite comfortable. Cornering brings out the lean so common to most cars of this era. Steering is light at

1949-51 Mercury Development

Late 1942—Styling work begins on postwar FoMoCo lines, this under E.T. Gregorie at instigation of Edsel Ford.

May 26, 1943—Edsel Ford dies.

Sept. 13, 1943—Ford's chief engineer, Larry Sheldrick, leaves.

Dec. 15, 1943—Henry Ford II elected Ford vice president on return from Navy.

Jan. 23, 1944—HF-II elected executive vice president of Ford.

March 3, 1944—Charles Sorensen, Ford production chief, leaves.

Sept. 21, 1945—HF-II made FoMoCo president. That same day Harry Bennett resigns but is allowed one more month on board of directors to save face.

July 3, 1945—Ford postwar passenger-car production resumes.

Oct. 22, 1945—Lincoln-Mercury becomes a separate division.

Nov. 1, 1945—Lincoln and Mercury production resume.

April 12, 1946—Light Car Div. established to produce inexpensive postwar compact by Oct. 1947.

July 1, 1946—Ernie Breech arrives at Ford; had previously been with Bendix and GM.

July 17, 1946—Harold Youngren arrives as director of engineering, had previously been with Oldsmobile and Borg-Warner.

Late July, 1946—Breech drives proposed "1948" Ford prototype, considers it too heavy and expensive.

Aug. 1946—Breech suggests to Ford policy committee to make Gregorie's proposed 118-inch Ford the 1949 Mercury and Gregorie's Mercury the Lincoln. Urges a crash program to design a new-from-scratch 1949 Ford. Committee agrees.

Sept. 1946—Ford Motor Co. begins to show profits on car sales for the first time since 1942.

Dec. 11, 1946—Policy committee votes between Gregorie's and Walker's proposed 1949 Ford designs. Walker's chosen.

Dec. 15, 1946—Gregorie resigns.

April 7, 1947—Henry Ford, aged 84, dies.

April 22, 1948—1949 Lincoln bows.

April 29, 1948—1949 Mercury bows.

June 8, 1948—1949 Ford bows.

1950 Mercury 8BA convertible coupe

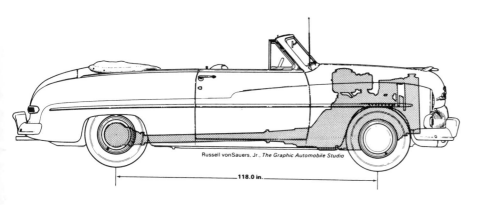

Russell vonSauers, Jr., *The Graphic Automobile Studio*

118.0 in.

1950 Mercury 8BA convertible

7.1 in.
58.5 in.

Price when new $2,412 f.o.b. Dearborn (1950).

Current valuation Xlnt. $1,630; gd. $830; fair $265.

Options Overdrive, radio, heater, whitewall tires.

ENGINE
Type L-head V-8, cast en bloc, water-cooled, 3 mains, full pressure lubrication.
Bore & stroke 3.1875 x 4.00.
Displacement 255.4 c.i.d.
Max. bhp @ rpm 110 @ 3,600.
Max. torque @ rpm 200 @ 2,000.
Compression ratio. 6.8:1.
Induction system 2-bbl. downdraft carb, mechanical fuel pump.
Exhaust system Cast-iron manifolds, crossover pipe, single muffler.
Electrical system 6-volt battery/coil.

CLUTCH
Type Single dry plate, woven asbestos lining.
Diameter 10.0 inches.
Actuation Mechanical, foot pedal.

TRANSMISSION
Type 3-speed manual with overdrive, column lever, synchro 2-3.
Ratios: 1st 2.82:1.
2nd 1.60:1.
3rd 1.00:1.
Overdrive 0.72:1.
Reverse 3.62:1.

DIFFERENTIAL
Type Hypoid.
Ratio 4.27:1 (3.91:1 std.).
Drive axles Semi-floating.

STEERING
Type Gemmer worm & roller.
Turns lock to lock 5.25.
Ratio 18.2:1.
Turn circle 43.0 ft.

BRAKES
Type 4-wheel hydraulic drums, internal expanding.

Drum diameter 11.0 in.
Total lining area 159.1 sq. in

CHASSIS & BODY
Frame Channel-section steel, central X- and front K-members.
Body construction All steel.
Body style 2-dr., 6-pass, conv. cpe.

SUSPENSION
Front Independent A-arms, coil springs, tubular hydraulic shocks, linkless stabilizer bar.
Rear Solid axle, longitudinal semi-elliptic leaf springs, tubular hydraulic shock absorber
Tires 7.10 x 15 tube type, 4-ply.
Wheels Pressed steel, drop-center rims, lug-bolt brake drums.

WEIGHTS & MEASURES
Wheelbase 118.0 in.
Overall length 207.0 in.
Overall height 69.9 in.
Overall width 76.9 in.
Front tread 58.5 in.
Rear tread 60.0 in.
Ground clearance 7.1 in.
Curb weight 3,710 lb.

CAPACITIES
Crankcase 5.0 qt.
Cooling system 22.25 qt.
Fuel tank 19.5 gal.

FUEL CONSUMPTION
Best 19-21 mpg.
Average 16-18 mpg.

PERFORMANCE (from **Motor Trend** test of 1950 Mercury sedan):
0-30 mph 4.55 sec.
0-40mph 7.80sec.
0-50 mph 1.00 sec.
0-60mph 15.98 sec.
0-70 mph 21.40 sec.
Standing 1/4 mile 20.88 sec. and 69 mph.
Top speed 83.75mph.
* Courtesy **Antique Automobile Appraisal**, Prof. Barry Hertz.

speeds above 25 mph, heavy below that, fairly slow, with a big wheel.

By 1949, Ford Motor Co. was back on solid ground—that great series of postwar crises had passed. Breech was right, of course, in insisting that the new Ford be lighter and smaller. Even with four inches' less wheelbase, the 1949-51 Merc would have made a poor Ford. The Gregorie Ford made a great Mercury, though: heavy, solid, substantial, rather luxurious actually, and a good-looking car in my opinion. Now if Ford could only have gone ahead with that wooden-bodied convertible station wagon.... ☞

Special thanks to Tony Nieto, South San Francisco, California; E.T Gregorie, St. Augustine, Florida; Thomas L. Hibbard, Camden, Maine; Henry Edmunds, Win Sears, and David Crippen of the Ford Archives, Henry Ford Museum, Dearborn, Michigan; Michael W.R. Davis, Chuck Mulcahy, and Bill Peacock of the Ford Motor Co.; Bob Doehler, Milwaukee; and members of the Ford-Mercury Club of America, Box 3551, Hayward, California 94544.

1950 MERCURY MONTEREY

by Alex Meredith
photos by Bud Juneau

WHEN automobile production ground suddenly to a halt with America's entry into World War II, the Mercury had hardly been around long enough to prove its case before the court of public opinion. True, it had done remarkably well for a new marque, holding eleventh place in the industry during 1939-40 and slipping only slightly to twelfth in 1941, the last full year of production before the ax fell. But still, its principal competitors, Pontiac and Dodge, were outselling the Merc by ratios of 3.5:1 and 2.7:1, respectively.

Even in the postwar world, when demand for automobiles far exceeded the supply, while Mercury moved ahead of Chrysler and Nash to take over tenth place, it had yet to hit its stride.

But then came the 1949 model, spectacularly restyled by E.T. "Bob" Gregorie and introduced to an eagerly waiting public on April 29, 1948. And what a revolution in design it represented, compared to its predecessors!

● The rigid axle was replaced by independent front suspension, while the transverse springs — a hold-over from the days of the Model T Ford — gave way to coils at the front and longitudinal semi-elliptic leaf springs at the rear.

● Hotchkiss drive took the place of the traditional torque tube and radius rod, providing a softer ride as well as a substantial reduction in unsprung weight.

● The engine was stroked a quarter of an inch, increasing its displacement from 239.4 to 255.4 cubic inches, and

LUXURY, ECONOMY

Originally published in Special Interest Autos #135, May-June 1993

— with the help of a slight increase in the compression ratio — raising its horsepower from 100 to 110.

- The excellent Borg-Warner overdrive, called "Touch-O-Matic" by Mercury, became a factory option.
- Sharing its body shell with the smaller Lincoln, the new car was far roomier, as well as more impressive-looking, than any previous Mercury.
- Although the wheelbase remained unchanged at 118 inches, the overall length was increased by five inches while the width grew by three and a quarter inches.
- Height, meanwhile, was reduced by nearly four and a half inches, which made the car look even longer than it really was.
- And although the new Mercury was 88 pounds heavier than its predecessor, its weight-to-horsepower ratio was improved from 33.68:1 to 30.78:1

Floyd Clymer, on behalf of *Popular Mechanics* magazine, drove a '49 Mercury club coupe on a high-speed test run from Omaha to Cheyenne, covering the 484-mile distance in seven hours,

15 minutes for an average speed of 66.6 miles an hour including stops. Along the way, Clymer recorded some of his impressions:

"Now I've reached the City Limits of Omaha, having averaged about 25 miles an hour so far. I think that out of about

mal position. This car has a very large radiator, certainly an improvement over the older Mercurys...."

Nearing Osceola, Nebraska: "In the past half hour I have covered 42 miles, that's about 84 miles an hour...."

And at Gothenburg, Nebraska: "It is

AND PERFORMANCE

25 traffic signals I have hit only two green lights...."

Later, passing through Wahoo, Nebraska: "The car is operating beautifully. There is no swaying or weaving. It's a sure-footed car and steers with very little effort. The front springs are very soft. I think the shock absorbers could be set up a little tighter, however they give a very comfortable ride. The heat indicator doesn't even get up to 'normal,' and even yesterday when it was quite hot it seldom reached a nor-

now 7:30 and the speedometer indicates that I have covered 243 miles. The last few miles were clicked off at about '95.' I cannot over-emphasize how nicely this car handles at high speed. It is all that anyone could ask for as it has exceptional stability and roadability...."

Finally, entering Cheyenne, Clymer notes, "In checking over the Union Pacific time-table I find my time with the Mercury, to my surprise, is only five minutes faster than the crack Union Pacific streamliner, *City of Los*

1950 MERCURY

Above: *Fog lamps on driveReport car are original factory accessory.* **Below:** *Vinyl top was one of the easily distinguishable styling touches on the Monterey.*

Angeles.... The time of the Mercury beat the regular Union Pacific train, the *Los Angeles Limited*, by two hours twenty-five minutes...."

Concluding his report, Floyd Clymer noted that out of 3,000 replies to a survey of 1949 Mercury owners, 83.6 percent rated it "Good" to "Excellent," while only 0.8 percent called it "Poor."

Endorsements such as these were soon reflected in the sales figures. Calendar year production, which had hit a postwar peak of 86,603 units in 1946, rose to 301,319 in 1949. By 1950 Mercury had edged past Kaiser/Frazer, Studebaker and even Dodge, to take over the industry's number seven spot, and in August of that year the one-millionth Merc came off the assembly line.

A record like that hardly calls for major changes in either engineering or styling, and the 1950 Mercury, though it was billed — no doubt correctly — as "Better than Ever," represented simply a refinement of its immediate predecessor. A new, "Econ-O-Miser" carburetor was designed to increase gas mileage; sound-proofing was more effective; there was a new heating and ventilating system (optional, but almost universally specified). A new dash panel layout, clearly inspired by that of the '49 Cadillac, was not only better looking, but more legible as well. And there were minor trim differences, but basically, the '50 Merc represented the continuation of a winning formula. Prices were unchanged.

From the start, Mercury had offered only one series. There was no optional engine, and no choice of wheelbase or

Mercury versus the Competition

(Since none of Mercury's competitors offered a model comparable to the Monterey, four-door sedans are used here for purposes of comparison.)

	Mercury Eight	Buick Special	De Soto Deluxe	Olds 88 Deluxe	Studebaker Commander Regal
Price, f.o.b.	$2,031	$1,952	$1,986	$2,056	$2,024
Wheelbase	118 inches	121.5 inches	125.5 inches	119.5 inches	120 inches
Overall length	206.7 inches	204.0 inches	206.7 inches	202.0 inches	207.9 inches
Shipping weight	3,386 lb.	3,720 lb.	3,525 lb.	3,520 lb.	3,265 lb.
Engine	V-8	Straight 8	6-cylinder	V-8	6-cylinder
Displacement	255.4	248.1	236.7	303.7	245.6
Compression ratio	6.80:1	6.30:1	7.00:1	7.25:1	7.00:1
Horsepower/rpm	110/3,600	115/3,600	112/3,600	135/3,600	102/3,200
Torque/rpm	200/2,000	212/2,000	195/1,200	263/1,800	205/1,200
Valve configuration	L-head	Ohv	L-head	Ohv	L-head
Clutch diameter	10 inches	10 inches	10 inches	10.5 inches	9.25 inches
Overdrive available?	Yes	No	No	No	Yes
Automatic available?	No	Yes	Semi	Yes	Yes
Steering ratio	18.2	19.8	18.2	19.0	17.0
Braking area (sq. in.)	159.1	161.5	173.5	191.7	178.0
Drum diameter	11 inches	12 inches	11 inches	11 inches	11 inches
Tire size	7.10/15	7.60/15	7.60/15	7.60/15	7.60/15
Horsepower/c.i.d.	.431	.464	.473	.445	.415
Lb./horsepower	30.8	32.3	31.5	26.1	32.0
Lb./c.i.d.	13.3	15.0	14.9	11.6	13.3

illustrations by Russell von Sauers, The Graphic Automobile Studio

specifications

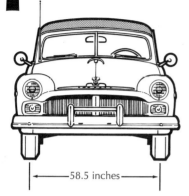

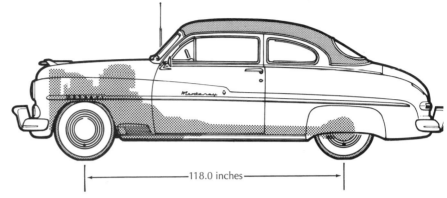

58.5 inches

118.0 inches

1950 Mercury Monterey

Price	$2,146 f.o.b. factory, federal excise tax included
Standard equipment	Leather seat facings, woolen carpeting, vinyl top, chromed inside window frames, fender shields, special steering wheel, dash painted to match exterior color, dual outside mirrors, wheel covers
Options on dR car	Touch-O-Matic overdrive, radio with rear seat speaker, heater, white sidewall tires, stainless steel curb buffers (trim beneath door), bumper guards, fog lamps, backup lamps, under hood light, trunk light, remote valve stem, gas filler door guard, 2-inch rear lowering blocks, window washers, heavy duty air cleaner, oil filter
After-market equip.	Dual exhausts, door handle trim

ENGINE
Type	90-degree L-head V-8
Bore and stroke	3.1875 inches x 4 inches
Displacement	255.4 cubic inches
Compression ratio	6.80:1
Horsepower @ rpm	110 @ 3,600
Torque @ rpm	200 @ 2,000
Taxable horsepower	32.5
Valve lifters	Mechanical
Main bearings	3
Fuel system	Dual downdraft carburetor, camshaft pump
Lubrication system	Pressure
Cooling system	Centrifugal pump
Exhaust system	Dual (originally single)
Electrical system	6-volt

CLUTCH
Type	Single dry plate
Diameter	10 inches
Actuation	Mechanical, foot pedal

TRANSMISSION
Type	3-speed selective w/overdrive synchro 2nd and 3rd speeds, column-mounted lever
Ratios: 1st	2.82:1
2nd	1.60:1
3rd	1.00:1
Reverse	3.62:1
Overdrive	0.70:1

DIFFERENTIAL
Type	Hypoid; Hotchkiss drive
Ratio	4.27:1
Drive axles	Semi-floating

STEERING
Type	Gemmer worm-and-roller
Ratio	18.2:1
Turns lock-to-lock	5.25
Turning diameter	43 feet, 0 inches (curb/curb)

BRAKES
Type	4-wheel internal hydraulic, drum type
Drum diameter	11 inches
Effective area	159.1 square inches

CONSTRUCTION
Type	Body-on-frame
Frame	Channel section steel with X-members and front K-members
Body construction	All steel
Body style	6-passenger coupe

SUSPENSION
Front	Independent A-arms, coil springs, linkless stabilizer bar
Rear	Rigid axle, longitudinal semi-elliptic leaf springs

Shock absorbers	Tubular hydraulic
Wheels	Pressed steel; drop-center rims
Tires	7.10/15 4 ply

WEIGHTS AND MEASURES
Wheelbase	118 inches
Overall length	206.7 inches
Overall width	76.5 inches
Overall height	64.8 inches
Front track	58.5 inches
Rear track	60 inches
Min. road clearance	6.8 inches
Shipping weight	3,626 pounds

CAPACITIES
Crankcase	5 quarts
Cooling system	21 quarts
Fuel tank	19.5 gallons
Transmission	3.5 pints
Differential	3 pints

CALCULATED DATA
Hp per c.i.d.	.431
Weight (lb.) per hp	33.0
Weight per c.i.d.	14.2
P.S.I. (brakes)	22.8

PERFORMANCE
Standing 1/4-mile	20.88 seconds
Acceleration 0-30 mph	4.57 seconds
0-60 mph	15.98 seconds
Top speed (in O/D)	83.75 mph*
Stopping distance	173 feet (from 60 mph)

*Test crew believed test run was too short for optimum results

(from *Motor Trend,* May 1950)

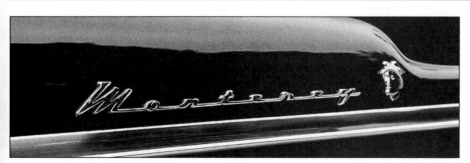

Model designation is spelled out in script on both doors.

The 1950 Mercury and the Grand Canyon Economy Run

For a number of years prior to World War II, California's Gilmore Oil Company sponsored an "Economy Run," in which the various makes and models of automobile were pitted against one-another for the purpose of determining which among them delivered the best fuel mileage. A number of classes were established, so that each contestant competed against cars in its own price range. The route, extending from Los Angeles to Yosemite National Park, provided a wide variety of conditions, including city traffic, open highway, and mountain driving.

The contest was suspended during World War II, for in those tight times when both gasoline and tires were severely rationed, no one could afford to engage in such frivolity. But as 1950 approached it was announced that the contest was about to be resumed, sponsored now by General Petroleum, producers of Mobilgas and Mobiloil.

Just to be sure that none of the participants could forget who was hosting the affair, the rules required that each entrant use Mobil motor oil and either Mobilgas Regular or Mobilgas Special for fuel. Transmissions and differentials were drained, flushed, and filled with the sponsor's lubricants. Even the cooling systems were similarly treated with Mobil products.

Since a Packard Super Eight, for example, could hardly be expected to achieve gas mileage comparable to that of a Studebaker Champion, ratings were based on ton-mpg, rather than the actual miles-per-gallon figure. The formula for computing that figure was as follows: weight of car (including actual passenger load) expressed in tons, times the number of miles traveled, divided by the number of gallons of gasoline consumed.

To cite a hypothetical example, suppose we take an automobile with a road weight of 3,550 pounds, carrying four passengers whose weight totals 700 pounds. If the route covers 850 miles and the car consumes 38.5 gallons of fuel, the ton-mpg would be 46.91, computed thus: 2.125 tons times 850 miles, divided by 38.5 gallons equals 46.91. Actual fuel consumption, computed by dividing the mileage (850) by the number of gallons used (38.5) would be 22.07 mpg.

All of which may not be quite as equitable as it sounds, for when such influences as wind resistance are taken into consideration, the formula tends to favor the heavier cars.

By the time the contest was resumed, in February 1950, the course had been substantially extended, routing the cars from Los Angeles north through Mojave, 55 miles southeast of Bakersfield, and thence to Lone Pine. Then the route headed eastward past Panamint Springs, across Death Valley and on through Las Vegas, Hoover Dam, Kingman, and finally to the south rim of the Grand Canyon. The planned distance of 751.3 miles was expected to take the contestants through elevations ranging from 178 feet below sea level to 7,005 feet above, with a correspondingly wide range of temperatures.

Among those who could see a potential publicity bonanza in the new Mobilgas Economy Run was Art Hall, Lincoln-Mercury dealer in Long Beach, California, and a long-time racing buff. Seeking factory sponsorship for his car, Hall contacted Lincoln-Mercury headquarters, where he was accorded a cool reception. Mercury had gone upscale commencing with the 1949 model, competing now with the Buick Super instead of in the Dodge/Pontiac class, and the factory people could see little benefit in an economy contest.

Hall then contacted Benson Ford, recently appointed head of Lincoln-Mercury, and got his approval — though truthfully, Ford showed little enthusiasm for the idea. And as far as financing the undertaking was concerned, that was entirely the responsibility of Art Hall's dealership.

In order to provide the Mercury with every possible competitive edge, Hall recruited veteran race driver Bill Stroppe and his partner, master mechanic Clay Smith, to take charge of the project. A brand new, overdrive-equipped Mercury Sport Sedan was taken from stock, and Smith undertook to work his magic on its engine. The rules required that all mechanical specifications were to remain strictly stock, but there was nothing to prevent Smith from seeing to it that the engine was perfectly balanced, with all tolerances held within precise limits.

While Clay Smith was preparing what must have been the best-running stock Mercury flathead ever built, Bill Stroppe attended to a few little matters on his own. He and Smith had determined that the engine's optimum running temperature was 200 degrees. Because of the wide variation in outside temperature that was expected during the run, the use of a "winter front" was permitted. Older readers will recall that this device was commonly used in order to restrict the flow of air through the radiator during cold weather.

Now, most winter fronts were simple canvas affairs, weighing two or three pounds at most. Stroppe, however, seeking to raise the Mercury's weight, borrowed a 60-pound metal rig from a GMC truck. This was entirely legitimate, for the contest rules had nothing to say about what sort of winter front was permissible. He also saw to it that the Merc was equipped with the heavy, optional bumper guard.

Then, making good use of his racing contacts, Bill Stroppe acquired from Firestone a set of perfectly round, 100 percent rubber tires. Alignment was adjusted to take out the normal toe-in, so that the car rolled absolutely straight. Springs were adjusted so that with four people aboard — Stroppe, Smith, crewman Les Viland

and an official American Automobile Association observer — the car would sit perfectly level. Again, all these preparations, though perhaps unusual, were entirely legitimate according to the rule book provided by the AAA.

Then the course was meticulously reviewed. In his biography of Bill Stroppe, *Boss: The Bill Stroppe Story*, Tom Madigan describes what was done:

"Every mile was plotted so Stroppe... would know exactly what was coming up. Every traffic light was timed to the second; they never once during the whole trip consumed extra gas while idling at a signal. Bill also hired a weather man and some of the hands back at the agency to hussle [sic] along in front of them with a wind indicator and flags. Stroppe could look out the window as he drove along and monitor the winds, backing off the throttle in a head wind and increasing speed with a tail wind. Bill even ground off the heel of his driving shoe so it would not wiggle or vibrate while running."

A couple of days before the run was to begin, all the cars were impounded. A rainstorm came up, drenching many of the cars including the Mercury. En route, Stroppe discovered to his dismay that the electrically actuated overdrive had shorted out. According to the rules, no parts could be changed, so Bill relied on free-wheeling to provide at least some measure of advantage. At one point the Merc came rolling down a mountainside at speeds topping 80 miles an hour, the tires screaming their protest on the curves and the passengers sitting tight-lipped and no doubt offering silent prayers. But thanks to his racing experience, Stroppe was able to negotiate the turns without once touching the brakes.

There was a fuel stop at Mojave, and there Clay Smith — unobtrusively, so as not to alert the AAA observer — reached for the fuse box and rolled the overdrive fuse back and forth, hoping that it would make contact. The effort was successful, and the overdrive was employed throughout the balance of the trip.

In the end, the Mercury won the sweepstakes, achieving 61.27 ton miles per gallon — 2.15 tmpg better than the runner-up, a Cadillac Sixty-Special. It even came in a close second in the actual miles per gallon: 26.52, compared to 26.55 for the little Studebaker Champion.

Lincoln-Mercury hadn't even sent an observer to witness the event, but when Art Hall telephoned Benson Ford to tell him the results of the contest, Ford quickly volunteered to underwrite Hall's expenses. And as far as Bill Stroppe was concerned, the Economy Run proved to be the beginning of a lengthy and mutually profitable relationship with Lincoln-Mercury.

1950 MERCURY

trim level, as there was in the case of the Pontiac, for example. Just four body styles had been catalogued for 1949: Sport (four-door) Sedan, Club Coupe, Convertible and Station Wagon.

For 1950, however, the line was expanded just a little. In 1949 Mercury had moved up-market, to be priced closer to the Buick Super than to its traditional rival, Pontiac, as shown in the following table:

	Mercury	Pontiac 8	Buick Super
1948	$1,645	$1,599	$1,987
1949	$1,979	$1,779	$2,059

Doubtless in order to supply the dealers with a reasonably priced entry-level car, a new coupe was introduced on November 15, 1949, several weeks after the four carry-over 1950 styles. Known simply as the Type 72A Coupe, it was $105 cheaper than the "regular" Type 72 Club Coupe, and differed from it in several respects. Fixed rear quarter windows were used, for instance, in place of the flip-out type, and there were no reveal moldings around the windshield or the rear or side windows. The electric clock was omitted, as were wheel trim rings. There is no available record of how many of these "bare-bones" Mercs were built, but to the best of the writer's memory they were not very popular.

Then at the other end of the scale, on June 20, 1950, a dressed-up Club Coupe called the Monterey was introduced. Evidently conceived in response to GM's popular new "hardtop convertibles," it featured one of the industry's first vinyl-covered roofs. A number of dress-up items were included as standard equipment: rear fender shields, popularly known as "skirts"; a gold-winged hood ornament; dual outside mirrors; grille guard; two-tone instrument panel, painted to match the exterior color scheme; custom steering wheel; chrome-plated interior window frames; carpets; artificial leather headliner, and leather and Bedford cord (or, for $10 extra, all-leather) seats. Three exterior color combinations were offered: black with yellow vinyl top; Cortaro Red Metallic with black top, and Turquoise Blue with dark blue top.

For such a lavishly equipped automobile, the Monterey was a bargain at $2,146 — just $167 more than the Type 72 Club Coupe. But once again, production figures are unobtainable; for reporting purposes Mercury lumped the three coupes together. Estimates of the number of 1950 Montereys produced range from 800 units to more than 5,000.

The 1950 Mercury established an enviable reputation for itself, in terms of

Above: Backup lamps are also factory accessory. *Below left:* Fuel filler hides neatly away under lift-up door in left rear fender. *Below right:* Radio with rear seat speaker is a scarce option in a 1950 car.

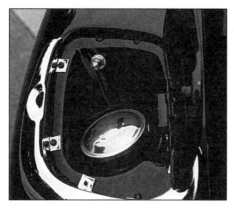

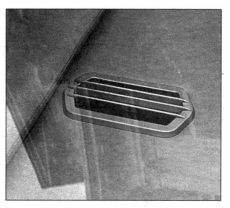

both economy and performance. Two NASCAR Grand National races were won by Mercs that year, and — as announced by Ed Sullivan on his *Toast of the Town* television show — a yellow Mercury convertible was selected to pace the Indianapolis 500. Then in the Mobilgas Economy Run — the first such contest to be held since the war — a Mercury Club Coupe driven by Bill Stroppe beat all comers, averaging 61.27 ton miles per gallon (see sidebar, page 68).

Walt Woron, editor of *Motor Trend*, took a 1950 Mercury Sport Sedan out for an eight-hour road test. His report, which was almost entirely favorable, made special mention of the car's roominess, comfortable ride, speed, acceleration, hill-climbing ability and stopping power. Accessibility in the engine compartment also drew favorable comment. Woron did admit, however, that the soft suspension detracted from the Merc's cornering ability.

Driving Impressions

Our driveReport subject, a beautifully restored 1950 Monterey belongs to Roy

Schneckloth, of Hayward, California. Roy had previously owned and restored a '51 Ford convertible — a beautiful car, but when the job was done he found that the car didn't satisfy him. "It drove lousy," he recalls. He wanted a heavier automobile.

Roy purchased the Merc a decade ago from Jerry Lew, whose own 1950 Mercury convertible has made two appearances in this publication (SIA #12 and #103). Lew, in turn, had acquired it from the original owner, an Oakland man who reportedly caught particular hell from his wife for having bought the car in the first place. It was the Monterey's premium price, evidently, that bothered the lady. "For that amount of money you could have had a Lincoln," was her complaint.

At the time Schneckloth acquired it, the Monterey's odometer registered 71,000 miles. But judging from the car's condition at the time, it is Schneckloth's guess that those numbers might possibly be making their second appearance on the dial, for it needed a great deal of mechanical work.

Roy was able to find another 1950 Merc with a virtually new engine in it; so

1950 MERCURY

Above: *driveReport car rides on lowering blocks at rear to give it a sleeker stance.* Below: *Interior boasts leather seat facings, chromed window frames.* Bottom: *Monterey dashboards were painted to match exterior color.*

a "transplant" took place. With the help of a friend, Roy overhauled the transmission and overdrive, and then went on to rebuild the front end and the brakes.

One door and the accompanying quarter panel had been damaged before the car came into Schneckloth's possession, and the repair had not been a good one. Both had to be replaced, as did all the moldings. The paint was shot and the vinyl top was checked and worn. Otherwise, however, the body was straight and solid.

Through *Hemmings Motor News,* Roy found someone to re-cone the radio speaker. Dale Wood, of Grass Valley, California, replaced the vinyl top and the leather-and-vinyl interior, closely matching the original materials. Woolen carpeting was imported from England. The engine compartment was meticulously detailed, even down to the cadmium plated bolts under the hood. And finally, Schneckloth — a body and fender man by trade — was responsible for the flawless black paint job, leaving the original finish on the firewall and door jambs.

From start to finish, the restoration took two and a half years. And then, at the 1991 Silverado Concours d'Elegance, the Mercury brought home a Third Place trophy. It was a good showing, for the competition was stiff, but when more detailing has been done, the car should do even better. There was one half-amusing, half-irritating sidelight to the concours: One of the judges insisted that Mercury hadn't built any Montereys until the 1952 model year. Not until Roy displayed a 1950 factory brochure showing the Monterey was the matter settled. (There's a moral to this, of course: When showing a car, especially if it is a comparatively rare model, take along any supporting documentation you can lay your hands on.)

Our brief tour behind the wheel of Roy Schneckloth's car served to confirm the judgment of the 1950 Mercury's contemporary reviewers. Since it was obviously intended to compete against the Buick, it's hardly surprising that its suspension provides a soft, floating ride, with — inevitably — some loss of the crisp handling that characterized earlier Mercs. It's a spacious car, with more adequate leg room than most club coupes. Seats are comfortable and supportive. The trunk is roomy, and the spare tire is mounted to one side where it is out of the way, yet easily accessible. A further convenience is supplied in the form of a remote pressure valve for the spare.

The clutch, whose action is very

Left: Flathead V-8's rated at 110 bhp. Below: Factory accessory tissue dispenser stows under dash. Bottom: Unusual remote valve stem hookup allows inflation of spare without opening trunk.

smooth, takes hold as soon as the pedal leaves the floor. Acceleration is brisk, and there's more top speed here than anyone in his right mind ought to use. Hills are taken with ease, thanks to the Merc's generous power and careful selection of the gear ratios. At highway speeds, with the overdrive engaged, the engine purrs along quietly and without strain, though the after-market dual mufflers aren't as quiet as the stock unit would be. Steering is light enough when the car is under way, though in parking one might wish for a power-assist.

Roy and his wife, Evelyn, have gone on club tours with this car, taking the scenic drive, for instance, up the Redwood Highway. It's the sort of automobile that, notwithstanding its 40-plus years, can be driven all day long at freeway speeds, without creating undue fatigue among its driver and passengers.

And of course, everywhere they go the Schneckloths are followed by admiring glances. ೋ

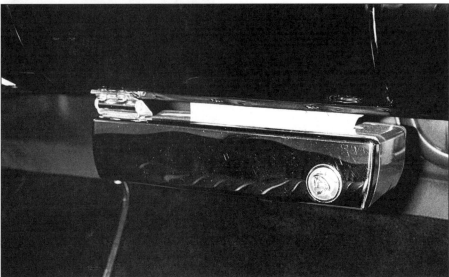

Acknowledgments and Bibliography

Automotive Industries, *May 1, 1948, and March 15, 1950; Dammann, George H. and James K. Wagner,* The Cars of Lincoln-Mercury; *Gunnell, John (ed.),* Standard Catalog of American Cars, 1946-1975; *Langworth, Richard M.,* Encyclopedia of American Cars, 1940-1970; *Lincoln-Mercury Division factory literature; Madigan, Tom,* Boss: The Bill Stroppe Story; Motor Age, *December 1949; Woron, Walter A., "Testing the Economy-Minded 1950 Mercury,"* Motor Trend, *May 1950; "Mercury Wins Economy Event,"* Motor Trend, *April 1950. Our thanks to Ralph Dunwoodie, Sun Valley, Nevada; Janet Ross, Librarian, National Automobile Museum, Reno, Nevada. Special thanks to Roy Schneckloth, Hayward, California.*

1954 MERCURY SUN VALLEY

LET THE SUNSHINE IN

By Tim Howley
Photos by the author

ANYONE who ever traveled in the old Vista-Dome trains would enjoy driving a 1954 Mercury Sun Valley. This and the 1954 Ford Skyliner, introduced a little later, were the first two mass-production cars to offer motorists a view of the sky above from a fully enclosed hardtop coupe. The Sun Valley concept was born out of Ford design research and experimental cars such as the Ford X- 100 and Lincoln XL-500. The roof above the Sun Valley's driver's compartment is made of 1/4-inch-thick transparent acrylic resin plastic tinted a blueish-green. The plastic was originally developed for use in military aircraft, and the ability to filter out heat rays was one of its basic specifications.

There are two myths about the Sun Valley:

1. Driver and front seat passengers cook on warm, sunny days. The Plexiglas roof filters out 60 percent of the sun's heat rays and 72 percent of the glare. Tests conducted in the Arizona desert between a Mercury Sun Valley and standard Monterey hardtop showed a difference in interior temperature of five degrees. If this was too much for driver comfort, an aluminized, zip and snap-in fabric shade screen was offered as an option, and Mercury offered air-conditioning for the first year.

2. The Sun Valley roof turns the passengers as green as Martians. While there is a slight green glow from the roof, it is more pleasant than annoying in the same sense as good quality sun glasses. The roof does not discolor faces, and there is no glare. For the most part, you hardly know the roof is tinted green unless you look up through it.

Since I owned the particular Sun Valley tested for a number of years, I can make some first-hand observations, comparing it with a 1983 Mustang with a sunroof, which my daughter owned until recently. In six years the Mustang sunroof (tinted blue) cooked the front seats and dashboard to the point of discoloration and permanent damage. It was quite uncomfortable driving the car on a hot summer day here in San Diego, even with the air-conditioning on. By contrast, the Sun Valley was always a joy to drive, even in the warmest California coastal weather. The car is now 35 years old, and the interior shows no signs of wear or fading from the sun through the top. The Sun Valley concept was brilliant, but evidently the public of the time was unwilling to accept it, as Mercury abandoned the concept after the 1955 model year. Ford Skyliners were continued into 1956.

While 1954 Ford Skyliners and 1955 Mercury Montclair Sun Valleys came in a wide choice of colors, 1954 Mercury Sun Valley color choices were quite limited. The basic body color was either a light mint green or cream, both with a dark green roof to match the tinted plastic front section. The interior was an extremely attractive, soft frosty green and cream. Standard seat inserts were a light green and silver weave nylon with green plastic as an option. Seat tops and backs could be ordered in high-quality leather, the same green and cream combination. Now, over the years I have seen 1954 Mercury Sun Valleys with other exterior body colors, such as white or black, but I believe these cars have been repainted. I have never seen a 1954 Sun Valley with interior colors other than those described here.

1954 was the last year of the three-year body design and, as such, the car received a major facelift. Grille, bumpers, side trim and wheel discs were all new. The car received a major tail lift as well, with reworked rear fenders and wraparound taillamps. With the wheelbase remaining at the same 118 inches as the 1953, the overall length went from 202.2 inches to 203.7 inches. The total effect was a car that looked

Originally published in Special Interest Autos #113, Sept.-Oct. 1989

Driving Impressions

The 1954 Mercury Sun Valley feels like no other car of that year except a 1954 Lincoln Capri coupe, junior size. The moment you step behind the wheel you know you are surrounded by something very special, with clean, straightforward interior styling and soft tones of green that accent the greenhouse roof. The car is a constant reminder to me of my teenage years, riding in the silver Vista-Dome Burlington-Zephyr trains that sped twice daily between Minnesota's Twin Cities and Chicago.

The most noticeable differences between the '54 and '53 Mercury are acceleration (especially in the lower speed range), speed, roadability and handling. Tom McCahill, in road testing a 1954 Sun Valley for *Mechanix Illustrated,* commented, "Where the new Mercury outjumps the big Lincoln is in its 0-30 mph performance. The standard synchromesh gets to 30 mph in 3.2 seconds. And the new Merc with Merc-O-Matic drive gets there in 3.4. Above 30 the automatic transmission slows this rig down considerably. It takes 15.6 seconds to get to 60. Top speed with synchromesh averages between 104 and 106 mph, but even with the automatic it will top 100 and averages around 102. After the initial burst of speed, the Lincoln will soon eat up the Mercury if the distance is long enough. In a one mile run from a standstill the 1954 Lincoln will beat the Merc by quite a few car lengths."

Science & Mechanics noted a flat spot in accelerating between 50 and 60 and said that the Merc-O-Matic, with its 3.54:1 rear axle ratio (same as the 1953) penalized he car's acceleration potential slightly.

Our driveReport car is equipped with a 292, which gives a lot of improvements in performance in the higher-speed ranges, and this engine change is definitely favored over the original 256. I should point out to purists that there are no noticeable outward appearance differences in the engines that would cost you points in a concours, but what a difference in high-speed performance the extra 27 horses make.

I can't say enough good things about Mercury's new ball-joint front suspension plus the power steering on this car. They team up to give you a silk-smooth, jolt-free ride over all but the roughest roads, and cornering ability is excellent even by today's standards. The car has a flat, sure ride, maybe a bit on the stiff side, but I personally prefer it that way to the Mrs. Plushbottom brands of the Fifties. The car hugs the road tightly even in serpentine turns, and side tilt is only minimal when making a 285-foot radius circle at 40 mph. As we photographed the car we watched driver Larry Fournier slam the car into 40-mph turns that would have made the '53 rear end break loose or go into a spin. On the '54 you don't even hear any tire squeal. The photographs tell the story of just how little lean this car has in the turns. That's my son, Michael, riding beside Larry. Michael can still remember co-piloting the car when he was only 8. Of course it didn't perform or handle like that back in those days, and it hasn't looked this new since its early years in San Mateo.

I only wish Mercury engineers hadn't made the steering response so slow. Five turns plus lock-to-lock is much too slow for such a fine handling car. And say

your prayers when you hit the brakes in a high-speed panic stop. While the braking is adequate at lower speeds, it leaves you holding your breath at any speed above 50. *Motor Life* recorded a stopping aistance of 178 feet at 60 mph. compared to 45 feet at 30. To realize how inadequate these brakes really are, all you have to do is turn off the engine and put your foot down on the pedal. Since Mercury was taking its engineering cues from Lincoln in the engine and suspension we wonder why they didn't follow through with the brakes. The problem was corrected in 1955 when the drums went from 11 to 12 inches for 30 more square inches of brake lining area.

Fuel economy is pretty good by 1955 ohv V-8 standards. The car runs okay on leaded regular, but prefers premium, and will deliver 15 mpg or better at a steady 60 mph, and nearly 20 mpg at a steady 30.

The ride is extremely comfortable and the driver can see the ends of all four fenders. The hood is typically high, a characteristic of all Ford-built cars of the era. The first 28 feet of the road in front of you is blocked off. Wind noise is low at highway speeds, even with the front vent windows open. The body is still tight and rattle free after all these years. Fortunately, this car was never hit. The gauges are all very visible, but the heater/vent controls on the shelf in front of you take some getting used to. Your arms are forever bumping into the steering column when you use them. Well, they're part of 1952-'54 Mercury charms. In the 1954 Mercury Sun Valley there are many more charms than annoyances. Fifties motoring memories are made of cars like this.

1954 MERCURY

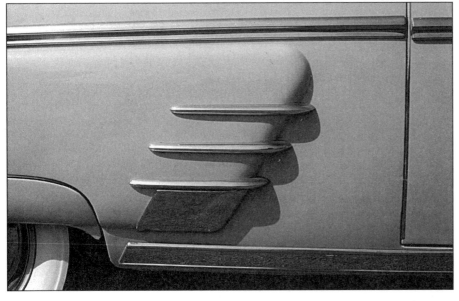

Among the changes from the '53 Mercs were a heavier, chromier grille, wraparound taillamps in the mode of the '54 Lincoln, and an additional rear fender accent stripe.

more like a Lincoln than a Ford, even though it shared the basic Ford body shell. The most noticeable interior change was the new "Interceptor" instrument cluster, which replaced the 1952-53 separate "pod" with a cluster handsomely integrated into the dash. However, the quadrant or tray of heater/vent controls was retained.

The 1954 Mercury body had the highest quality assembly, with careful soldering of body joints and meticulous attention to fit and finish inside and out. A new hood-lock support plate was added to reduce vibrations of the front sheet metal. A new steering column support did the same thing for road vibration.

For the first time Mercury offered MacPherson strut ball joint front suspension, which the famous Mexican Road Race Lincolns had featured since 1952. Ball joint suspension, touted by Ford as being all new at the time, was anything but. Lancaster experimented with such a system in 1900; Porsche in 1933; Daimler-Benz in 1932; Sizaire in 1933. Thompson Products experimented with ball joints in the early forties, and Ford began serious research into the system in 1945. By 1954 ball joints were favored by Jaguar and the Aston Martin DB3 and DB3S.

Ford called their system MacPherson-strut, named after the corporation's head of engineering who developed it. Ball joint front suspension had enormous advantages for cars of the fifties. It created more room for even bigger engines. It helped eliminate 12 of the previous 16 grease fittings. The system is far easier to service than older king-pin systems, although the savings in labor will never show up on your repair bill. The ball joint design is amazingly resistant to loss of correct wheel alignment. And, most important of all, there is a world of improvement in high-speed handling.

The chassis of the 1954 Mercury has the strength of Gibraltar. It is a ladder type, beefed with a massive X bracing for the convertible. A tubular cross-member is so located in the forward portion of the frame that the oil pan can at last be removed directly, without dismantling other parts of the car. *Cars* magazine observed: "The frame side members are full box section and they do something new at the front end. The old problem in frame construction for others as well as for Mercury, has been designing the frame around the spring pockets. A new approach to this problem has been made possible by ball joint suspension, and the box section side members are now split so they surround the spring pockets, transforming

what was one of the most critical fatigue-sensitive parts of the frame into one of the strongest."

But the biggest Mercury news for 1954 was the engine. "So new in fact," quipped *Motor Trend*, "that designers could have carried the Sun Valley idea a little further with a Plexiglas hood to let the public in on the brand new engine." Ford development on an ohv V-8 began in 1948, and production was first realized on the 1952 Lincoln. The new 1952 Ford ohv 6 was developed out of the same engineering. This was followed by a series of brand new truck, tractor and industrial engines, and finally Mercury and Ford in 1954.

The new Mercury and Ford ohv V-8, while perhaps not quite as quiet and smooth as the old flathead at idle and low speeds, was remarkably quiet and smooth in its own right, especially at higher speeds. And the Mercury and Ford versions with solid tappets were almost as quiet as the Lincoln version with hydraulic lifters. It was a more economical engine than the old flathead for a number of reasons. A shorter stroke meant reduced friction. There was improved thermal efficiency because less heat was lost in the cooling system. The fuel worked more efficiently because the compression ratio was higher. The engine breathed more freely, due to a new induction system and exhaust system. In place of the old three-port exhaust manifolds, the new manifolds provided an exhaust outlet for each cylinder. The engine also boasted the first four-venturi carburetor available for a standard transmission car.

Such a radical new engine was not without its problems. The 256 cubic inches were not nearly enough to haul over 3,500 pounds of automobile. And even though the car had a respectable acceleration ratio (0-60 mph in 15.6 seconds with Merc-O-Matic) and a top speed in excess of 100 mph, the car cried for a bigger engine. The 292, which Mercury brought out a year later, was a vast improvement. In restoring a 1954 Mercury, one should give serious consideration to going to a 292 or 312,

Grille design is clean and horizontal in appearance. Wheel covers carry a representation of the mythical Mercury. Car looks particularly smooth and sleek from out back.

Our Sunny California Sun Valley

Rarely does a driveReport writer/photographer have the opportunity to select a car with a history known from the day it left the showroom. Even more rare is the case where the reporter once owned the actual car. But such is the special situation with this much loved automobile.

The car was purchased new by a San Mateo, California, man who loved it so much he kept it for about 15 years. After around 35,000 miles he found the original 256 was not quite as wonderful as the initial road reports and Mercury publicity had led him to believe. So he had a local garage install a low-mileage 292 out of a wreck. He continued driving the car daily up until 1969 and about 110,000 miles. The man, then retired, offered the car to the late and well known East San Francisco Bay collector, Owen Owens. Owens bought the car and simply put it away in his large Emeryville warehouse with nearly 100 other cars. This is where I discovered the car in 1972 and purchased it from Owen.

The engine was tired and sludged up, but we enjoyed the car anyway in sunny San Rafael. In 1977 we moved to San Diego and brought the Mercury down. A long engine project ensued, which I will not detail here. In 1982 we moved back to the San Francisco Bay area briefly and sold the uncompleted project to San Diego

collector Larry Fournier. I knew that Larry had restored it, so when I began writing up the Sun Valley story for *SIA* in early April 1989 I gave Larry a call. He suggested that I come right over because he was planning to sell the car at the Imperial Palace Auction in Las Vegas, April 22-23.

By this time a lot of professional work had been done on the car: engine and transmission rebuild, paint, complete rechrome, carpeting and lots of detailing. The original upholstery, still good after 35 years, simply needed a good cleaning, and the original Sun Valley Plexiglas top bad not crazed or cracked. It had been a long road for the Sun Valley, and a lot of very fine work had been done on the car.

We both lamented the selling of the Sun Valley as Dean Kruse slammed down the gavel at $10,250—right on the money for a Number Two condition car. This is the nicest really original 1954 Sun Valley I have ever seen in the Western United States. It is dent free, bondo free, rust free, and had never been altered down through the years. As Larry and I both lamented, "Somebody bought one awfully nice car." We are both delighted that we will be able to relive our memories of it through this *SIA* driveReport. I had tears in my eyes and a lump in my throat when I wrote up this one.

specifications

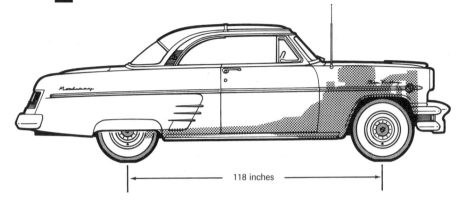

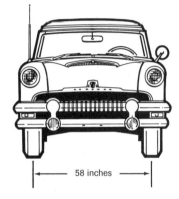

118 inches

58 inches

1954 Mercury Sun Valley Hardtop Model 60F

Price when new	$2,582 f.o.b. Dearborn
Options	Radio, heater, power steering, power brakes, Merc-O-Matic, deluxe steering wheel, fender skirts, stainless steel rocker panels, door-handle plates, white sidewall tires

ENGINE
Type	OHV V-8, water-cooled, cast-iron block, 5 main bearings, full pressure lubrication
Bore x stroke	3.62 inches x 3.10 inches
Displacement	256 cubic inches
Max. bhp @ rpm	161 @ 4,400
Max. torque @ rpm	238 @ 2,200-2,800
Compression ratio	7.5:1
Induction system	4-bbl. downdraft carburetor, mechanical pump
Exhaust system	Cast-iron manifolds, single exhaust
Electrical system	6-volt battery/coil

TRANSMISSION
Type	Merc-O-Matic 3-speed hydraulic torque converter with planetary gears
Ratios: Drive	1.48, 1.00*
Low	2.44*
Reverse	2.00*

* Plus torque converter

DIFFERENTIAL
Type	Hypoid, spiral-bevel gears
Ratio	3.54:1
Drive axles	Semi-floating

STEERING
Type	Power-assisted worm and roller
Turns lock-to-lock	5.1
Ratio	26.4:1
Turn circle	41.5 feet

BRAKES
Type	4-wheel hydraulic drums, internal expanding, vacuum assist
Drum diameter	11 inches
Total swept area	159.08 square inches

CHASSIS & BODY
Frame	Ladder type, box section side-rails, K-member braces
Body construction	All steel
Body style	2-door, 6-passenger coupe with Plexiglas roof section

SUSPENSION
Front	Independent A-arms, ball joint spindles, coil springs, tubular hydraulic shocks, anti-roll bar
Rear	Solid axle, semi-elliptic longitudinal leaf springs, tubular hydraulic shocks
Tires	7.10 x 15
Wheels	Pressed steel discs, drop-center rims, lug-bolted to brake drums

WEIGHTS AND MEASURES
Wheelbase	118 inches
Overall length	203.7 inches
Overall width	74.4 inches
Overall height	62.2 inches
Front track	58 inches
Rear track	56 inches
Ground clearance	6.75 inches
Shipping weight	3,535 pounds

CAPACITIES
Crankcase	5 quarts
Cooling system	20 quarts
Fuel tank	19 gallons

FUEL CONSUMPTION
Best	20.5 mpg
Average	15.1 mpg

PERFORMANCE
0-30	3.4 seconds
0-50	11.3 seconds
0-60	15.6 seconds
0-70	21.1 seconds
Top speed	104-106 mph w/overdrive; 102 with Merc-O-Matic
Speedometer error	At 60 mph on speedometer, actual speed 55 mph

(from *Mechanix Illustrated* road test of 1954 Mercury Sun Valley with Merc-O-Matic)

This page: DriveReport car sports accessory door handle guards. *Facing page, top:* Plexiglas roof panel is accented by stainless trim. *Far left:* Sun Valley roof gives plenty of visibility, yet filters the rays effectively. *Center:* Mercury is also found hiding in trunk latch. *Center right:* Plenty of shiny stuff accents the roof pillars. *Middle:* Mercury began the short-lived false hood scoop craze in the fifties. *Bottom:* Model identification is spelled out on front fenders.

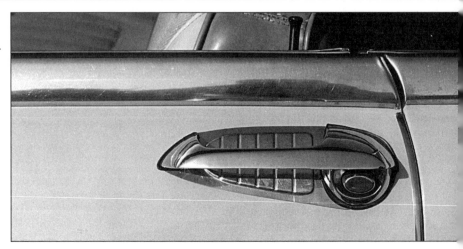

1954 MERCURY

which were identical in outward appearance to the 256. Moreover, a rebuildable 256 today is nearly impossible to find, and even the 292s and 312s are getting mighty scarce.

Even though the 1954 engine had more torque than the 1953, the Merc-O-Matic transmission remained unchanged, and the overdrive ratio was

still .70 to 1. However, the standard transmission had its clutch diameter increased from 10 to 10.25 inches, total plate pressure was increased, and the clutch linkage was redesigned to reduce pedal pressure approximately seven percent.

Most 1954 Mercurys were equipped with Bendix power steering and power brakes, which were offered for the first time in 1953.

The choice of models was the same as in 1953, with the addition of the Sun Valley. In the Custom series, there was a two- and four-door sedan and a hardtop. The fancier Monterey models had a four-door sedan, standard hardtop, Sun Valley hardtop, convertible and station wagon with simulated wood trim. The Custom models have mostly broadcloth and other fabric upholsteries. Functional but not fancy. The Monterey models sport quite elegant and often colorful two-tone interiors, in the Lincoln tradition. Lincoln-Mercury advertising of the year boasted, "Designed for Modern Living." Interiors were done in durable and frequently bright-colored vinyls, including even vinyl headliners. Seat faces and backs had nylon weave inserts. All vinyl seats or leather seats were optional. Vinyl headliners were standard in the hardtops, optional in the sedan. The Monterey models also had more interior chrome and painted metal trim. Outside, the Monterey models can be distinguished by their plastic medallions on the front fenders and "Monterey" script on the rear fenders.

The 1954 Mercury Sun Valley listed for $2,582, as compared to $2,452 for the standard Monterey hardtop. Most Sun Valleys were shipped from the fac-

The 1954 Mercury Engine

The faithful Ford flathead V-8 introduced in 1932 remained the basic Ford arid Mercury powerplant through 1953, Ford's 50th Anniversary year. By the early Fifties, much of the original machinery was still in operation and, having produced over 20 million engines, it was about worn out. This obsolescence coincided with Ford's corporate decision to phase out flathead design completely in favor of modern ohv V-8s and 6s for all passenger cars and trucks.

The new engine project began in 1948. The idea was to produce a whole family of ohv V-8s and a six, which ultimately became the 317.5-c.i.d. 1952 Lincoln engine, the 215-c.i.d. 1952 Ford six, the 239-c.i.d. l954 Ford V-8 and the 256-c.i.d. 1954 Mercury V-8. Before any of these designs became firm, 640 experimental test engines were built and completely rebuilt an average of eight times. Over 90,000 drafting and engineering hours were charged to the project and over a quarter million hours went into dynamometer testing alone. The prototypes of the production engines were subjected to more than 3½ million road miles of road testing.

The '54 Merc does not have the same block as the 1952-'55 Lincoln, but it is engineered along the same design. It is a compact, nickel-chrome-iron alloy casting. Its most unique feature is a crankcase that extends almost three inches below the crank centerline, providing the five main bearings of the stiffer, lighter crankshaft with support over a 240-degree area rather than the former 180 degrees. The deep-skirt crankcase not only permits stronger crankshaft and transmission support, it also ensures more positive bearing and oil pan seal. The bottom of the crankcase flares out towards the rear, providing anchorage points for the bell housing on each side of the flywheel and nearly three inches below the centerline. These connections, plus the normal ones over the flywheel, make the engine-transmission assembly extremely rigid.

Like all Ford crankshafts, the Merc crankshaft is made of forged steel. Ford's crankshaft casting process and the alloys used were unique to the industry. The 1954 Mercury crankshaft is 20 pounds lighter than the 1953 unit. It is so rigid and well balanced that a vibration damper is not employed. Pistons and connecting rods are much re-engineered due to the new oversquare design.

Motor Trend, in writing up the 1954 Mercury Sun Valley in its January 1954 issue, explained Ford's new combustion chamber design: "It follows the route pioneered by Ricardo [Sir Harry R. Ricardo, a noted automotive engineer-designer]. It's kidney shaped, with a large quench (or squish) area at the end farthest from the spark plug. When the piston comes up on the compression stroke, the mixture is caught and squished out into the main volume, creating the turbulence necessary for even burning. As the flame front progresses away from the plug, it compresses the gases ahead. Conditions are ripe for detonation, but the squish area now

becomes a quench area. The unburned gases are confined and cooled by contact with the cylinder head and piston. Proponents of the hemispherical combustion chamber argue that this works too effectively; the remaining gases, they say, aren't burned at all. At any rate, Ford-Mercury engineers certainly had their choice. They have made many a tank engine with hemispherical combustion chambers, but have chosen the squish type for passenger cars."

Ford began experimenting with chamber design when they started developing their ohv V-8s. They tried hundreds of varieties of shapes before they arrived at the final design. They came to the conclusion that for the infinitely variable requirements of passenger cars, the kidney shape that offered maximum squish was the answer. It was purely a matter of preference. Others had equal success with wedge shapes, half-round shapes and hemispherical chambers. And Ford certainly had plenty of success with its hemi tank engines during World War II.

The overhead valves are driven by rocker arms acting off pushrods and solid tappets controlled by a precision-molded camshaft. The rockers are fitted with adjusting screws and are lubed by pressure oil, which flows through the rocker shafts. There are two holes in each rocker through which oil is delivered to the valve stem and pushrod socket. The method of oiling is probably the greatest weakness of the engine design. The pinholes in the rockers are prone to clogging up. Also, the main oil supply lines to the rocker shafts tend to clog up. Thus, you would see a lot of Fifties Fords/Mercs with outside oilers added after 70,000 or so miles. Another problem was oil pumps that failed early on. Finally, oil sludging and caking at the bottom of the oil pan covered the screen and rendered the entire system useless. Any or all of these problems could occur as early as 30,000 miles, as was the case with the original engine in our driveReport Sun Valley. However, this writer has learned from years of personal experience with this family of engines that pulling the oil pan,

cleaning the oil screen, installing a new oil pump and cleaning out the rocker arm assemblies does wonders for these cars without ever going to the expense of an engine overhaul or rebuild.

Other noteworthy features of the 1954 Mercury engine include a completely new intake manifold of an over-and-under design. Its most important aspect is the balanced length of each runner which leads from the carburetor to each port. The construction also allows extremely large and uniform port areas for breathing, never achieved in the old flatheads.

Crowning the manifold is the first four-venturi carburetor in Mercury's price class and the first which adapts well to conventional transmissions. In previous engines, the throttle valves in both the front and rear venturis had always been linked mechanically, so that opening the auxiliary throttles had been a function of foot pressure on the accelerator. While this worked very well for automatics, it did not prove at all satisfactory on standard-transmission cars, when opening the secondary venturis.

In the Mercury setup, the front main throttle valves are operated by the accelerator pedal. Then, air flow through the main venturis creates a vacuum, which acts upon a diaphragm linked to the secondary throttle valves. Thus there is no mechanical linkage between the front and rear throttles—only vacuum connects them.

There were a number of other improvements, including chain-driven camshaft, radical redesign of the cooling system, better ventilation of the carburetor and a greatly improved electrical system, although still six volts in 1954. It is unfortunate that Ford designers chose to place the distributor at the back of the engine where it is most difficult to service. But, all things considered, the new Merc 256 and its companion, the Ford 239, were remarkable improvements over the flatheads, not so much in dependability and smoothness as in performance, economy and ease of servicing the valves. These engines paved the way for the Ford 272.

1954 MERCURY

tory heavily loaded with options, and were priced in dealer showrooms close to $4,000, nearly as much as a Lincoln. Total 1954 Mercury production was 259,305, putting Mercury slightly behind Pontiac, which still retained the antiquated L-head six and eight and kingpin front suspension; but Mercury was well ahead of Dodge, which offered the even more advanced Hemi ohv V-8, packaged in coffin-like styling. Take your pick.

Nine thousand, seven hundred sixty-one Mercury Sun Valleys were built for 1954, a mere 1,787 for 1955. No production figures were offered for 1956, but I have been told that a few hundred were actually produced. ✍

Acknowledgments and Bibliography
"Mercury Sun Valley Road Test and Ford-Mercury ohv V-8 Story," Cars, *March 1954;* "Greenhouse on wheels," Motor Trend, *January 1954;* "1954 Mercury Monterey Hardtop Road Test," Science & Mechanics, *June 1954;* "Tom McCahill Tests the 1954 Mercury Sun Valley," Mechanix Illustrated, *March 1954;* "Griff Borgeson Tests the 1954 Mercury," Motor Life, *May 1954;* "1955 Ford Crown Victoria," Special Interest Autos #37, *Nov.-Dec. 1976,* and "1952 Mercury Monterey," Special Interest Autos #43, *Jan.-Feb. 1978. Special thanks to Larry Fournier, LaMesa, California, for furnishing the Sun Valley for photos and road test.*

1956 MERCURY MONTCLAIR
"A Mercury is to see yourself in."

by John F. Katz
photos by Vince Wright

THE little boy is maybe five years old, but his short, medium-brown hair lies perfectly combed and Brylcreemed; his black leather shoes shine like mirrors. He's crouching low, head comfortably cradled in his hands, admiring his own distorted image in the massive chrome bumper of a new '56 Montclair. The ad copy continues:

"A Mercury is a lot of glittering moments. A Mercury reflects you. A Mercury is power shined up to GO."

It's a charming old *Saturday Evening Post* sort of advertisement, evoking sweet memories of a childhood spent infatuated with the big, shiny cars of the fifties. But it unintentionally summarizes Mercury's struggle in those days to

establish an identity. Stretched too thin between the low-priced Ford and the luxury-class Lincoln, Mercury reflected an image that never quite came into focus. Like the words of the ad, it suggested power and glitter but stabbed haphazardly at meaning—and ultimately said nothing at all.

The '56 Mercury deserved better.

"The problem with Mercury," recalled Carl Pfeiffer, product planning manager for Mercury from 1954-60, "was it had a problem making up its mind what kind

of Mercury it wanted—whether it wanted to be a full-sized car to compete with Oldsmobile or Buick, or whether it wanted to be a dressed-up Ford." For the most part, the finance crew liked a Ford-based Mercury requiring minimum investment; the car was not a hot seller, they reasoned, so why pour money into it? On the other hand, the product men argued that a more unique Mercury could *become* a hot seller by competing more effectively against GM's upper-middle divisions.

This ongoing disagreement alternately tugged the Mercury up-market and down. Born in 1939 as an upgraded Ford, the Mercury shared the smaller of two Lincoln bodies in 1949-51 and then

Originally published in Special Interest Autos #161, Sept.-Oct. 1997

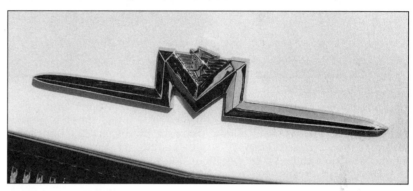

Above: "Lightning bolt" side trim was new for '56. **Right:** "Big M" theme was carried prominently up front. **Below:** Big bumper guards are integral part of front end design. **Below right:** Aircraft-style hood ornament was first seen on '55 Mercs.

returned to a Ford shell in '52. How much all this waffling actually hampered Mercury in the sales race is debatable. Mercury inevitably lagged behind mighty Buick and Pontiac, but consistently out-distanced DeSoto and—after 1949—all of the independents, too. And in a good year, Mercury could threaten a flagging Dodge or Oldsmobile. But the image issue clearly troubled Ford insiders as much as it irked the pundits of the press, who complained that they were never sure whether a Mercury was a "big Ford" or a "baby Lincoln."

The '54 Mercury did little to answer this question—although it heralded some significant engineering advances, including the first ball-joint steering in the medium-price field, and a neat 256-cubic-inch overhead-valve V-8 that made 162 bhp, or about 30 percent more than the fabled flathead it replaced. A "Sun Valley" hardtop with a huge, tinted Plexiglas panel in its roof drew positive attention, even if it sold poorly.

But the product planners saw a real opportunity in the 1955 model year. Management had budgeted for extensive revision of the 1952-54 Ford/Mercury body shell and mechanical package. Both the Ford and Mercury studios deserve credit for deftly squeezing an all-new look out of the three-year-old body, adding a fashionably curved windshield, flashy new side trim, and mostly new sheet metal all around.

But the Mercury stylists, led by Design Director Gene Bordinat and Studio Chief Don DeLaRossa, also managed to put some more visual distance between their car and the Ford—by emphasizing everything that had made a Mercury a Mercury since 1952. The double-bar bumper grille grew squarer and bolder; and the headlamps, merely Frenched before, now peered out from below sharply peeked hoods. Both Ford and Mercury had worn the vestiges of a separate rear fender in '52-54, but while this form all but disappeared from the '55 Ford, on the Mercury it grew into a

bold *faux* scoop, creeping up almost to the level of the door handles. An uncharacteristically modest press release called the changes "evolutionary"; in truth, they transformed the car completely.

"That was a major departure for the Mercury," said Pfeiffer. "We really tried to camouflage the Ford and make a different car out of it." The '55 Merc, he continued, "had more unique styling features, more unique sheet metal, and was upgraded in ride and handling and performance. At the time the '55 model was approved, the company still didn't know what the Mercury wanted to be. But we did persuade them to invest a little more money to make it more of a B-body [Buick and Oldsmobile] competitor."

The chassis *was* all-new, stretched one inch in wheelbase and three inches in rear track. (Wagons, which shared Ford rear quarters, retained the old chassis dimensions.) The ball-joint front suspension was significantly revised,

and the rear shocks installed at a more horizontal angle. Brakes now featured increased lining area. "We tried to upgrade the car in noise and harshness and vibration," added Pfeiffer, "so it would be a noticeably better car [than the Ford]." He credits engineers Neil Blume and Joe Felts with tuning a chassis that entertained the road testers while "the basic four-door sedan [remained] a comfortable, middle-aged couple's car."

Meanwhile, engine designer Victor Raviolo reshaped the combustion chambers for better valve cooling (and hence, resistance to knock) while adding aluminum pistons, a higher-lift cam, and an improved Holley carburetor. Metallurgical changes to the camshaft, tappets, and pushrods prevented the scuffing and galling that had flawed the '54s; while changes to the air cleaner, rocker covers, timing chain, and oil pump all

reduced the noise level of the already quiet engine. Bored and stroked to 292 cubic inches, the top Mercury motor now produced 198 bhp and 286 foot pounds of torque. Performance improved dramatically; for the first time ever, a showroom-stock Merc could break 100 mph.

Backing up the revised engine was an almost completely redesigned "MX" Merc-O-Matic transmission, with a new case for strength and new hydraulic controls for smooth shifts and more responsive kickdowns. And with passing gear more readily available, the engineers switched to a numerically lower final drive for better economy while cruising. Full-throttle starts now engaged first gear, while previous Merc-O-Matics had started in second unless the driver manually selected first.

Mercury ads bragged about the new "exclusive styling" and assured would-

be buyers that "you don't have to look twice to tell it's a Mercury." *Motor Life* noticed the Mercury's improved handling, and *Motor Trend* added that "you'll search a long time before you find a better-handling car than this one." The crisp roadability of the new Merc reminded Tom McCahill of the Carrera-Panamericana Lincolns. And in a year-end wrap-up, *MT* tied the Mercury with the all-new '55 Chevy as America's "best-handling and most roadable cars"—displacing the '54 Ford for the title. Yet perhaps the most welcome accolade of all came from *Motor Trend* Editor Walt Woron, who wrote that the new Mercury "looks and feels entirely different from the '55 Fords."

Even so, Mercury had saved its masterstroke for the mid-winter doldrums. At the Chicago Auto Show in January, Mercury debuted the "low-silhouette" Montclair, a two-door hardtop with a chopped windshield and a sleeker, flatter roofline. A panel of contrasting color below the side windows emphasized its long, low shape; while dual exhausts with oval extensions completed the package at the rear. The Montclair stood only 58.6 inches high, a full two inches lower than a Monterey sedan. Mercury also showed a Sun Valley Montclair with a Plexiglas roof panel, and a Montclair convertible with the same cut-down windshield as the hardtops.

The Montclair hardtop shared its greenhouse with the Fairlane Crown Victoria, and the Fairlane Sunliner convertible used the same windshield. In April, however, Mercury debuted a completely unique product: a Montclair four-door sedan just 0.2 inches taller than the hardtop. Its notched beltline stepped down slightly just aft of the windshield, then kicked back up again at the rear door handle to meet the quarter panel—so that the side windows appeared to be countersunk into the body. According to Pfeiffer, this "involved a lot of unique sheet metal and quite an investment." Mercury called the Montclair four-door a "hardtop," and camouflaged its window frames and center roof pillar with chrome plating. It wasn't a true hardtop, of course, but *Motor Trend* called it "1955's best-looking four-door sedan."

Mercury took another important step away from Ford that April. Since 1952, Dearborn management had discussed reorganizing the company, with more separate divisions to better compete with GM and Chrysler. Product planner Francis C. "Jack" Reith proposed positioning a lower-middle-class "Edsel" and an upper-middle Mercury between Ford and Lincoln. Management approved this plan on April 15, establishing a separate Mercury Division with Reith as general manager.

As if to confirm the wisdom of this de-

cision, Mercury built a record 43,354 cars that month, and made the model year its best yet, too, with 329,808 cars produced. Seventy-five percent of them were high-buck Montereys or Montclairs, and 85 percent packed automatic transmissions. In November, Mercury announced that it would boost the capacity of its St. Louis assembly plant by 25 percent; then build an all-new facility in Rosemead, California, and—an industry first—a plant dedicated to station-wagon assembly in Wayne, Michigan.

The 1956 Mercury models that debuted on September 29, 1955, were not radically changed but were significantly refined. Raviolo continued to develop the ohv engine, now bored an additional .05 inch and stroked an additional .14 for 312 cubic inches. A new camshaft, new rockers, larger ports and passages, "full vacuum" spark control, and an even larger carburetor all contributed to faster starts and improved response to the throttle. And Mercury switched to 12-volt electrics.

Manual-shift Mercs came with 8:1 compression and 210 bhp at 4,600 rpm—more than the most powerful 292 had produced in '55. Customs with Merc-O-Matic came with 8.4:1 compression and 215 bhp, while Merc-O-Matic Montereys and Montclairs featured 9:1 compression and 225 bhp. Custom buyers could also specify the 225-horse engine, but only with automatic transmission. According to some sources, a 235-bhp V-8 appeared on the option list late in the model year. Dealers sold a 260-bhp dual-carburetor kit over the counter—ostensibly for stock-car racing.

The chassis guys softened the shocks for '56, but *Motor Trend* could detect no appreciable change in ride or handling. The '56 Merc still leaned only moderately in the sharpest turns, and understeered until all four wheels started to drift—a situation easily corrected with ample applications of throttle and steering. New fixed-anchor brakes didn't improve stopping performance but they did simplify production; too many '55s had left the factory with their brakes mis-adjusted.

Styling changes included a new grille and rather more elaborate taillights, although both followed well-established Mercury themes. The crest-like medallion that adorned the hood of '55 Mercs gave way to a simple, bold, "M," which fit well with Mercury's new "Big M" advertising campaign. ("We drove THE BIG M around in circles night and day—so you can take any curve with ease," boasted one ad. "We took THE BIG M up the steepest mountains," bragged another, "so you can sail up any hill with ease.")

But the most noticeable change was in

Facing page, top: Clever use of two-toning makes Merc look even longer and lower than it is. *Bottom:* Texture at top of grille harks back to '49 Mercurys. **This page, above:** Spinner style wheel covers were standard on Montclairs. **Below left:** Medallions on fender trim began with 1954 models. **Right:** Like all of Clyde Horst's cars, this one has a correct vintage sticker.

The Mercury Family for '56

	Price	Shipping Weight	Production
Medalist			
Two-door sedan	$2,254	3,430 pounds	20,582
Four-door sedan (1)	$2,313	3,500 pounds	6,653
Two-door hardtop (1)	$2,389	3,545 pounds	11,892
Phaeton (2)	$2,458	3,530 pounds	6,685
Custom			
Two-door sedan	$2,351	3,505 pounds	16,343
Four-door sedan	$2,410	3,520 pounds	15,860
Two-door hardtop	$2,485	3,560 pounds	20,857
Phaeton (3)	$2,555	3,550 pounds	12,187
Convertible	$2,712	3,665 pounds	2,311
Station Wagon	$2,722	3,790 pounds	17,770
Monterey			
Four-door sedan	$2,555	3,570 pounds	26,735
Two-door hardtop	$2,630	3,590 pounds	42,863
Sport Sedan (4)	$2,652	3,550 pounds	11,765
Phaeton (3)	$2,700	3,800 pounds	10,726
Station Wagon	$2,977	3,885 pounds	13,280
Montclair			
Two-door hardtop	$2,765	3,620 pounds	50,562
Sport Sedan (4)	$2,786	3,610 pounds	9,617
Phaeton (3)	$2,835	3,640 pounds	23,493
Convertible	$2,900	3,725 pounds	7,762

1) available after February 1.
2) available after March 9.
3) available after January 2.
4) available until January 2.

specifications

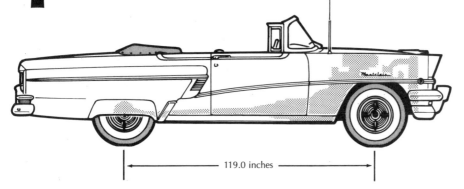
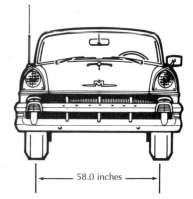

← 119.0 inches →

← 58.0 inches →

1956 Mercury Montclair convertible

Base price	$2,900
Standard equipment	Flo-Tone paint, spinner wheel covers, deluxe interior, clock, oil-bath air cleaner, dual exhausts with extensions
Options on dR car	Merc-O-Matic transmission, power steering, power brakes, power windows, windshield washers

ENGINE

Type	V-8
Bore x stroke	3.80 x 3.44 inches
Displacement	312 cubic inches
Compression ratio	9.0:1
Bhp (gross) @ rpm	225 @ 4,600
Torque (gross) @ rpm	324 @ 2,600
Taxable horsepower	46.2
Valve gear	Ohv
Valve lifters	Mechanical
Main bearings	5
Induction system	1 Ford 4-v
Fuel system	Mechanical pump
Lubrication system	Pressure
Cooling system	Pressure with centrifugal pump
Exhaust system	Dual with reverse-flow mufflers
Electrical system	12-volt

TRANSMISSION

Type	3-speed automatic with 3-element torque converter, air-cooled
Ratios: 1st	2.40:1
2nd	1.47:1
3rd	1.00:1
Reverse	2.00:1
Max. torque converter	2.10:1 @ 1,590-1,790 rpm

DIFFERENTIAL

Type	Hypoid, semi-floating
Ratio	3.15:1

STEERING

Type	Worm and roller with Bendix hydraulic linkage booster
Turns lock-to-lock	5
Ratios	20.0:1 gear; 25.4:1 overall
Turning circle	43.2 feet (curb/curb)

BRAKES

Type	4-wheel hydraulic with vacuum servo
Type, front	11 x 2.5-inch drum
Rear	11 x 2.0-inch drum
Effective area	190.9 square inches
Parking brake	Mechanical, on rear service brakes

CHASSIS & BODY

Construction	Separate body on ladder frame with box-section side rails, five crossmembers and one X-member
Body	Welded steel stampings
Body style	6-seat convertible coupe

SUSPENSION

Front	Independent, ball joints, upper and lower control arms, coil springs, link-type anti-roll bar
Rear	Live axle on semi-elliptic leaf springs
Shock absorbers	Hydraulic, direct-acting, front and rear

Tires	Originally 7.60 x 15, now 7.10 x 15 Goodyear Super Cushion 4-ply
Wheels	Steel disc, 15 x 5.5K

WEIGHTS AND MEASURES

Wheelbase	119 inches
Overall length	206.4 inches
Overall width	76.4 inches
Overall height	58.8 inches
Front track	58.0 inches
Rear track	59.0 inches
Min. road clearance	6.6 inches
Shipping weight	3,725 pounds (without options)

CAPACITIES

Crankcase	5 quarts (refill, less filter)
Transmission	21 pints
Rear axle	3.5 pints
Cooling system	20 quarts (with heater)
Fuel tank	18 gallons

CALCULATED DATA

Horsepower per c.i.d.	.72
Weight per hp	16.6 pounds
Weight per c.i.d.	11.9 pounds
P.S.I. (brakes)	19.5

PERFORMANCE*

Acceleration: 0-30 mph	4.0 seconds
0-60 mph	11.0 seconds
Standing 1/4 mile	18.2 seconds/78 mph
Max. speed	102.6 mph (average of 4 runs)

* Montclair 2-door hardtop with 225-bhp engine and Merc-O-Matic, tested by *Motor Trend*, March 1956.

Right: Trunk has flip-up key access. Fuel goes into central filler behind license plate. *Facing page, top left:* Deeply hooded headlamps originated on XM-800 show car. *Top right:* Mercury head on rear seat lights up when doors are opened. *Below right:* Door panels follow exterior "lightning bolt" theme. *Bottom:* Elaborate taillamps have been dubbed "gel caps" by today's collectors.

the side trim. In '55, a bright spear had swept back from the top of the grille opening, pointing at the fake air scoop in the rear quarter. A second spear extended from the bottom of the scoop to the bottom of the taillight. Whereas in '56, the front spear arched gently downward to actually meet the bottom edge of the bolder-textured scoop, while the rear spear trailed off the *top* edge of the scoop straight back to the *top* of the taillight. The result was an elongated "Z" of chrome, like a lightning bolt down the side of the car. Many observers considered it an improvement, and it certainly provided a convenient dividing line for two-tone paint schemes. Montclairs now featured "Flo-Tone" paintwork, with one color for the roof, the panel below the windows, and the body side below the "Z"; and a contrasting color on the hood, the deck, and upper part of the body.

Custom and Monterey hardtops now shared the lowered roof line of the two-door Montclair, and a Monterey "Sport Sedan" borrowed the countersunk greenhouse of the Montclair four-door. As if to confound future historians, Mercury also lowered the roof line of the standard Monterey and Custom sedans, though only by three quarters of an inch. The sun finally set on the slow-selling Sun Valley, while Mercury expanded down-market with the Medalist — a bare-bones two-door sedan wearing 1952 hubcaps and comparatively little chrome. For $107 more than a Fairlane V-8, it offered the power and refinement of a Mercury.

Motor Trend praised Mercury for sticking with a winning formula. "We haven't found a better road car in '56," wrote Sports Editor Al Kidd. "But don't expect the softest ride on the market." Like McCahill before him, he likened the Merc to the Mexican Road Race Lincolns. Performance had improved where it counted the most, shaving a full second off of 1955's 50-80 passing time. Kidd also noted improved quality control and the Mercury's better-than-average resistance to brake fade.

Once again, Mercury brightened the winter months with some mid-year model changes. On January 2, the division introduced a true four-door hardtop to replace the Montclair and Monterey Sport Sedans. But if the low-profile four-door sedan had been a "hardtop," then the new hardtop could be a "Phaeton"—and it said so, in gold letters, just above the rear door handles.

Still, 1956 proved a slow year generally for auto sales, particularly in the medium-price range. Mercury responded on February 1 by expanding the entry-level Medalist series with a four-door sedan and a two-door hardtop, and at the same time dressing up all Medalist models with the full lightning-bolt trim. A Medalist Phaeton arrived on

March 9, along with a Custom convertible dressed in all-vinyl upholstery and rubber floor mats. The plain-Jane convertible sold just 2,311 examples, but the expanded Medalist range found nearly 46,000 buyers. In a year which saw Oldsmobile and Buick sales drop 17.6 and 22.5 percent, respectively, Mercury's output declined by just 1,856 units, to 327,943.

Of course, Buick and Olds still outsold Mercury by a comfortable margin. "The '55-56 Mercury came out pretty well," concluded Pfeiffer. "But Mercury

Safety Surge in '56

Nineteen fifty-six, of course, was the year that Ford Motor Company discovered safety. All '56 Mercs came with a dished, collapsible steering wheel; a ball-jointed rear-view mirror that would yield on impact, with a tape-backed safety glass to resist shattering; seat belt anchors; and improved door locks designed not to pull apart as the body stretched and bent in a collision. Padded sun visors and a 1.875-inch pad of cellular plastic for the dashboard were offered as options. Dealers could install the dash pad as well as seat belts when the customer desired.

Other novel features included "safety-beam headlamps" with a new filament shield claimed to keep more light on the road while less escaped into the treetops. Mercury said the lights had taken five years to develop, and that they illuminated up to 80 more feet of pavement on low beam than the conventional lamps they replaced. Even Mercury's new 312-c.i.d. engine became the "Safety Surge V-8" with "flashing acceleration and power reserve that make highway passing quicker and safer."

Interestingly, *Motor Trend*'s editors found the Mercury's dished steering wheel uncomfortably high, and noted that "you can replace the "dished-in" wheel with a standard straight-crossbar wheel and get it right down in your lap."

didn't have the clout, didn't have the dealer strength, and didn't have the image to compete with the bigger guys."

For 1957, Mercury would at least have its own body shell. Reith wanted far-out, provocative styling, and DeLa-Rossa, backed by Design Vice President George Walker, was happy to comply. Their overwrought creation arrived just in time for the bottom to drop out of the medium-price market. Lincoln and Mercury re-married into a single division in September 1957, and new General Manager James J. Nance launched the

Mercury in yet another direction altogether.

Driving Impressions

Clyde Horst, whom I profiled in *SIA* #133, collects 1956 convertibles of every US nameplate. He found our drive-Report Mercury in California in 1988, in very rough condition despite only 50,000 miles on its odometer. "The top was in shreds," he recalled, but the body remained solid and most of the

original parts were undisturbed. Clyde completed the restoration in the summer of 1995, reproducing the Merc's original Classic White and Persimmon "Flo-Tone" paint job.

The front bench seat feels soft and laid back (perhaps a little *too* laid back), and the four-way power adjuster jacks it up from kinda high to really, really high, relative to the Montclair's cut-down windscreen. The top mechanism is identical to a '56 Fairlane's, except that the exposed metal framework that is painted glossy black in the Ford is chrome-plated in the Mercury. In a mid-fifties context, it looks more expensive than garish.

Kudos to the interior studio for an exceptional instrument panel. Although it lacks the classic round-gauge simplicity of the '56 Ford layout, the Mercury's fan-shaped gauge cluster puts all the needles where you can read them at a glance; and the striking, black-on-white color scheme contributes to the exceptional brightness of the interior without sacrificing legibility. Accessory sliders for climate control are easily reached and used, once deciphered. Even the centrally mounted radio, with its "town" and "country" buttons, is easy to reach. The deep-dished steering wheel feels huge and pleasantly heavy; it's bigger than it needs to be on a car with power steering, but it's happily positioned where it doesn't intrude on personal space.

Typical of a convertible, the back seat is somewhat less hospitable, with decent leg room but a skimpy lower cushion and a stiffly upright backrest. The top well intrudes heavily into elbow room, and while the integrated armrests

End of the Lube Racks?

Well, maybe not. When *Motor Trend*'s editors ran the above headline in April 1955, their prediction of the grease gun's imminent demise was still—as Mark Twain would say—greatly exaggerated. But the Lincoln-Mercury Division had taken an important step toward simplified chassis maintenance.

All 1955-56 Lincolns and Mercurys offered an option called the "Multi-Luber," which allowed drivers to pump vital lubrication to eleven points in the chassis by simply holding down a button on the dashboard. Similar "one-shot" chassis lubers (the Bijur was the best known) had appeared on Packards and other fine cars of the twenties and thirties, but American car buyers hadn't seen anything like the Multi-Luber since before World War II.

The Multi-Luber was manufactured by the coincidentally named Lincoln Equipment Company of St. Louis. Prewar systems had usually relied on a mechanical plunger and the driver's own muscle, but

the Multi-Luber used engine vacuum to direct a supposedly leak-resistant mixture of 95 percent SAE 90 and 5 percent soap through a network of nylon tubing. To activate the system, the driver simply pressed a button next to the radio dial and held it until a light on the other side of the dial went out. This could take as little as three to five seconds in warm weather or well over a minute in oil-thickening cold. L-M recommended pushing the button once a day or every 50 miles. A reservoir in the engine bay held enough lube for 225 applications, and the plumbing was designed so that a leak at one point wouldn't empty the entire system. But the prop shaft's universal joints still required occasional hand-lubing.

The Multi-Luber could be installed at the factory or by a dealer; it could even be retro-fitted to any older Lincoln or Merc with ball-joint front suspension. But our driveReport car doesn't have it, and we don't know how many Lincolns and Mercurys actually did.

look neat, they aren't where my arms want to be.

Any deficiency in the back seat, however, is quickly forgotten once the engine is lit. The 225-bhp V-8 chugs conspicuously at idle and breaks into a rorty, *look-at-me! look-at-me!* rumble with the gentlest prod at the throttle. Clearly, Mercury didn't build cars for shy people. Acceleration from a second-gear start won't peel any rubber off of the tires, but it's plenty satisfying nonetheless. (In deference to the car's age, I did not try a full-throttle standing start—the only kind that will engage first gear.) The Merc-O-Matic's single upshift is noticeable but not uncomfortable.

The '56 Ford was a pretty good road car, and the '56 Mercury drives like a more comfortable Ford, eliminating a lot of the Ford's busy ride motions. The Mercury's ride is soft yet poised; its power steering smooth and responsive, with a weight behind it that inspires confidence. Understeer is under control. It's mainly the slippery vintage tires that limit the Mercury's handling. Take a look at the cornering photo: We had to throw the Merc hard into an off-camber turn to get it to lean that far—and even then it felt quite manageable. The surprisingly modern power brakes provide good feedback, delicate modulation, and a generous quantity of real stopping power.

While reviewing my notes on the Mercury, I found I'd used the word "satisfying" again and again—about the steering, the throttle response, the overall impression of quality. The Merc retained the best features of its companion Ford, while at the same time adding a sense of solidity and value. The planners hit their target dead on. 🔧

Acknowledgments and Bibliography

Books: John A Gunnell, 55 Years of Mercury; John A. Gunnell (editor), Standard Catalog of American Cars 1946-1975.

Periodicals: Fred Bodley, "'55 Mercury," Motor Trend, April 1955; Al Kidd, "'56 Mercury Road Test," MT, March 1956; Tom LaMarre, "Banner Years for the Big M," Automobile Quarterly, Vol. 25, No. 2; Don MacDonald, "Spotlight on Detroit," MT, January and February 1955; Walt Woron, "Driving Around with Walt Woron," MT, January 1955; Walt Woron and Don MacDonald, "The '56 Mercury," MT, November 1955; "End of the Lube Racks?" MT, April 1955; "The Top Cars of 1955," MT, September 1955.

Thanks to Mike Lamm; Kim M. Miller of the AACA Library and Research Center; Carl Pfeiffer; Henry Siegle; and of course to Clyde Horst.

Facing page: Despite body lean, Merc's chassis sticks well in hard cornering. **Above:** *225-horse V-8 can match the performance of many new cars.* **Below:** *Graceful instrument panel combines modern appearance and good functionality.*

Medium-Priced Convertibles in 1956

	Mercury Montclair	Buick Special	DeSoto Firedome	Dodge Cus. Royal	Olds Super 88	Pontiac Star Chief
Base price	$2,900	$2,740	$3,032	$2,878	$2,726	$2,853
Wheelbase	119 inches	122 inches	126 inches	120 inches	122 inches	124 inches
Bore and stroke	3.8″ x 3.44″	4.0″ x 3.2″	3.72″ x 3.8″	3.63″ x 3.80″	3.88″ x 3.44″	3.94″ x 3.25″
C.i.d.	312	322	330	315	324	317
Compression	9.0:1	8.9:1	8.5:1	8.0:1	9.25:1	8.9:1
Bhp @ rpm	225 @ 4,600	220 @ 4,400	230 @ 4,400	218 @ 4,400	240 @ 4400	227 @ 4800
Weight	3,725 pounds	3,880 pounds	4,230 pounds	3,630 pounds	3,947 pounds	3,917 pounds
Stroke/bore	0.90	0.80	1.02	1.05	0.89	0.82
Bhp/c.i.d.	0.72	0.68	0.70	0.69	0.74	0.72
Lb./bhp	16.6	17.6	18.4	16.6	16.4	17.2
Production	7,762	9,712	2,646	na	9,561	13,510

Mechanical specifications are for base V-8 engine with automatic transmission.

GIZMOBILE

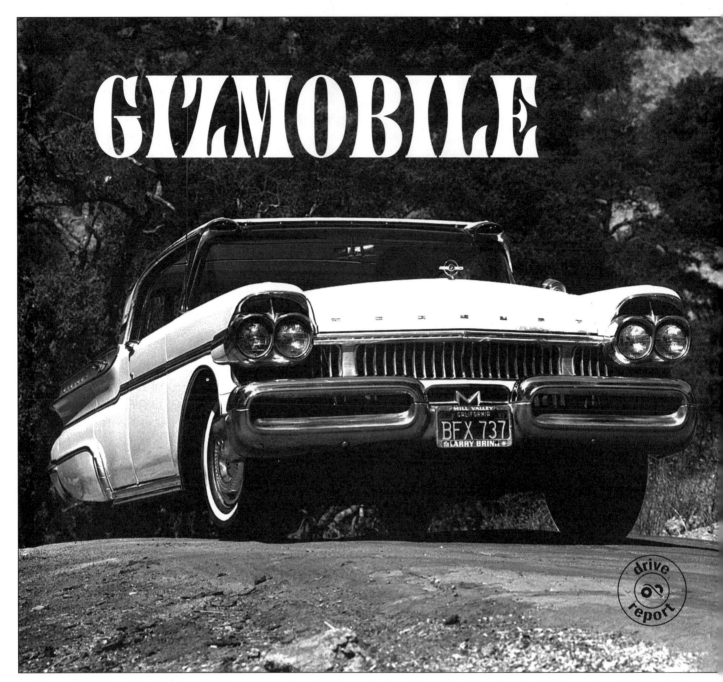

Mercury's Turnpike Cruiser, in its excess of gadgets and gingerbread, epitomizes left-wing extremist car design.

by Michael Lamm, *Editor*

You've noticed, I'm sure, that auto design, like politics and fashion, oscillates between periods of conservatism and radicalism. It's a pendulum that sometimes swings far left, then centers itself, then goes right—back and forth.

I view the 1930s as fairly far left. The '30s gave rise to "streamlining" generally and to such radical production cars as the Chrysler Airflow, Lincoln Zephyr, Aerodynamic Hupp, and 1934 La Salle. The 1940s, on the other hand, took on an air of quiet conservatism for the most part. Then the 1950s moved from liberality early in the decade to downright left-wing radicalism toward the end. The 1960s leveled off again, middle of the road, and now the 1970s seem to be entering another conservative period.

The historic peak of styling radicalism—I call it extreme left-wing car design—crested in 1957-58, the outgrowth of tailfins, 3-tone paint jobs, great expanses of chrome and anodized aluminum, jukebox interiors, wraparound windshields, and dual and quadruple everything. The extreme far left climaxed with cars like the 1958 Buick Limited and the 1957-58 Mercury Turnpike Cruiser (TC for short).

The time for such cars looked right enough. An economic boom after the Korean War led to record car sales in 1955, "Ford's best year ever" according to its annual report. It also led Detroit's market researchers to predict a

steep rise in the demand for medium-priced cars. That's where the future lay, said the analysts, and Ford Motor Co. immediately got to work on the E-Car (Edsel), because research showed that the market in small imported cars was a passing fad, and buyers who'd been driving Fords, Chevys, and Plymouths would soon be moving up into E-Cars, Pontiacs, Mercurys, De Sotos, Oldses, Dodges, and Buicks. Surveys showed that people wanted more horsepower, more conveniences, more power accessories, and more gadgets. Americans now had the money and the will to pamper themselves.

The researchers and analysts might have been right, too, if the Eisenhower recession of 1958 hadn't hit. That recession pushed buyers into imports and made Rambler the third-best-selling U.S. car of 1960-61, mostly by virtue of the American. Detroit crash-programmed the Corvair, Falcon, and Valiant in 1957-58 for a super-quick turnabout.

But in 1955, Ford Motor Co. was still gearing up for the E-Car, and putting its eggs into the medium-price basket. It was a period of musical chairs at Ford, with new divisions being formed almost daily and general managers being kicked upstairs, downstairs, and all around Dearborn. Lincoln became a separate division in May 1955, as did Continental, Mercury, and Special Products. Ford was already a separate division under Robert S. McNamara.

The newly created Mercury Div. was handed to Francis C. (Jack) Reith,

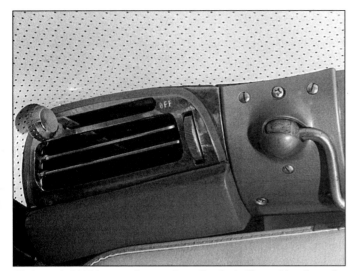

Air from windshield vent pods enters here. Despite baffles and handle to shut passage, rain water leaks in. Sunvisors are double-jointed.

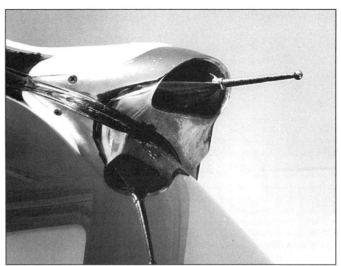

Fake aerials precede pods. These vents were an afterthought when designers found need for something to strengthen high windshield peak.

Midsection of backlight rolls down electrically, gives flow-through ventilation. Mercury revived the breezeway roof idea during 1963-67.

a Ford v.p. and one of FoMoCo's 10 original Whiz Kids. Reith had come to Ford with Tex Thornton and McNamara and a group of other bright, young, ex-Air Force officers right after WW-II. Reith, who was 38 in 1955, had grown up in Des Moines, where his first car was a jumbo-tired 1932 Hudson. He liked cars, but his work with Ford had involved mostly finance and organization. He was tall and had played a lot of tennis before polio left him with a limp. Reith spent 1952-54 in France with Ford S.A.F. and was awarded the French Legion of Honor for his work in helping save Ford of France from receivership.

Reith's assignment after his successful two years in France had been to study the E-Car, to digest its research data and the various proposals for it, and to present a summary to Ford's Product Planning Committee. This he did on April 15, 1955. He showed, among other things, that the Ford Motor Co. needed a third body shell to compete with other companies' mid-priced cars. At that time, Ford and Mercury were sharing one basic shell, and Lincoln had another. Thus 97.7% all of FoMoCo products were built on the Ford shell, and only 2.3% on the Lincoln shell. That didn't give Ford much flexibility against Buick-Olds-Pontiac and De Soto-Chrysler.

So Reith suggested the following range of body shells for future (post-1956) FoMoCo products:

A-body—Mainline and standard Fords.
A¹-body—Big Ford and small Edsel.
B-body—Standard Mercury and big Edsel.
C-body—Lincoln and Turnpike Cruiser.

The committee went along with Reith's recommendations except for the TC, which reverted to the B-body shell. I must hasten to add. too, that Reith *wasn't* primarily responsible for the Edsel's birth; it's just that he did make this very successful and convincing presentation, and the Edsel figured into it.

Designers overlooked absolutely nothing. Tach and other instruments have rubber bezels, and dashboard is thickly padded with expanded vinyl.

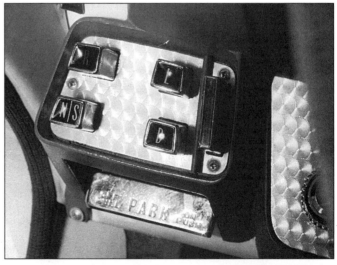

Merc-O-Matic console uses cables. Driver must push NEUTRAL/START before engine cranks. Left-side placement makes shifting difficult.

Aluminum plate identifies TC V-8. It's a destroked Lincoln at 290 bhp. In 1958, Mercs could be ordered with 400-bhp Super Marauder.

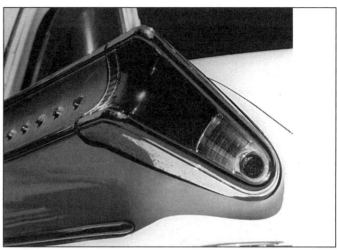

Gold anodized insert leads to canted wraparound taillight. Lens can be seen from side at night. 1957 Cruisers came as hardtops or convertible.

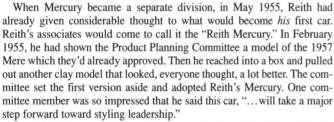

Big M graces deck, with keyhole behind Mercury's head. Similar M stands in grille. Cruiser was top offering in '57, demoted for 1958.

Turnpike cruising is its specialty, and air-filled rubber spring eyes help give very cushy ride. Power everything makes driving soporiferous.

When Mercury became a separate division, in May 1955, Reith had already given considerable thought to what would become *his* first car. Reith's associates would come to call it the "Reith Mercury." In February 1955, he had shown the Product Planning Committee a model of the 1957 Merc which they'd already approved. Then he reached into a box and pulled out another clay model that looked, everyone thought, a lot better. The committee set the first version aside and adopted Reith's Mercury. One committee member was so impressed that he said this car, "...will take a major step forward toward styling leadership."

Don DeLaRossa, manager of Mercury exterior and interior styling in 1954-55 under Elwood Engel, had a major hand in designing the 1957-58 Mercury, including the TC and the Mercury XM Cruiser showcar. DeLaRossa recalls this period vividly, and I'll let him tell it:

"Jack [Reith] had a great amount of enthusiasm for the product. He had a lot of ideas and, of course, at this particular time, the automobile business was giving strong indications that the medium-priced car had an almost unlimited future as far as volume was concerned.

"We had, when Jack entered the scene in April 1955, what I think we could safely call a very, very effective 1955-56 Mercury off the Ford body, but it was primarily looking at Pontiac as its major competitor. Jack, for obvious reasons, wanted to go after Olds and Buick, too, and for that he thought Mercury shouldn't be basically a Ford. so he talked upper management into approving a unique body shell for the 1957 Mercury—in other words, one shared with neither Ford nor Lincoln. Jack won his case, and 1957 marked the first and only year since 1940 that Mercury didn't share bodies with some other division.

"This was just the beginning. He expanded on this, reasoning that the public who buys medium-priced cars also buys upper-medium-priced cars, and it was in that context that he envisioned an effective Turnpike Cruiser emerging—a kind of a super Mercury."

I interrupted Don to ask whether the same sort of market research went into the 1957 Mercury as had gone into the E-Car.

"No, it really didn't. Jack believed in gut feel, right or wrong, and as I look back on it, I don't think he would have tolerated market research, par-

Everywhere you look there's this lavish attention to detail. The use of texture makes passengers want to touch things while driver tries gadgets.

ticularly if it didn't agree with his judgments. As I recall Jack, he was devoted to the product—in all phases. He was concerned with everything: ride and handling, the aesthetic execution right down to the smallest detail. He *participated*. In fact, at times we used to wonder who was minding the store as far as general management was concerned. But if there was an area that didn't have something going on, he would recommend...if not a solution, at least he would call our attention to it and head us in the direction of filling that void. Which we did in a pretty unrestrained way."

I next asked Don what he thinks of the Turnpike Cruiser now, looking back on it from this distance.

"I call this period the Dark Ages of auto design, frankly. Looking back, I

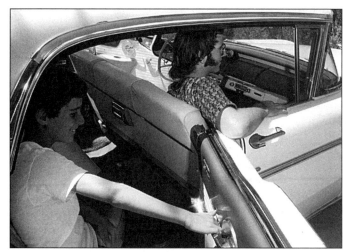

We found out the pinchy way that passenger shouldn't rest his elbow while rear door is being shut.

Interior is tremendously light and roomy.

Power seat's memory can be set with small dial atop dash. Trip-tally clock contains odometer, with practice helps compute average speed.

XM Cruiser showcar of 1956 was designed after 1957 Merc's lines had been approved. Ghia-built XM was driveable, had special glass trailer.

don't understand the total lack of discipline, but it was there. It showed up in our cars. It showed up in General Motors, too, and you could see how we could get the reputation as real hacks and chrome merchants, because looking at those cars, it would be darned hard to deny."

I had never sat in a Turnpike Cruiser before, and I must say my first reaction was mixed. On one hand, I had a tremendous urge to try out all the gadgets—the high-level air vents, the memory seat, to touch and push the rubber instrument bezels, to figure out how to work the trip-averaging odometer/clock, to flip the rear window up and down. All these gizmos were telling me to come play with them, but at the same time they were also

telling me, "Here's the sort of self-amusing decadence that American society came to in 1957." It was a kid's fascination mixed with an adult's realization that these expensive toys were ego props.

I don't mean to say I dislike the Cruiser. I don't. The gadgets fascinate me, but I worry about what they represent. Does the buyer of a car like this think so little of his own worth that he needs a raft of mechanalia to buoy up his self-esteem? The topper came in 1958 with the 400-bhp V-8.

Getting in for the first time, I found the TC very airy and bright. All the windows were down, and that gave the interior a tremendous feeling of spaciousness. No pillars except the one I konked my knee on as I slid into the driver's seat. I noted the flat-topped steering wheel and the windshield distortion in the corners. It was the first time, too, that I realized how far into the roof the center of the windshield peaked.

I reached up to move the sunvisors so I could check out the high-level air intakes. The pods on the outside, with their aerial-spear centers, keynote the car. Inside, the visors are double jointed, so they can be set either above or below the intakes. The intake grilles themselves open with little finger tabs.

I learned later that these air intakes were afterthoughts, necessitated by the steep windshield wrap-over. The header needed structural breaks above the pillars, and the pods gave the breaks. But solid pods didn't make sense, so the designers turned them into high-level air intakes. And while these vents seemed a good idea at first, they didn't work out.

It's generally agreed by auto designers that cool air should enter a car near face level. (Heating air should enter near ankle level.) In combination with the lowerable rear window, the upper intakes should theoretically do a good job of ventilating.

Unfortunately they don't. First and most important, Mercury never could figure out a way to keep them from letting in rain water. There was no way to drain them indirectly. These vents leak even with the grilles shut. Second, air hits front-seat passengers at scalp level, so it ruffles hairdos.

When I first turned the ignition key, there was no sound from the starter, but the seat started to move up and forward. This, I realized, was the memory seat doing its thing. More about that in a moment. It took me a couple of minutes to figure out how to start the engine. The Mere-O-Matic uses pushbuttons, and it finally dawned on me what the N/S button means, namely NEUTRAL/START. So to crank the engine, first turn on the key, then punch N/S.

At 290 bhp from the Lincoln V-8, the Cruiser has ample power, but it's not neck-snapping. It's very quiet, though, and the car rides extremely smoothly, thanks in part to air-cushioned spring shackle eyes for the rear leaves (not to be confused with air suspension, which Mercury catalogued in 1958 but never sold). These shackle eyes are 6-inch rubber donuts on

Cruiser's king-sized trunk makes a spacious playpen. Steep window angle allows huge decklid to open wide. The upright spare tire, though, stands too near center and breaks up the floor area.

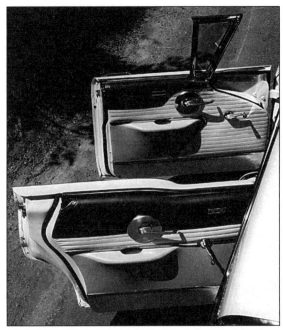

Thick, heavy doors don't rattle. Power windows, a delete item, were deleted in this car.

Big reflectors stand inside bumper ovals. Cruiser corners fairly well, but it's not the sort of car you corner hard. It's best going straight.

Hood ornament (left) and decklid ornament are completely different. In this car, the front ornament's clear plastic center had been broken out.

each end of both rear springs. Their hollow centers are permanently inflated at the factory. I'd read about them and was curious to see how they stood up in a 15-year-old car with over 100,000 miles on it.

Fine, I discovered. We traveled over both freeways and rough, twisty roads, and the TC never bottomed nor made fussy noises. Ride felt pillowish, but cornering didn't suffer: some oversteer, some bobbing of the front end, lots of tire scrub, yet the engine gives plenty of power to stay square through turns.

Tom McCahill called this "a space-age design for earth travel." There's a 6,000-rpm tach on the dash, but what good is it? Standard equipment includes Merc-O-Matic, power steering/brakes/windows/backlight/seat, the memory seat feature, quad headlights, and a clock/odometer with twin dials that lets you compute average trip speed.

This clock is complicated enough to discourage all but the most ardent gadgeteer. Briefly, it includes the car's trip odometer in the bottom of the face. A knurled knob at the top of the clock sets the regular bands. Another knob at the bottom clears the odometer to 000.0 when you push it in and sets the elapsed-time indicator dial when you pull it out and twist it. You pull out, set the e.t. dial to the hour hand of the regular clock, and then at the end of your turnpike trip, you see how long and how far you went. From those data, you can calculate your average traveling speed. Not that it would matter. And if you didn't follow this paragraph, never mind. (The Cruiser's owner's manual, by the way, includes two pages listing all the turnpikes in the country as of 1957.)

Now to the Seat-O-Matic memory power seat. Settings can be dialed by first clearing everything (move the central knob on dash to 7). Now determine your most comfortable driving position. Fore and aft comes by twisting the 1-2-3 dial, with up and down on an A-B-C dial. Then, if you leave the pointers on, say, 4-F, that's the position the seat will return to every time you switch on the ignition. When you turn the key off, the seat sinks automatically to a full-rearward, full-down position, making it easier to get in and out.

Two hazards here: First, if you're in the habit of buckling up before you turn on the ignition, you might find yourself appendectomized by the seatbelt. Second, these seats nearly all went flooey after a time, and owners rarely bothered to get them fixed.

The Cruiser had its share of gadgets, but much less publicized was the fact that it also contained more than a normal amount of safety items. Seatbelts were optional, as was a child's pullover safety jacket. Standard features included a deeply padded dash, padded visors, rubber-bezeled instruments, deep-dish steering wheel, front-hinged hood, and sliding door locks. Taillights wrapped around both rear fenders and were visible from the sides, and two huge reflectors stood inside the massive rear bumper ovals.

In 1958, the big Edsel borrowed the Merc's new body shell, yet Edsel and Mercury shared no exterior stampings, and their styling themes were done independently in different studios, with no overlap.

It would be reasonable to assume that the 1957 TC's lines were laid down by the experimental Mercury XM Cruiser. Not so. The XM went on view in late January 1956, but by that time the production TC's design had already been set. The XM was built by Ghia in Italy during late 1955 as a roadable showcar, but it was designed *after* the 1957 Merc had been okayed by top FoMoCo management. Don DeLaRossa, who went to Turin and oversaw the XM's construction, says that the design group enjoyed a freer hand with the XM than with the TC because Jack Reith wasn't so concerned with the showcar as with production models. The XM turned out quite a bit cleaner than the 1957 Mercury, and while it didn't influence the '57s' design, it did influence the extensively facelifted '58s, particularly the hardtops in the 1958 Park Lane series.

For 1958, the Turnpike Cruiser was considerably demoted. It no longer ranked as a separate series but now merely represented a model in the middling Montclair series. While in 1957 it had been available in three body

specifications

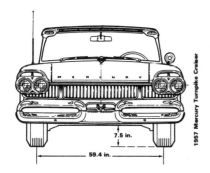

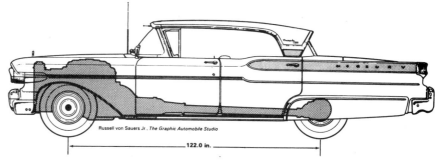

7.5 in.

59.4 in.

1957 Mercury Turnpike Cruiser

Russell von Sauers Jr., The Graphic Automobile Studio

122.0 in.

1957 Mercury Turnpike Cruiser 75A 4-door hardtop

Price when new	$3,849 f.o.b. Dearborn (1957)
Current valuation*	Xlnt, $740; gd, $310; fair, $125

ENGINE

Type	Ohv V-8, cast-iron block, water-cooled, 5 mains, full pressure lubrication
Bore x stroke	4.0 inches x 3.66 inches
Displacement	368.0 cubic inches
Horsepower @ rpm	290 @ 4,600
Torque @ rpm	405 @ 2,800
Compression ratio	9.7:1
Induction system	One-bbl, downdraft carburetor, mechanical fuel pump
Exhaust system	Cast-iron manifolds, twin mufflers and pipes
Electrical system	12-volt battery/coil

TRANSMISSION

Type	Merc-O-Matic, 3-speed automatic torque converter with planetary gears
Ratios	1st: 2.40:1; 2nd: 1.46:1; 3rd: 1.00:1; Reverse: 2.00:1
Overdrive	0.72:1

DIFFERENTIAL

Type	Hypoid, spiral-bevel gears
Ratio	3.22:1
Drive axles	Semi-floating

STEERING

Type	Power, recirculating ball & rack
Ratio	24.0:1
Turns lock-to-lock	5
Turn circle	43.3 feet

BRAKES

Type	4-wheel hydraulic drums, internal expanding, vacuum assist
Drum diameter	11 inches
Total swept area	233.4 square inches

CHASSIS & BODY

Frame	Ladder type with box section siderails, 5 crossmembers
Body construction	All steel
Body style	4-door, 6-pass. hardtop

SUSPENSION

Front	Independent, unequal A-arms, coil springs, balljoints, tubular hydraulic shock absorbers, link-type stabilizer bar
Rear	Solid axle, longitudinal leaf springs, tubular hydraulic shock absorbers
Tires	8.00 x 14 tubeless, 4-ply
Wheels	Pressed steel discs, drop-center rims, lug-bolted to brake drums

WEIGHTS AND MEASURES

Wheelbase	122 inches
Overall length	211.1 inches
Overall width	79.1 inches
Overall height	56.6 inches
Front track	59.4 inches
Rear track	59.0 inches
Ground clearance	7.5 inches
Curb weight	4,222 pounds

CAPACITIES

Crankcase	5 quarts
Cooling system	24 quarts
Fuel tank	20 gallons

FUEL CONSUMPTION

Best	14-16 mpg
Average	12-13 mpg

PERFORMANCE (from **Motor Trend,** 3/57)

0-45 mph	6.0 sec.
0-60 mph	9.8 sec.
Standing 1/4 mi.	17.2 mph and 80.0 mph
Top speed (av.)	110 mph

* courtesy **Antique Auto Appraisal**, Prof. Barry Hertz

styles (2- and 4-door hardtops plus a convertible), for 1958 the convertible was dropped. And Mercury's top 1958 line became the new Park Lane.

Under their hoods, 1957 Mercurys offered two engines: the 312 at 255 bhp and the Lincoln 368 at 290 bhp. In 1958, all Mercurys used Lincoln engines, and these were two versions of the big Lincoln 430. The smallest was destroked from 3.7 to 3.3 inches and displaced 383 c.i.d. This V-8 came in two ratings—312 and 330 bhp. The 430 was likewise available in two ratings—360 (standard in the Park Lane) and 400 bhp (optional in all 1958 Mercurys). This last had 10.5:1 c.r. and three 2-barrel carbs. It was called the Super Marauder, and it came with finned aluminum rocker covers and air cleaner.

A total of 16,861 Turnpike Cruisers were built in 1957 and 6,407 in '58. Mercury registrations as a whole went from a record 1955 high of 371,837 to 136,162 in 1958. Mercury registrations hadn't been that low since 1947. Ford Motor Co. made some more quick managerial and corporate changes. On July 1, 1957, Lincoln and Mercury divisions merged again, and on December 2, Edsel became part of that group, creating Mercury-Edsel-Lincoln (M-E-L) Division.

Reith's prestige within the corporation had been eroded, through no fault

of his. Mercury's sinking sales were simply a reflection of the shifting auto market and the 1958 recession. Medium-priced cars were now being squeezed from above and below and were the hardest-hit segment during the Eisenhower recession.

James J. Nance, fresh from Studebaker-Packard's undoing, replaced Jack Reith as general manager of Mercury Div. and lasted exactly one year. Reith went to the Crosley Div. of Avco in Cincinnati as its president in October 1957, but things didn't go well for him there, either.

The Cruiser isn't yet what you'd call a hot collector's item, which means that the small remaining number in good condition is fast dwindling. But it's an important car historically, epitomizing that last great gasp of automotive excess. With turnpikes spreading and cars shrinking, it's hard to see anything like the Cruiser coming down the freeway for a while. ☙

Our thanks to Michael WR. Davis, Chuck Mulcahy, William Harris, Cara Benson, Don DeLaRossa, and George Muller, all of the Ford Motor Co., Dearborn; Elwood Engel, Bloomfield Hills, Michigan; Robert Lieben, Lafayette, California; James J. Bradley, Detroit Public Library, Detroit; and the Ford Archives, Henry Ford Museum, Dearborn.

WAY-OUT WAGON

1959 Mercury Commuter

by John F. Katz
photos by Roy Query

WITH hindsight, we see that it had to happen. The furious styling flurry of the 1950s had to produce a hardtop station wagon. After the four-door hardtop sedans of mid-'55 and '56, a pillarless wagon was the next obvious step.

Still, it often takes a visionary to see the obvious. And while Chevrolet may have introduced frameless windows to wagons with the '55 Nomad, credit for the first true hardtop-style family hauler belongs to American Motors, which launched its pillarless four-door Rambler wagon in January 1956. Buick, Olds, and Mercury followed with their own hardtop wagons in the fall.

Among these, however, the Mercury deserves a certain distinction. Olds, Buick, and Rambler cautiously kept a pillared variant in production alongside their pillarless wagons, while Mercury alone built every one of its wagons as a

hardtop, from 1957 through 1960. Mercury also made the industry's only two-door-hardtop wagon, which was incidentally the only two-door wagon of any kind offered in the medium-price field.

"Any car looks better as a hardtop than with a solid B-pillar," commented A.B. "Buzz" Grisinger, who headed Ford's Advanced Studio before moving to Mercury-Edsel-Lincoln in early 1958. The Mercury wagon, he emphasized, was already in the pipeline before the Rambler appeared. The designers wanted to build hardtop wagons exclusively, he recalled, "to try to stay a step ahead." The hardtop-only policy also saved tooling dollars and simplified production.

Mercury looked like a marque on the

move at the start of the '57 model year. After sharing a body shell with Ford in 1952-'56, the Big M finally rated a body of its own, sporting the longer, lower "horizontal-plane styling" and heavily sculptured "dream car design" that had been previewed in 1956 by Don DeLaRossa's Ghia-built show car, the XM Turnpike Cruiser (see *SIA* #43). Mercury even borrowed the Turnpike Cruiser label for a new flagship model, introduced mid-season and distinguished externally from other Mercurys by the air scoops over its compound-curved windshield, its reverse-slanting roofline, and its retractable rear window.

As an option, Mercury adopted the Lincoln 368-c.i.d. V-8, with hydraulic lifters and a neat thermostatic system that regulated the temperature of the intake air. Automatic Mercs — which accounted for 96 percent of production — featured a "keyboard drive selector," a

Originally published in Special Interest Autos #154, Jul.-Aug. 1996

Top left: "The Big M" was Mercury theme in late fifties, and it's reflected in hood ornament. *Above left:* Wheel covers are worthy of an Eldo. *Above:* Front end theme is all rectangles. *Below left:* Perfect name for a wagon to serve suburbia. *Right:* Traditional flip-down tailgate adds to Merc's impressive carrying capacity.

mechanical push-button system similar to Chrysler's. Unfortunately, lapses in quality control tarnished the image of Mercury's new models — just when the public seemed to be tiring of show-car flash and raging horsepower. The Big M held on to its seventh-place rank in the industry, but sold only 286,163 cars, its poorest showing since 1954.

Just as the '57s went on sale, however, ex-Packard chief James J. Nance took over as general manager of Lincoln-Mercury. Nance envisioned a somewhat different image for Mercury: solid, conservative — a fine luxury car for a middle-class price. Mercury would become, in effect, Ford's Clipper.

But automakers, like sailing ships, do not change course quickly, and 1958 brought more of the same. Externally, a massive combination bumper-grille and rather fussy side trim distinguished the '58 Mercs from the '57s. Internally, an all-new family of "Marauder" engines provided the power, ranging from a 312-horse, 383-cubic-incher with a single four-barrel on up to a 430-c.i.d. "Super Marauder," pumping out 400 bhp via three deuces. These more modern engines featured "in-block combustion," with the firing chambers formed by a ten-degree offset between the block and head. Mercury claimed that this arrangement subjected the head to less heat and left little opportunity for carbon buildup. Valves were arranged so that no two exhaust ports lay adjacent to each other, again for even heat distribution. The power steering pump, when ordered, mounted directly to the crankshaft, the brakes were self-adjusting, and "Multi-Drive" transmission control offered "High Performance," "Cruising," and "Hill Control" ranges at the touch of a button.

Mercury's model line-up expanded both up-market and down. The new Edsel Corsair and Citation shared Mercury's previously exclusive body shell, with a wheelbase of 124 inches to Mercury's 122. So to maintain its seniority, Mercury debuted the Park Lane, whose unique rear quarters stretched over a wheelbase of 125 inches. Then, late in calendar-year 1957, Mercury revived the Medalist name — and the old solid-lifter 312-c.i.d. V-8 — for a stripped-down, entry-level model that sold for about the same price as the smaller, Ford-bodied Edsel Ranger and Pacer. Edsel wagons also shared the Ford wagon's (pillared) body shell; so the Mercury wagon body, with its hardtop roofline, remained a Mercury exclusive.

Overall, Mercs outsold Edsels more than two-to-one. But that wasn't much of an accomplishment, and Mercury finished the season in eighth place, with production at a ten-year low of only 133,271 units.

Meanwhile, the product planners scrambled to eliminate the disastrous overlap in Mercury and Edsel pricing. For 1959, all Edsels shared the Ford body shell — so Mercury once again enjoyed a body that was exclusively its

Above Commuter was based on Monterey series; weighed in at well over two tons. ***Above right:*** *"Panoramic skylight windshield" could probably fry an egg on a hot day.* ***Right:*** *All '59 Mercs had wild canted taillamp design.* ***Facing page, left:*** *TMore flash for Merc buyers' cash.* ***Right:*** *Taillamps are pumped-up version of the '57-'58 design.*

1959 Mercury

own. The separate Edsel dealer network was phased out, as Mercury dealers adopted the E-car as a price-leading replacement for the short-lived Medalist. Mercury jettisoned a number of other model-and-body-style combinations as well, including the spacey Turnpike Cruiser. There would be no more pretenders to the Park Lane's throne.

Styling showed evolutionary but significant changes. A return to a distinct bumper, below a handsome die-cast grille designed by Grisinger, visually lightened and simplified the Mercury's face; and the rear-quarter "projectile" now blended better with the side trim. All hardtops were now called "Cruisers" (they had been "Phaetons" in '57-58), and featured a new roofline, terminating in a graceful, all-glass semi-fastback.

More significantly, the 1959 Mercury was a bigger and substantially redesigned automobile. To further assert Mercury's seniority over the Edsel, an extended nose stretched the Monterey and Montclair to 126 inches in wheelbase, and the Park Lane to 128. With the longer wheelbase came a new and stronger frame of the "cow belly" design, pioneered on the '56-57 Continental Mark II. Front tread spread 0.6 inch on all models, while rear tread increased one inch on Montereys and Montclairs and three inches on Park Lanes. In overall length, Montereys and Montclairs grew by four inches, and wagons by four and a half, while the already lengthy Park Lane gained only two inches. All models measured one-half to one full inch lower, and about one inch wider as well.

The engineers put the extra length to good use, pushing the engine forward to pull the transmission out of the passenger compartment, and tilting the entire engine/transmission assembly downward at the rear. These changes combined to reduce the size of the transmission tunnel by half. At the same time, the design department moved the cowl forward six inches and down two and a half, further enlarging the front seating area. The lower cowl allowed a larger windshield (60 percent larger, Mercury literature claimed), radically com-pound-curved and curled over at the top. For all its wild appearance, though, this impressive piece of glasswork actually fitted against significantly straightened windshield posts — which, combined with the four-door models' four-inch-wider doors, opened up the space between the windshield dogleg and the center door post by a full six inches. Rear doors also measured wider than before.

Improved power steering reduced

The Mercury Family for '59			
	Price	**Weight**	**Production**
Monterey			
Two door sedan	$2,768	3,837	12,694
Four-door sedan	$2,832	3,902	43,570
Two-door hardtop	$2,854	3,852	17,232
Four-door hardtop	$2,918	3,917	11,355
Convertible	$3,150	4,068	4,426
Commuter			
Two-door wagon	$3,035	4,292	1,051
Four-door wagon	$3,105	4,414	15,122
Montclair			
Four-door sedan	$3,308	4,158	9,514
Two-door hardtop	$3,357	4,129	7,375
Four-door hardtop	$3,437	4,179	6,713
Voyager			
Four-door sedan	$3,793	4,467	2,496
Colony Park			
Four-door wagon	$3,932	4,474	5,959
Park Lane			
Two-door hardtop	$3,955	4,338	4,060
Four-door hardtop	$4,031	4,388	7,206
Convertible	$4,206	4,506	1,257

Mercury Power for '59

Cyl.	C.i.d.	Bore x stroke	Compression	Carburetor	Bhp @ rpm	Torque @ rpm	Std. in:
V-8	312	3.80 x 3.44	8.75:1	2v	210 @ 4,400	325 @ 2,200	Monterey
V-8	383	4.30 x 3.30	10.0:1	2v	280 @ 4,400	400 @ 2,400	Commuter
V-8	383	4.30 x 3.30	10.0:1	4v	232 @ 4,600	420 @ 2,800	Montclair*
V-8	430	4.30 x 3.70	10.0:1	4v	345 @ 4,400	480 @ 2,800	Park Lane

* including Voyager and Colony Park

Note: The 345-bhp V-8 was optional in all models; the 322-bhp V-8 optional in Monterey and Commuter; and the 280-bhp V-8 optional in Monterey.

parking effort by 50 percent, with 15 percent less tug required in highway maneuvers. The front suspension's upper control arms were now angled for anti-dive geometry, which was just as well, with so much weight ahead of the windshield. Rear springs now stretched a full 60 inches long and two and a half inches wide. And new "tandem" windshield wipers shadowed each other's motion and overlapped in the middle, for 43 percent better clearance.

Engine choices retreated from the excess of previous years. With the Medalist gone, the Monterey now listed the "little" 312, re-tuned for regular gas, as its base power plant. The optional 383 could now be ordered with a two-barrel carburetor, and the triple-carb Super Marauder vanished, along with the Turnpike Cruiser. A lightweight, alu-minum-cased, two-speed automatic transmission, mistakenly attributed to Mercury in the December 1958 *Motor Trend*, was in fact intended for the Ford and Edsel. Mercury retained the familiar three-speed Merc-O-Matic, now with a conventional lever selector instead of push-buttons — although a "Dual-Range" option (standard on Park Lane) salvaged some of the versatility of 1958's "Multi-Drive" keyboard system.

Mercury sales literature could now accurately boast that "Mercury for '59 is the only car in its class which does not use a dressed-up body, shared with a low-priced car." The single-body program that GM had rushed into production that year included no pillarless station wagons — so for '59 only Mercury and Rambler offered wagons in the hardtop mode.

Since Mercury hardtops were now

tion that year included no pillarless station wagons — so for '59 only Mercury and Rambler offered wagons in the hardtop mode.

Since Mercury hardtops were now

Mercury Meets the Competition

Mercury marketing for '59 aggressively attacked the medium-range makes from both GM and Chrysler. One piece of sales literature quoted a half-dozen former Mopar owners, explaining in their own words why they had switched to the Big M. Another convincingly compared Mercury engineering to that of the new-for'59 GM line. The Mercury's box-section perimeter frame, said the brochure, "can stand as much force as a 12-inch steel I-beam"; and it sure did look sturdy next to the siderail-less X-frame "used by Pontiac and some other cars." Another illustration flaunted the three arched braces inside the roof of a Mercury hardtop, vs. the single flat brace used in pillarless GM models. Mercury eschewed the "plastic sealers" and "applied metal panels" employed by GM, relying instead on good, old-fashioned solder. And Merc touted its "Super-Enamel" paint as more resistant to weather, gas spills, and stone chips than the lacquer still used by the General. Tables and charts demonstrated how Mercury offered a longer wheelbase, wider front

door openings, more windshield area, and bigger brakes than competitive models from GM and Chrysler.

Motor Trend conducted a somewhat less biased comparison in March 1959, matching a Mercury Montclair against a Dodge Custom Royal and a Pontiac Catalina. The Mercury indeed scored high marks for interior space, ease of entry and exit, visibility, low mechanical noise, and for its ability to smooth out rough pavement; but it drew mixed reviews for its eccentric instrument panel, and boos for excessive wind noise. In fuel economy, the Merc finished ahead of the thirsty Pontiac but behind the thrifty Dodge.

But the proof, of course, is in the driving. The Mercury edged out both of its rivals in acceleration and equaled the Pontiac for braking; but disappointed *MT*'s editors in the handling tests, leaning and understeering significantly more than the nimble Dodge or the glued-to-the-road Pontiac. And neither the Merc nor the Dodge could touch Pontiac's wide-track ride.

illustrations by Russell von Sauers, The Graphic Automobile Studio

© copyright 1996, Special Interest Autos

specifications

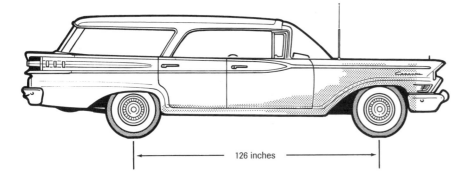

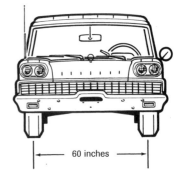

126 inches

60 inches

1959 Mercury Commuter

Base price,	$3,105 (4-dr wagon)
Std. equipment inc.	280-bhp Marauder V-8, oil filter, Safety-Sweep two-speed electric wipers, hardtop-style roof, concealed under-floor storage compartment, Flush-Fit tailgate with retractable window, Super-Enamel paint
Options on dR car	Automatic transmission, AM radio, heater/defroster, forward-facing third seat, power tailgate window, accessory brake booster

ENGINE

Type	V-8
Bore x stroke	4.30 inches x 3.30 inches
Displacement	383 cubic inches
Compression ratio	10.0:1
Horsepower @ rpm	280 @ 4,400 (gross)
Torque @ rpm	400 @ 2,400 (gross)
Taxable horsepower	59.2
Valve gear	Ohv
Valve lifters	Hydraulic
Main bearings	5
Carburetor	1 Ford 5752004A 2-bbl
Fuel system	Mechanical pump
Lubrication system	Pressure with oil mist to piston pins, gravity feed to timing chain
Cooling system	3-stage pressure-vent
Exhaust system	Single with crossover and reverse-flow muffler
Electrical system	12-volt

TRANSMISSION

Type	Merc-O-Matic three-speed planetary with torque converter
Ratios: Low	2.40:1
Intermediate	1.47:1
Drive	1.00:1
Reverse	2.00:1
Max. torque converter	2.10 @ 1,500-1,650 rpm

DIFFERENTIAL

Type	Hypoid, semi-floating with straddle-mounted pinion
Ratio	2.71:1

STEERING

Type	Ford recirculating ball
Turns lock-to-lock	5.4
Ratio, gear	N/A
Ratio, overall	29.0:1
Turning circle	43.9 feet, curb to curb

BRAKES

Type	4-wheel hydraulic, self-adjusting, with vacuum servo
Type, front	11 x 3-inch ribbed iron drum
Type, rear	11 x 2.5-inch ribbed iron drum
Swept area	205 square inches
Parking brake	Mechanical, on rear service brakes

CHASSIS & BODY

Construction	Box-section perimeter frame with separate body
Body	Welded steel stampings
Body style	9-seat, 4-door station wagon

SUSPENSION

Front	Independent, upper and lower control arms, coil springs, link-type anti-roll bar
Rear	Live axle, semi-elliptic leaf springs
Shock absorbers	Double-acting hydraulic, concentric with coil springs in front
Tires	8.50 x 14
Wheels	Steel disc, 14 x 6JK

WEIGHTS AND MEASURES

Wheelbase	126 inches
Overall length	218.6 inches
Overall width	80.7 inches
Overall height	57.8 inches
Front track	60.0 inches
Rear track	60.0 inches
Min. road clearance	6.0 inches
Shipping weight	4,414 pounds (w/out options)
Estimated weight	4,540 pounds (as equipped)

CAPACITIES

Crankcase	5 quarts (less filter)
Transmission	20 pints
Rear axle	4.5 pints
Cooling system	22 quarts (with heater)
Fuel tank	20d gallons

CALCULATED DATA

Horsepower per c.i.d.	0.73
Weight per hp	16.2 pounds
Weight per c.i.d.	11.8 pounds
Lb. per sq. in. (brakes)	22.1

Right: Original selling dealer is long gone from Staten Island. ***Far right:*** Fuel filler access hides behind rear panel. ***Facing page:*** Merc corners remarkably well for softly sprung heavyweight.

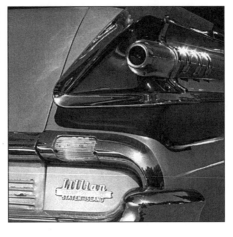

1959 Mercury

Cruisers, wagons became Country Cruisers. And as they had since '57, Mercury wagons wore unique nameplates not shared with Mercury sedans. The basic Country Cruiser, for example, was the Commuter, which carried Monterey-level trim but packed the 383 two-barrel V-8 as standard equipment. The mid-range Voyager paralleled the Montclair exactly in both trim and power; while the top-of-the-line Colony Park was essentially a Voyager with wood-grain side trim.

Mercury advertised its '59 wagons with every bit as much vigor as its sedans. Since that year's trunk-backed Mercs featured "space-panned" interiors, wagons were naturally "family-planned" (although one wonders, with all that family planning going on, why they still needed a nine-seater option). Mercury wagons offered "two-car convenience at a single-car price," and, with no apologies to Jaguar, "a tasteful blend of grace and space."

Overall, the '59 Merc was widely recognized as a move up-market — which was, of course, exactly what Nance intended. Recognizing the new Mercury's rightful place at "the upper end of the medium-price field," *Car Life* called it "a car that a great deal of brain power has

been put into." Sales recovered somewhat, rising to around 150,000 units. Still, other marques recovered faster, and Mercury's ranking in the industry sank to ninth.

And as the Edsel turned into a debacle, the front office told Mercury to tighten its belt. 1960 brought the compact Comet, of course, but also some further pruning of Mercury's full-size line-up. The two-door wagon was gone, and the Park Lane now shared the 126-inch wheelbase of the Monterey and Montclair. All-new sheet metal from the belt line down lent what Grisinger called a "more integrated, less appliqued" look. Grisinger is justifiably proud of the handsome '60 Mercury, which was really the last of a breed. 1961 began "the long drought when McNamara dictated that the Mercury have high interchangeability with the Ford." Meaning Ford body shells — again.

That, of course, spelled the end of Mercury's hardtop station wagons. Coincidentally, Rambler also built its last hardtop wagon in 1960. But that very same year Chrysler dove headlong into the pillarless wagon business, and continued to offer both Chrysler and Dodge hardtop wagons through 1964.

Driving Impressions

Our driveReport Commuter Country Cruiser was purchased new from Lillian Mercury on Staten Island. The original owner opted for a third seat and automatic transmission, but skipped power

steering and power brakes. A few years later, he developed a heart condition, and was advised by his doctor not to drive a car without power steering. So it is not surprising that he bought himself a brand-new 1963 Mercury, this one with servo assistance for the directional control. Curiously, however, he did not trade in his '59. Instead, he added an aftermarket brake servo and consigned it to his large, two-car garage. "He must have had a fondness for it," mused current owner Sal Conti, "because for all those years he would take it out just a couple of times a year — and one of those trips was to the gas station to get it inspected." When Sal bought the car in 1989, it was a bit worn and faded, but essentially intact, with only some 43,000 miles on the clock. Sal replaced the exhaust and some rusted brake lines, and rebuilt the fuel pump and carburetor, but otherwise left the Mercury in its original condition. For several years he convoyed to car shows with a friend who owned another hardtop wagon, a '60 Chrysler New Yorker,

The compound-curved windshield is a remarkable thing to see, but its bottom corner restricts the space available for getting in or out of the car. Surprisingly, perhaps, it looks less dramatic from the inside, where its wrapped-over top can go easily unnoticed. The instrument panel, on the other hand, is pure science fiction. While most dashboards jut outward at the driver and passenger, this one curves dramatically inward,

1959 Mercury

creating what architects would call a "great space" in the front seating area. The Mercury's dashboard wears the same Bermuda Sand paintwork as the outside of the car, so that it seems to flow continuously into the engine hood, interrupted only briefly by the windshield.

Seeming to float in front of this vast, curving expanse, the instrument pod itself stares back like a narrow-eyed robot. A ribbon-style speedometer crawls across the top, with small but legible gauges for fuel and temperature underneath. Separate side pods bring controls for lights, wipers, and climate just a finger's length away. As if it were an afterthought, however, the radio is relegated to the center of the concave dash, where neither driver nor passenger can reach it easily.

One other glitch mars the Mercury's otherwise outstanding ergonomics: A collar at the near end of the steering column houses the shift quadrant, and a funny, cup-like indicator cradles the P, R, N, D, or L. It works fine as long as the car is aimed dead ahead, but as the steering wheel turns, the spokes obscure the letters. The wheel itself is typically thin-rimmed, but provides spokes at the ten, two, and six o'clock positions, maximizing leverage while offering a handy place to hook your thumbs.

The relationship of the wheel to the pedals feels natural, although the driver's seat itself leaves much to be desired. While I liked the generous height of the cushion, I found the backrest at once too upright and too soft for comfort. The problem was probably aggravated by age and wear, as the back seats are in fact firmer and far more comfortable. (They don't look very inviting, with all the exposed framework that allows them to fold, but they feel just fine. Incidentally, it's also easier to get in and out of the back seat, and once you're in you'll find plenty of sit-up-straight-and-stretch-your-toes room.)

With 126 inches of wheelbase and unassisted steering, the Commuter feels awkward in low-speed maneuvers. Out on the road, however, the steering lightens considerably, demanding very little effort yet not requiring a lot of cranking, either. On-center road feel is minimal — a typical complaint in cars of this era — yet once dialed into a turn, the steering serves up just enough information to inspire confidence. More remarkably, that confidence would not be misplaced; the big Merc corners flat and neutral, with a sure-footed grip on the road. Driving briskly, but with respect for the car's age, I noticed none of the understeer that so troubled *Motor Trend*. Yet the old Merc rides quietly and comfortably, neither pillow-soft nor European-hard, but a very nice compromise between the two.

Like the chassis, the engine responds eagerly to the driver's commands. This is no rumbling hot rod; but open the throttle wide, and it accelerates convincingly, gathering itself up with a rushing, al-most electric hum. The transmission, I should add, did its job unobtrusively at all times. Deceleration

The Dance of the Divisions, 1955-59

The 1957-60 Mercurys emerged from a broad product strategy, one designed to improve Ford's representation in the medium-price field. GM had five divisions, from proletarian Chevrolet to glittering Cadillac; and when Chrysler launched the Imperial as a separate marque for 1955, it, too, offered five different nameplates under one corporate banner. So it's easy to understand why Ford product planners felt short-changed, with only two divisions producing just three distinct car lines.

So Ford's self-transformation began, innocuously enough, with William Clay Ford's Special Products Operations, created in July 1952 to develop a successor to the Continental. Around the same time, corporate planners circulated proposals for a premium Mercury based on the Lincoln body shell. By may 1954, the Lincoln-Mercury Division had given this embryonic product a name: Edsel. Nurtured by planner Francis C. "Jack" Reith, the Edsel evolved into a separate marque, selling two lines of cars, one based on the Ford body shell and the other on the all-new Mercury shell due for 1957. At this point the plan still included a Lincoln-based car in the upper-middle price range, but now that car would be a Mercury.

Senior management approved the Reith plan on April 15, 1955. Reith himself was named general manager of the newly separated Mercury Division, headquartered at 6200 West Warren Avenue in Detroit. Lincoln would be headed by Ben D. Mills. Special Products (itself a separate division since October 1953) handed the Continental over to Bill Ford's new Continental Division, and then assumed responsibility for the Edsel.

However, this experiment in divisionalization ended as rapidly as it began, as it quickly became apparent that neither Lincoln, nor Mercury, nor Continental sold enough cars to justify three separate divisions. So Continental was re-absorbed by Lincoln in July 1956 (with Mills in charge), which in turn re-merged with Mercury in September 1957—this time headed by ex-Packard chief James J. Nance, with Mills as his assistant. Then, as Edsel sales failed to materialize, it, too, was rolled into an omnibus Mercury-Edsel-Lincoln (M-E-L) Division in January 1958, headquartered at 3000 Schaefer Road in Dearborn. Meanwhile, the "Super Mercury" or "Olympian" emerged as the Park Lane, using a stretched Mercury body rather than a Lincoln shell.

Nance held the reins at M-E-L until September 1958, when Mills succeeded him. Then, with the demise of the Edsel in November 1959, the divisional title returned once more to Lincoln-Mercury—as it has remained now for 36 years.

Facing page, left: 383 V-8 pulls out 280 horses. **Right:** *Three-segmented instrument pod floats science-fiction style in front of driver.* **Below:** *Rear styling is positively subdued compared to the rest of exterior treatment.* **This page, above and below:** *Commuter offers wide variety of seating and cargo combos.*

is equally impressive, with firm, informative brakes that are very strong for their time — if not quite up to modern standards. In all, this massive hauler from a bygone time proved itself a surprisingly able and agile road car, with a crispness in its reflexes that belies its age and era. ൭

Acknowledgments and Bibliography

Books: Thomas E. Bonsall, The Lincoln Motor Car; Geo. H. Dammann & James K. Wagner, The Cars of Lincoln-Mercury; John A. Gunnell, 55 Years of Mercury; John A. Gunnell (editor), Standard Catalog of American Cars 1946-1975. Periodicals: Bill Callahan, "Mercury for '59," Motor Trend, December 1958; Tom LoMarre, "Banner Years for the Big M," Automobile Quarterly, Vol. 25, No. 2; Don MacDonald, "57 Mercury," MT, December 1956; Charles Nerpel, "3-Way Comparison Road Test: Pontiac, Mercury, Dodge," MT, March 1959; Paul Sorber, "Mercury Road Test," MT, March 1957; Joe H. Wherry, "Mercury's Turnpike Cruiser Drivescription," MT, March 1957.

Thanks to Kim M. Miller of the AACA Library and Research Center; Ford Motor Company designers A.B. Grisinger and Rhys Miller; Henry Siegle; Vince Wright of Infinity Unlimited Productions; and, of course, special thanks to owner Sal Conti.

Originally published in Special Interest Autos #162, Nov.-Dec. 1997

1964 Mercury Marauder
Twenty-Fifth Anniversary Car

by Tim Howley
photos by the author

IN the late thirties Ford desperately needed a car between the highest priced Ford at approximately $900 and the Lincoln-Zephyr in the $1,300-$1,600 range. After considering over 100 names, Mercury, the Roman god of commerce and gain, was chosen. The car was designed entirely in Ford's infant styling department located in a corner of the Ford engineering lab. It was designed by E.T. "Bob" Gregorie working very closely with Edsel Ford. The same people who styled this car styled the 1939 Ford and 1940 Lincoln Continental. Only 19 people worked in Ford styling at the time, and it is reasonably safe to assume that they all worked on all three makes.

The first Mercury had a Ford-based chassis extended from 112 to 116 inches. All of the increased four inches in the wheelbase was put in the hood. The Mercury had the same transverse springing as the Ford. Hydraulic brakes were standard in 1939 for all 1939 Ford-built cars. While the Mercury body looked much like a '39 Ford it was not the same. Except for some inner body panels it was completely different sheet metal. The engine was a 239.4-c.i.d. flathead V-8, the Ford 221 bored out a sixteenth of an inch. This gave it 95 horsepower, or five more horsepower than the Ford. The 1939 Mercury was offered in five body styles including a two-door coupe sedan with thin-pillared chromed window frames, making it very close to, but not quite a hardtop. This same type of coupe was offered on the Lincoln Continental a year later.

The Twenty-Fifth Anniversary Mercury was a far cry from the original. The chassis had now grown from a 116-inch wheelbase to 120 inches and the overall length had gradually grown from 195.9 inches to 215.5 inches. Whereas in

Long and low in appearance and in reality, Marauder's length is accented by strong horizontal chrome trim application.

1964 Mercury Marauder

1939 there were only five models in one series, in 1964 there were 18 models in three series: Monterey, Montclair and Park Lane. This does not count the mid-sized Comet, Comet Caliente and Cyclone. The basic Mercury engine was the 390, rated at 250, 266, 300 and 330 horsepower.

A lot of Mercury history went down between 1939 and 1964. A completely restyled Mercury without running-boards was introduced for 1941. In 1942 Mercury, along with Lincoln, introduced the ill-fated Liquamatic automatic transmission. 1941-48 Mercurys were Fords on a longer wheelbase with upgraded trim. In April 1948 Mercury introduced the car that should have been the 1949 Ford. With the team of Bill Stroppe and Clay Smith, Mercury started making a name for itself in the Mobilgas Economy Runs. In the 1951 Mexican Road Race, Troy Ruttman finished fourth in a hopped-up '48 Mercury club coupe. For 1952, Mercury adapted the GM look, then in 1954 got ball-joint front suspension and a transparent plastic top model. This was followed by bigger cars in 1955 and the Turnpike Cruiser in 1957. 1959-60 models were nearly as big as Lincolns. Then for '61, Mercury pulled back to share its bodies with Ford, and then add the compact Comet. 1963 saw the Breezeway rear window revived, plus the introduction of the smart, scatback Marauder hardtop in 1963½.

In 1963, after an absence of more than five years, Bill Stroppe returned his Mercurys to competitive events. Despite initial troubles in NASCAR, the Mercury pit crews and drivers earned a respectable reputation on stock car circuits. Rounding out the '63 season, Parnelli Jones drove a Mercury to a new record for stockers at Pikes Peak.

The 1963 Mercury received a new body, which would be carried over into 1964. There is an interesting story about this body among old-time Ford stylists. It is believed that the 1964 Ford was supposed to be the 1963 Mercury, and the 1963 Mercury the 1964 Ford. For whatever reason, the two studios switched bodies; hence it is fairly safe to say that the 1963 Mercury, much like the '49, started out as a Ford. Actually, there were not all that many differences between the two makes, especially in 1964. 1964 Fords had a 119-inch wheelbase and were 209.9 inches overall. The quality of both makes was outstanding that year, arguably the best of the entire decade.

Beginning in 1963, the full-sized Mercury no longer shared a six-cylinder engine or 292 or 352 V-8 engine with Ford. The base engine was the 390, rated at 250 horsepower. There were two more 390s at 300 and 330 horsepower. Additionally, there were two 406 engines, pegged at 385 and 405 horsepower. The 427 was a mid-year introduction, which eventually replaced the 406.

In 1963, Mercury reintroduced the reverse-slanting "Breezeway" rear window which had been introduced on the 1957 Turnpike Cruiser, then was picked up by the 1958 Lincoln Continental. Another new model was the Marauder, a mid-year two-door fastback hardtop.

The Bill Stroppe Connection

Since the Mexican Road Race days in the early fifties, the name of the late Bill Stroppe has been closely associated with Ford performance. In 1957, Ford and Chevrolet agreed to officially pull out of racing. But Ford did give drivers cars free and clear to run any way they wanted, provided that no official Ford sponsorship or team support was even hinted at. Bill Stroppe, in his Long Beach, California, shop, prepared many of the cars, while Holman and Moody did the same in Charlotte, North Carolina.

Then in 1963, Ford indirectly returned to racing, staking Bill Stroppe to organize a Mercury racing team. Stroppe was now able to sign top drivers: Troy Ruttman, Roger Ward, Parnelli Jones, Darel Dieringer, Billy Wade, Dave MacDonald, Chuck Daigh, Whitey Gerken, and Louie and Bobby Unser. The car that Stroppe prepared was the Mercury Marauder, and the driver who made the Marauder a legend was Parnelli Jones. Actually his first ride was a 1962½ model, which opened the season at the first Riverside 500 road race for stock cars in January 1963.

Jones, driving #15, a Mercury Marauder, for Bill Stroppe, was just incredible. He won eight major stock car races in 1964. He was mean and he was fast. The team of Stroppe & Jones finished the season by winning the 1964 USAC Championship. Jones and Stroppe also went to Pikes Peak, Colorado, in 1963 and 1964, winning the stock car division title in 1963 in a 1963 Mercury Marauder, and setting a new record. His time up the famous mountain was 14 minutes, 17.4 seconds. That's driving a distance of 12.42 miles from an altitude of 9,402 feet to 14,110 feet. He was a tough act to follow. In 1964, he repeated his 1963 win in a Stroppe-prepared 1964 Mercury Marauder, shaving 35.2 seconds off his 1963 time up the hill.

The 1963 and 1964 Mercury Marauders that raced were completely disassembled in Stroppe's shop and rebuilt for racing. The engine was not the 425-horsepower 427 with dual four-barrel carburetors which was used for drag racing, but the 410-horsepower 427 with a single, four-barrel carburetor. The 427 had special main-bearing cap reinforcement, added ribs in the block's bulkhead, special head gaskets, lighter pistons, grooved main-bearing journals, selected and gauged rod bearings, and special connecting rods. In addition, there was a finned oil cooler at the left front of the engine compartment, aluminum intake manifold, specially designed exhaust manifolds, and heavy duty fan belt. These were not Stroppe modifications, but the way the 427 came from the factory.

Stroppe tore down the engines, balanced and magnafluxed every moving part, then dynamically balanced the reassembled engines. Frames were rewelded, suspensions reworked and beefed up, Mercury drums were replaced with Lincoln drums, interiors were almost but not quite gutted, roll bars were added, 22-gallon fuel tanks were installed with a steel firewall welded between the fuel tank and the rear seat area. Finally, the cars were painted red, white and blue.

*Above: There's a lot of Lincoln influence in rear fender and taillamp treatment. **Below:** Front end, however, is distinctly Mercury but with a bit of T-Bird thrown into fender shape.*

The Marauder was not necessarily a high-end car with a big engine and front bucket seats. It came in the Monterey series, Monterey Custom series and as an S-55 with front bucket seats. The S-55 was a sub series of the Monterey Custom.

Racing did indeed help sell big Mercurys in 1963. Model year production of the full-sized cars was 120,000, the highest figure since 1960. However, total Mercury production, including Comets and Meteors, was down from 1962.

1964 Mercurys were mildly facelifted '63s. The Veed grille now protruded out instead of in. Veed front fenders accented the grille. Rectangular taillamps replaced the round taillamps of 1963, and the taillamp back panel was redesigned. As in 1963, three taillamps were carried on each side, the inner ones carrying the back-up lamps in their center. Also as in 1963, stainless peaked the fender tops that ran the entire length of the car and there were very short, pointed tailfins. Chromed signatures on the rear fenders identified each series. Marauder identification additionally carried checkered flag fender emblems on the front fenders.

1964 Mercurys were offered in the Monterey, Montclair and the new Park Lane series with separate Marauder and Breezeway sub series. Two and four-door fastback Marauders were offered in all three series. The four-door fastback Marauder hardtop was a new addition in 1964, replacing the four-door Breezeway hardtop. Breezeway two-door hardtops, two-door pillared sedans and four-door pillared sedans were offered in all three series. There were two convertibles, a Monterey and Park Lane, plus two wagons, a Commuter and Colony Park. This gave buyers a choice of 18 models with 16 solid colors and 27 optional two-tone color combinations. Incidentally, the Marauder began as a January 1963 convertible put on the show circuit, then in the spring became a production model in fastback but not convertible form.

The standard engine for the Monterey

and Montclair was the 390 ohv V-8 rated at 250 horsepower. Standard for any Montclair with Multi-Drive and the Colony Park wagon with Multi-Drive was the 390 rated at 266 horsepower. Standard for any Park Lane, optional for the Monterey and Montclair, was the Marauder Super 390 rated at 300

horsepower. Optional for any full-sized 1964 Mercury was the 390 Marauder Interceptor rated at 330 horsepower. The 427 was optional for all but the station wagons, and it was rated at 410 and 425 horsepower. A three-speed manual transmission was standard for all models. Three-speed manual with

Mercury Breezeway Sedan

The Breezeway sedan with its reverse-slant rear window first appeared on the 1957 Mercury Turnpike Cruiser and then was adopted by the 1958-60 Lincoln Continental, including the convertible. The idea reappeared on the 1963-66 Mercury. 1964 Mercurys were divided into the Monterey, Montclair and Park Lane series with the Breezeway and Marauder sub series. Breezeways were pillared two- and four-door sedans, with the Breezeway rear window. Additionally, there was a Breezeway pillarless two-door hardtop, and a Breezeway four-door hardtop in 1963, but not 1964. Marauders were fastback two- and four-door hardtops, the latter being a new addition in 1964.

In addition to giving the rearseat pas-

sengers more head room, the reverse-slanting Breezeway rear window gave shade from the roof's rear overhang, plus excellent ventilation without air-conditioning. The Breezeway window is power-operated by a dash control. To give the window maximum performance, all you had to do was open the dash-controlled cowl vents and put the Breezeway window halfway down. If you put the window all the way down at high speeds, there would be too much turbulence. With the Breezeway window, there is no need to open the wind wings, which cause wind noise.

The idea of a rear window that rolls down was nothing new. Such windows were common in the thirties but faded out of existence once streamlining took over.

specifications

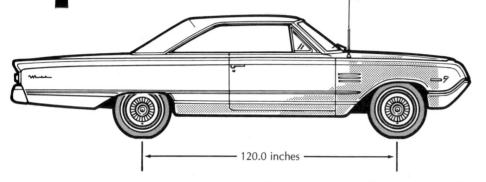
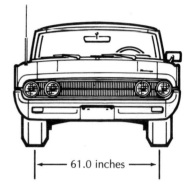

120.0 inches

61.0 inches

1964 Mercury Montclair Marauder two-door fastback hardtop

Base price $3,127
Price as equipped Approximately $4,100
Options on dR car 330-horsepower Marauder Interceptor engine, dual exhausts, power steering, power brakes, Multi-Drive Merc-O-Matic, aftermarket stereo radio with cassette player, twin rear view mirrors, color keyed padded instrument panel, deluxe wheel covers, vinyl top

ENGINE
Type Ohv V-8
Bore x stroke 4.05 inches x 3.78 inches
Displacement 390 cubic inches
Compression ratio 10:1
Horsepower @ rpm 330 @ 5,000
Torque @ rpm 427 @ 3,200
Induction system 4-bbl downdraft carburetor
Ignition system 12-volt
Fuel system Camshaft-driven vacuum pump
Exhaust system Dual
Valves Mechanical lifters
Main bearings 5

TRANSMISSION
Type Multi-Drive Merc-O-Matic single stage torque converter with 3-speed automatic planetary gear train
Ratios: LO 2.40:1
D2 1.47:1; 1.00:1
D1 2.40:1; 1.47:1; 1.00:1
Reverse 2.00:1

DIFFERENTIAL
Type Hypoid
Ratio 3.0:1*
Drive axles Floating
* Standard rear axle ratio is 3.0:1. Other axle ratios are 3.25:1, 3.50:1, 3.89:1, or 4.11:1

STEERING
Type Recirculating ball and nut, power assisted
Turns lock-to-lock 3.9
Turning circle 41.6 feet

BRAKES
Front Hydraulic, duo-servo, self-adjusting, power assisted, cast-iron drums
Drum diameter 11 inches
Total lining area 212.5 square inches

CHASSIS & BODY
Construction Body-on-frame
Frame Ladder-type frame with full-length boxed side rails and 5 crossmembers
Body construction All steel
Body style 2-door hardtop

SUSPENSION
Front Independent ball joint type, coil springs, tubular shock absorbers, upper and lower wishbones, stabilizer bar
Rear 5 semi-elliptic leaf springs, tubular shock absorbers
Tires 8.00x14 4-ply tubeless

WEIGHTS AND MEASURES
Wheelbase 120 inches
Overall length 215.5 inches
Overall width 80 inches
Overall height 56.7 inches
Front track 61 inches
Rear track 60 inches
Curb weight 4,500 pounds (approximately)

CAPACITIES
Crankcase 6 quarts (with filter)
Cooling system 20 quarts
Fuel tank 20 gallons
Merc-O-Matic 11 quarts

PERFORMANCE
Top speed 107 mph (130 plus for the 330-horsepower 390)
Acceleration: 0-60 mph 12.8 seconds
0-45 mph 7.6 seconds
0-30 mph 4.1 seconds
Standing 1/4 mile 17.6 seconds, 71.5 mph
Fuel mileage 16-18, best; 10, average
Source: *Motor Trend*, October 1963, testing a 1964 Mercury Marauder 4-door hardtop with the 266-horsepower 390 engine

Right: Marauder's doors are king-size and well appointed inside. **Facing page, top:** Marauder handles turns with initial understeer, changing to oversteer at higher speeds. **Below:** Dash is a riot of circles, rectangles and bright trim.

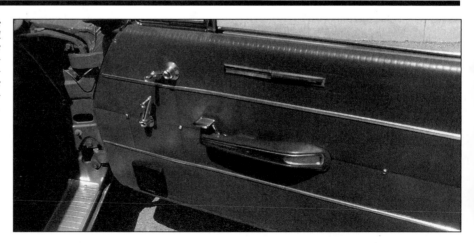

1964 Mercury Marauder

overdrive, four-speed manual and Multi-Drive Merc-O-Matic were optional. New features for 1964 included new universal joints, "piloted" wheels with true concentricity, and a vacuum-piston automatic choke with water-warmed control mechanism.

Bill Stroppe again figured prominently in NASCAR events, and the big Mercurys won four events. Sales of big Mercurys were down slightly to 110,000 units.

Driving Impressions

Marauders of any year are just about impossible to find today because they were so popular as stock cars and later were destruction derby favorites. We found a Carnival Red Marauder Montclair with a 330-horsepower police interceptor engine in the Los Angeles area. It could be the only one like it in existence.

In their October 1963 issue, *Motor Trend* commemorated Mercury's Twenty-Fifth Anniversary by doing a drive comparison between a 1939 Mercury and a 1964 Mercury Montclair Marauder with a 266-horsepower 390 engine and Merc-O-Matic transmission. The Marauder did 0-60 in 12.8 seconds and attained a top speed of 107 mph. It took the '39 Merc 19.5 seconds to get up

to 60. Top speed was 85 mph. The '39 beat the '64 only in gas mileage, 21-23 mpg average compared to 16-18 mpg for the '64. This Marauder with the 330-horsepower engine will do 0-60 in slightly under 10 seconds, is much quicker than the standard engine past 60, and has a verified top speed of 130 mph.

It is owned by Joe Skarda, a highly decorated Vietnam veteran. Joe was an Army helicopter gunner in the 116th Assault Helicopter Company. He is one of only four out of 21 door gunners in his command who came home. Fifty-four names from the 116th are now on

the "Wall" in Washington, D.C. Joe personally went down in helicopters 13 times, and today is on permanent disability due to neck injuries. The Mercury Marauder was near new when bought by his dad. Joe isn't sure what year he bought the car. His dad was a life-long Mercury fan who was in the process of restoring the car when he died in 1982. Joe then picked up the restoration where his father left off, and now shows the car in memory of his dad. At 134,000 original miles, the car has a new 330 engine, new paint and

1964 Mercury Marauder

vinyl top, and Joe has nearly $9,000 in repair receipts dating back to 1978. This car was originally equipped with a 330-horsepower engine.

The Mercury Marauder is a big car. At 215.5 inches overall, it is nearly as big as the 1964 Lincoln Continental and bigger than the 1963 Lincoln Continental. It is within an inch of the 1964 Chrysler and the Buick and is the second widest car on the road next to the Imperial. In the 250-horsepower version with Merc-O-Matic, it will go from 0-60 in 11.3 seconds and do the standing quarter mile in 18.5 seconds at 75.5 mph. Top speed is slightly over the century mark. This was about average for a car of its size in 1964, but its weight begins to tell at the top end. Better choices for performance are the 300 or 330-horsepower engines.

Joe has had 130 mph on his car verified by the CHP. Several years ago, while "blowing out the Merc" on the way to his mother's home in Simi, A "Chippie" in a new 5.0 Mustang got on Joe's tail and pulled him over. When the officer, who was about half Joe's age, pulled Joe over he said, "Son, do you know how fast you were going?" "No, sir, she pegs out around 120 mph," Joe replied. The officer told Joe that his patrol car was doing 130 and the Merc was walking away from him. Then the officer asked, "Is this a real Marauder?" "Know of another Mercury that goes 130 mph?" Joe replied. The patrolman just so happened to be a big Merc Marauder fan. He only gave Joe a warning, "If I ever catch you doing even 56 mph, I'll put you in jail!, he warned."

Handling on this car is a mixed bag. Air-shocks greatly improve the suspension, but the front end and steering box are tired, making a true evaluation of handling difficult. Joe says that at 70-80 mph with the power booster it is very easy to oversteer. Our own impression is that the car handles much like a 1964 Ford. On the Interstate the car is as steady as the QEII, and hardly reacts to crosswinds. In the high-speed turns, the car wants to keep going straight when the driver wants to go right or left. The ride is excellent, no longer on the soft side due to heavy-duty air shocks. The fact that Bill Stroppe was able to make a formidable racing car out of this family

1964 Mercury and the 1964 Riverside 500

Both Ford and Mercury were well represented at the Second Annual 1964 Riverside 500 held at the Riverside, California, Raceway on January 19, 1964. While the Fords finished first, second, fourth and fifth, the Stroppe-prepared Mercurys were plagued with bad luck. On the thirty-seventh lap Parnelli Jones broke an axle, which was quickly repaired, but he was never in contention again and later went out permanently with clutch problems. Other members of the Mercury team weren't faring much better. Roger Ward went out early with transmission troubles. Dave MacDonald broke an axle on the twenty-third lap, had it fixed, then experienced brake lock-up. That was quickly fixed, then he lost his brakes completely. In trying to downshift, his clutch linkage broke, so he pushed the Mercury up against the crash wall to stop the car and bring it into the pits permanently. Darel Dieringer in another Mercury had plenty of problems but managed to finish sixth.

The saddest Mercury experience of all was that of Joe Weatherly, the Clown Prince of Auto Racing, now going for his third Grand National Title. Joe had pitted on the tenth lap with transmission trouble. On the thirtieth lap he had more transmission trouble, pitted, and his crew changed the transmission. Then on the one hundred first lap something really went wrong. Observers believed that the throttle stuck. The Merc went up on the bank on the inside of the track entering turn six, then came off it, crossed the track and went straight for the wall. Joe was an outstanding and cautious driver. He suffered mortal head injuries, and died on the way to the hospital. Upon examining the wreck, nothing was found to be wrong with the car. To this day, exactly what caused the wreck remains a mystery. That race was ultimately won by Dan Gurney in a 1964 Ford. Near the end of the 1964 stock car season, Mercury pulled out of racing for the second and last time. But the Ford Division came to Stroppe's rescue, then Holman-Moody-Stroppe was formed in 1965 and continued racing in both NASCAR and USAC events for five more years. After that, Stroppe crewed a car for Bobby Unser in 1969, then moved into off-road racing.

hauler showed the potential this car has.

Power steering takes 3.9 turns lock-to-lock, which is moderately quick. You can turn the car in a 41.6-foot circle. Power-assisted brakes will stop the car in a good straight line. But one good panic stop will require a cooling period of several minutes before the brakes will perform at maximum efficiency again.

We love the full instrumentation on all 1964 Mercs, as opposed to the Ford's and Lincoln Continental's famous idiot lights. The biggest drawback to the 1964 Mercury is gas mileage, 16-18 mpg best with 250 horsepower, and less than 10 average. With the 330-horsepower 390, you can take about two mpg off those figures at all speeds. But then, nobody ever bought a '64 Mercury to win any economy runs. ✑

Acknowledgments and Bibliography.

Thomas, Wayne, "1963 Mercury Road Test," Motor Trend, March 1963; Thomas, Wayne, "Merc Goes Racing," Motor Trend, March 1963; Wright, Jim, "1964 Mercury Road Test," Motor Trend, October 1963; "25 Years With Mercury," Motor Trend, October 1963; Wright, Jim, "Motor Trend's 2nd Annual Riverside 500," Motor Trend, April 1964; Dammann, George H. and Wagner, James K., The Cars of Lincoln-Mercury; Lamm, Michael and Lewis, David L., "The First Mercury," Special Interest Autos #23, July-August 1974.

Special thanks to Joe Skarda, Granada Hills, California, for furnishing our drive-Report car.

Facing page: Robust 390 V-8 is rated at 330 bhp. **Above:** With 330 engine, top speed could bury the needle. **Below:** Scads of room for both luggage and passengers. **Bottom:** Lots of shiny stuff out back, too.

1967 MERCURY COUGAR XR-7

More Than a Mustang?

P ITY the Cougar. When it was brought out by Lincoln-Mercury in 1966, it was billed by some auto writers as "a Mustang in a Cougar suit." Still other new car reviewers dubbed it "a miniature Thunderbird."

The contrarian of ponycars, the Cougar vied for a place in the sun beside such close cousins as the Mustang and Thunderbird. Ultimately the Cougar was in a class all by its dashing self, despite the fact that it began life as a Mustang with a T-Bird-like front end.

Code-named T-7, this first Cougar was a designers' exercise, not yet sponsored by Lincoln-Mercury, in February 1963. Its vertical grille won immediate favor with Ford management and remained the nucleus of subsequent proposals. Mercury's advertising theme, which would surface four years later— that it was "the Man's Car"—was also

By Linda Clark
Photos by the author

unfolding. When Ford gave L-M the green light for the T-7's development in April 1964 (the month the Mustang was introduced), their goal was to give it straightforward, or what Ford called *masculine*, lines.

There were eight subsequent design exercises until the last one, the bold but tailored '67 Cougar as we came to know it, was approved on February 18, 1965. Its vertical bars over the taillights harmonized perfectly with the vertical front-end design. More remarkable still, the Cougar was a vivid example of refinement. It was lower, sleeker and ultimately more sophisticated than the Mustang. In Ford management's eyes, it had achieved its goal of a "man's car, which Mustang owners could step up to."

To the disappointment of convertible fans, the Cougar was offered in only one body style, a four-passenger hardtop coupe, until 1969. Given the Cougar's 14-carat personality, this void is sorely felt by Cougar collectors today.

Money and quality-control were the reasons, according to Frank Zimmerman, Lincoln-Mercury general sales manager during the sixties. Although it shared the inner skin, deck lid and roof with the Mustang, the Cougar cost some $40 million to tool; a convertible would have added another $8 million. It was also a lot easier to screw-in quality with a single body style, according to Zimmerman. A still-fresh wound called Edsel also made a reading on the Mustang essential before taking an all-out plunge.

The first proposal for the Cougar's interior featured bucket seats, a T-Bird-like central console and four large, round dials on the instrument panel. The first clay model finally produced from the design had only two instrument panel pods. A proposed horizontally lined texture running the width of the instrument panel was also replaced by a simple padded dash.

While the Cougar's theme was "scaled-down luxury," rather than sportiness, it had a good dose of both. The Cougar's concealed headlamps, Thunderbird-like sequential turn signals, cloth (leather in the XR-7) interior and Lincoln-like quietness were upscale refinements. But the Cougar shared most of the Mustang's running gear, portions of its sheet metal and every bit of its youthful zest.

There were no six-cylinder Cougars. The base 289-cubic-inch V-8 two-barrel engine delivered 200 horsepower. A three-speed manual floor-shifted gearbox was standard, and either a three-speed automatic or four-speed manual was available at extra cost. Standard rear axle was 2.79:1, and a 3.00:1 came with the optional transmissions.

A 225-hp version of the 289 V-8 was optional, using a four-barrel carburetor and needing premium fuel for its 9.8:1 compression. Transmission availability was the same as the 200-hp engine. All rear gearing was 3.00:1.

By September of 1967 a 320-hp 390-cubic-inch GT V-8 was also optional, in four-barrel form with 10.5:1 compression requiring premium fuel. All transmissions were available, but rear gearing was 3.25:1. The GT V-8 could be ordered alone or in conjunction with the GT Performance Group option, which included wide tires and heavy-duty suspension.

To expand its convenience or tire-burning abilities, Cougar owners had no less than 52 power-train and comfort options to choose from. The Cougar was *Motor Trend's* "Car of the Year" in 1967, and when 170,879 Cougars in all forms sold that first year, it surprised even Lincoln-Mercury, who had aimed for

Left: *XR-7 identification badges are attached to rear sides of Cougar's roof.*
Below: *Traditional Mercury symbol is found in center of grille.*

only 100,000. Cougar buyers, L-M reasoned, were generally college-educated upstarts buying a second or third car in the family. L-M's check of the first 3,200 Cougars sold revealed that 47 percent had no trade-in.

In February 1967 Lincoln-Mercury introduced the XR-7 and XR-7S models. The first was a Cougar with any of the engine options already available, but set off by a walnut-grained custom instrument panel—patterned after the likes of Jaguar or Aston-Martin— leather upholstery, an overhead console, deluxe wheelcovers and identifying trim on the dash, roof pillars and rocker panels. To go the full route, though, Lincoln-Mercury pitched the XR-75.

Also known as the Dan Gurney Special, this chrome-bedecked Cougar with a fiberglass dual-scoop hood, modified grille, racing mirrors, dual exhausts, Kelsey-Hayes mag wheels and XR-7 luxuries was promoted at auto shows throughout the country as a sort of "King Cougar." It was to come standard, according to pre-production ads,

with Ford's brutish seven-liter (428-cubic-inch) mill.

It never did. But Cougar lovers bought Dan Gurney Specials (the name XR-7S never materialized either) to the tune of 19,986. They came equipped with the Cougar's base 289 V-8, but an unconfirmed 200 are presumed to have been sold with extra-cost 427- and 428-cubic-inch engines.

While some Cougar historians speculate the Dan Gurney Special was a test-market prototype of the Cougar GT-E model Lincoln-Mercury brought out in 1968, one baffling fact remains. In 1968 exactly 12,506 Cougars were still sold under the model name Dan Gurney Special.

There was little styling news on '68 Cougars. The major difference was side marker lights, which served to identify '68s from '67s. The new GT-E model, bearing a cosmetic resemblance to the Gurney Specials, was the high-performer with automatic transmission and a 427-cubic-inch, 390-hp V-8 as standard. It also had its own distinctive two-

Above: Cougar appears longer than the Mustang and it is, by nearly seven inches. It's a whisker wider, too. *Right:* XR-7's door upholstery is quite plush, with such amenities as leatherette pull handle, safety light, and map pocket. *Below:* Taillamps also have their own "grilles." XR-7 shared sequential turn signals with T-Bird.

1967 MERCURY

tone paint with hood scoop, and Super Competition suspension. The Cougar's base engine was the 302-cubic-inch V-8, up from the prior year's 289.

In its Phase I compliance with federal anti-pollution laws, Ford adopted the IMCO (IMproved COmbustion) emission control system on automatic transmission equipped cars in 1968. Rather than burning the exhaust gases in the exhaust manifolds, as in the Thermactor system Ford used on models sold in California since 1966, the IMCO system reduced carbon monoxide and hydrocarbons through more complete combustion in the combustion chambers. Stick-shift models still used the Thermactor air-pump system until 1970.

The '68 Cougar maintained its highly touted smooth riding characteristics, due to rubber insulation eliminating metal-to-metal contact in the suspension and 123 pounds of sound-deadening material in the roof, floor and engine compartment.

Cougar Production Figures

	Htp. Cpe.	Conv. Cpe.	XR-7 Htp. cpe.	XR-7 Conv.	GT	GT-E	Dan Gurney Special XR-7S	Eliminator
1967	116,260	-	27,221	-	7,905	-	19,986	-
1968	81,014	-	32,712	-	4,054	264	12,506	-
1969	66,331	5,796	23,918	4,024	N/a	-	-	2,411
1970	49,479	2,322	18,565	1,977	N/a	-	-	2,200
1971	34,008	1,723	25,416	1,717	723	-	-	-
1972	23,731	1,240	26,802	1,929	N/a	-	-	-
1973	21,069	1,284	35,110	3,165	-	-	-	-

Note: N/a = Figures not available.

- = Model not available

Source: Ford Motor Company

Trans Am Cougars

Could Mercury's classy little Cougar find victory on the Sports Car Club of America's Trans-American racing circuit? As a matter of fact, yes.

In 1967 Mercury ended up with four wins and enough second, third and fourth place finishes to give them second in the final standings. Team Cougar was sponsored directly by the factory (the cars prepared by Bud Moore Engineering of Spartanburg, South Carolina) and captained by international driving ace Dan Gurney. The team also had the driving acumen of Indy winner Parnelli Jones, NASCAR champ Dave Pearson, Ed Leslie of Carmel, California, and the late Peter Revson.

The Trans-Am Cougars were equipped with 289-cubic-inch engines tuned to deliver 341 bhp at 5,800 rpm, and vied against such cars as Camaros, Mustangs, Darts and Barracudas.

In 1968 the Bud Moore Cougars were sold and the factory pooled its efforts behind the Mustang Team. A dual-quad introduction system that was developed for the Trans Am cars also became available for street Cougars.

*Left: Console holds radio and clock. Transmission position indicator is lighted both day and night. **Below:** Instrument panel bears resemblance to that of '67 Mustang; contains 6,000-rpm tachometer.*

Safety loomed large on Cougars, too. Impact-absorbing steering column, padded seat backs, dual brake system with pressure-loss indicator and a lane-changing feature on the directional signals to avoid driving with them blinking were just a few standard items. Four-way flashers, disc brakes and Wide Oval tires were some of the optional safety extras.

While Ford entered the muscle-car market in 1969 with its Mach I and Boss Mustangs, Lincoln-Mercury quickened its own image with the Cougar Eliminator in March of that year.

Inspired by Dyno Nicholson's quarter-mile "Eliminator" Cougar, which set a new world record in 1968, the name Eliminator became magic on the quarters of a special production Cougar. It was a package rather than a body style, but its acceleration was riveting and its front and rear spoilers, racing mirrors, and colorful graphics surpassed less dynamic muscle cars to become a striking sight on any road.

The heart of the Eliminator was its standard 351-cubic-inch four-barrel Windsor engine. At extra cost, owners could opt for the 390 four-barrel, 428 four-barrel or 428 four-barrel Ram Air engine. Exclusive to the Eliminator, the 302-cubic-inch four-barrel HO (high output) Boss powerplant, sold only with a four-speed transmission, was also available.

Standard axle ratios were 3.50 with four-speeds, 3.25 with automatics. Boss 302s were delivered with 3.91 gears, and a 4.30 ratio incorporating the Detroit Automotive ratcheting rear end (better known as the "Detroit Locker")

was optional. Mercury's new "Street Scene" performance logo went into the Eliminator by way of higher spring rates and front and rear anti-sway bars. A "Competition Handling" package was optional. Staggered shocks, used successfully on high-performance Mustangs, were standard with 3.91 or higher axle ratios.

Eliminators only came in white, blue, yellow or orange. Fender-to-quarter side stripes, in either white or black, ended in the word ELIMINATOR. It was the only Cougar that year with high-back bucket seats, available in either black, blue or white vinyl. Carpets came in blue or black. All Eliminators had a black dash with XR-7-like instruments.

The Cougar convertible premiered in 1969 and continued until July 5, 1973,

when Ford's (presumed) last convertible, a '73 Mercury Cougar, left Dearborn. Treasured among Cougar collectors today, the sportif convertible came standard with L-M's "Decor Group." This same year also saw the debut of Ford's electrically operated sunroof. At $459.80 extra, it found its way onto 642 Cougars in 1969.

Taking a potent last stand in 1970 before government safety and emissions requirements halted Detroit's high-performance pursuits, the Cougar Eliminator got brighter as the muscle car's significance got weaker (see sidebar, page 115). Sales of all Cougars dropped noticeably this year, too. A divided grille marked 1970's styling changes.

The trim and sporty Cougar entered a

specifications

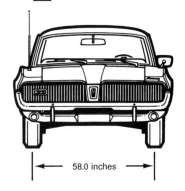

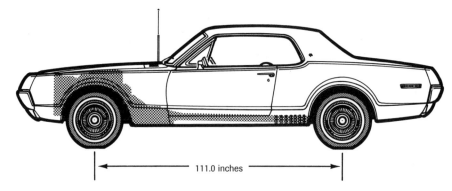

58.0 inches

111.0 inches

1967 Mercury Cougar XR-7 Hardtop Coupe

Price when new	$3,081 f.o.b. Dearborn, Michigan
Standard equip.	V-8 engine, self-adjusting brakes, front stabilizer bar, heater, defroster, bucket seats, walnut-grained steering wheel, front and rear seatbelts, courtesy lights, door-operated instrument panel light, dual sunvisors, 2-speed windshield wipers, remote control outside mirror, padded dash, collapsible steering column, padded-frame breakaway rear-view mirror, 4-way emergency flasher, sequential turn signals, concealed headlamps, wheel-opening moldings, XR-7 identifying emblems on roof pillars and dash, 7 diecast chevrons on rocker panel forward of wheel opening, leather upholstery, walnut-grained vinyl instrument panel, overhead warning and map-light console, deluxe wheelcovers
Options on dR car	Automatic transmission, power steering, AM radio, sports console, white sidewall tires, rear bumper guards

ENGINE
Type	90-degree ohv V-8, water-cooled, cast-iron block, 5 mains, full-pressure lubrication, push-rod-operated overhead valves, hydraulic lifters
Bore x stroke	4.0 inches x 2.87 inches
Displacement	289 cubic inches
Max. bhp @ rpm	200 @ 4,400
Torque @ rpm	282 @ 2,400
Compression ratio	9.3:1
Induction system	One Autolite 2100 2-barrel
Exhaust system	Cast-iron manifolds, single trans-

Electrical system	verse muffler with integrated tailpipe, reverse flow w/resonator 12-volt 42 amp-hr battery/coil, alternator

TRANSMISSION
Type	Merc-O-Matic 3-speed, torque converter with planetary gears
Ratios	1st: 2.46:1; 2nd: 1.46:1; 3rd: 1.00:1; Reverse: 2.20:1

DIFFERENTIAL
Type	Hypoid, Hotchkiss drive
Ratio	20.3:1 overall
Drive axles	Semi-floating

STEERING
Type	Semi-reversible, Bendix recirculating ball, power assist
Turns lock-to-lock	3.6
Ratio	20.3:1 overall
Turn circle	39.24 feet

BRAKES
Type	Dual-line hydraulic, self-adjusting, duo-servo shoes, cast-iron drums, hand-operated emergency brake lever below steering column
Drum diameter	10 inches
Total swept area	251.3 square inches

CHASSIS & BODY
Frame	Unitized platform incorporating underbody siderails, torque boxes, front end enclosures, floor pan, rear-end sheet

	metal and full-length floor tunnel
Body construction	Integrated, unitized steel shell
Body style	2-door, 4-passenger hardtop

SUSPENSION
Front	Independent with upper and lower control arms, coil springs, impact-absorbing fore/aft strut joint, tubular hydraulic shocks, stabilizer bar
Rear	Rigid axle, semi-elliptic leaf springs, impact-absorbing articulated strut, tubular hydraulic shocks
Tires	F70 x 14, Firestone Wide Oval nylon tubeless
Wheels	14-inch steel disc, 5-lug

WEIGHTS AND MEASURES
Wheelbase	111 inches
Overall length	190.3 inches
Overall width	71.2 inches
Overall height	51.8 inches
Front track	58.0 inches
Rear track	58.0 inches
Ground clearance	5.9 inches
Curb weight	3,119 pounds

CAPACITIES
Crankcase	4 quarts
Cooling system	15 quarts
Fuel tank	17 gallons

FUEL CONSUMPTION
Best	19 mpg
Average	15 mpg

1967 MERCURY

balloon stage in its career in 1971 when its sheet metal expanded to sit on a 112-inch wheelbase. It was still a striking car, though decidedly moving away from its ponycar heritage. But Cougar sales continued to plummet. Its buyers, too, were no longer hard-core performance seekers. Of the 62,864 Cougars sold in

1971, only 723 had the GT option, and the four-speed transmission accounted for a mere one percent of total Cougar sales. The XR-7 remained the top-of-the-line model.

Minor styling changes marked the '72 Cougars, while an across-the-industry de-emphasis on horsepower ratings signaled the decline of the prior decade's performance race. With the Cougar now enduring its third straight year of flagging sales, Mercury was forced to follow the Mustang's lead (since they shared

frame and basic body) in abandoning the ponycar market.

Camaro and Firebird successfully shared a joint-but-separate market, but Ford deemed it best to allow the Mustang and Cougar diverse ones. So while Ford was planning to recapture the original Mustang image by shrinking it for 1974, Lincoln-Mercury planned for a "bigger and better" Cougar that would compete in the mid-size specialty-car class against the likes of the Monte Carlo and Grand Prix.

There was no reason for Mercury to build a Cougar off the new Mustang when they had the Capri, but Mercury never considered eliminating the Cougar altogether, according to William Benton, then Mercury General Sales Manager.

And for the Cougar, at least, bigger (4,275 pounds, up from 3,119 in 1967) worked. The 1974 version, though different, was well received. Sporting the most sweeping changes since 1967, it sat on a 114-inch wheelbase, sharing its basic design with the Thunderbird and Mark IV—opera windows, hood ornament, vinyl roof and all. And its interior was a far cry from previous ones. The dash still housed a speedometer, tach, ammeter, fuel, temp and oil gauges, but they were now clustered on one panel directly in front of the driver. The seats resembled the Thunderbird and Mark IVs, but optional velour upholstery was available only on the Cougar.

Though the base engine was still the 351 (a 400 and 460 four-barrel were optional), extra weight and new suspension made the ride more refined than 1973's. Most road testers likened it to the Mark IV's. An improved "sound package' also kept the Cougar's interior whisper quiet.

When Ford Motor Company celebrated its seventy-fifth anniversary, the Cougar was trotted out in "1978 Anniversary

Eliminator

Striking out at the luxury (read European) end of the ponycar market during the performance-mad Sixties, the Cougar marched to the tune of a different drummer. Finely fit and polished, and comfort and gadget-laden, the Cougar put more flash than dash even into its performance-touted Dan Gurney Special. Having no other American car quite in the Cougar's class, said Ford engineer Tom Feaheny in a 1967 *SAE Paper*, only European makes can be numbered among its competitors.

The boldly-packaged Eliminators of 1969-70, though, radiated a buoyant enthusiasm for the typically *American* style of brash fire-brand. The Eliminator's bright colors, loud graphics, fat tires, noisy engines, stark interiors and aggressive scoops and spoilers were the spirit of Detroit. And what was under the hood during that era is what the baby boom that is now losing its hair marked their youth by . . . Hemi, Rat, Boss, Six Pak, Cobra Jet and, in the '70 Eliminator's case, Cleveland.

This new 351-cubic-inch four-barrel engine was standard in the '70 Eliminator. It delivered 300 hp, up 10 horsepower from the prior year Eliminator's 351-cubic-inch four-barrel Windsor. Performance-minded Cougar fans loved it, and *Hot Rod* told them how to get the most out of it. It could be teamed with any of the

transmissions already available, the same rear axles listed in '69, staggered shocks and Traction-Lok or Drag-Pak rear ends.

Optional powerplants included the 428 four-barrel Cobra Jet (discontinued in 1971), Boss 429 and Boss 302 (available only with a four-speed.) The former engines could be teamed with Select-Shift automatic or the four-speed manual with Hurst shifter assembly. Standard axle ratios were 3.25 with automatics and 3.50 with speeds. Records reveal only two Cougars sold with Boss 429s in 1970.

Green, gold and pastel-blue were added to the Eliminator's "Competition" paint colors. Fender-to-quarter striping, still either black or white, was re-designed, and the word ELIMINATOR was added to the rear-deck spoiler. Two hood stripe styles, only subtly different, were offered. A blacked-out grille, black vinyl front spoiler and non-reflective hood air-scoop suited the Eliminator's direct, no-nonsense persona. Chromed Cougar emblems appeared on the hood directly above the grille and on the gas tank door.

"Mercury" hubcaps with bright trim rings and a black XR-7-like dash remained standard on Eliminators.

Sports Car Graphic tested a Boss 302-equipped Eliminator and recorded a quarter-mile time of 14.40 at 98 miles per hour. Top speed was 110 mph, and gas consumption a heady eight mpg.

Cougar shared Ford's reliable thin-wall 289 V-8. Like the Ford version, it produced 200 horsepower at 4,400 rpm; also developed 282 foot-pounds of torque.

Overhead console was standard on XR-7, holds warning lights and map light.

1967 MERCURY

Edition" trim, available in two- and four-door models. Even this formal Cougar never totally abandoned its early sporting background. Bucket seats, racing mirrors, paint stripes and a sport instrumentation group were on the option list.

The Cougar was re-engineered and redesigned for 1980 when fuel economy and aerodynamics became the defining anthems of modern motoring. The length was trimmed 15 inches, the weight reduced 700 pounds, and a six-cylinder (V-8 in the XR-7) engine was standard. Rack-and-pinion steering, strut-type front suspension, steel-belted radial tires and an electronic instrument panel were just a few of the changes.

By 1983 the Cougar was a dim shadow of its original self. Sixteen years had brought radical changes. Electronic fuel-injection, a Tripminder computer and a voice-alert system now define, in part, the former American ponycar. But for those who measure time and memories with cars, the original Cougars remain a bright shuttle across the years.

Driving Impressions

When Mercury boasted, in Cougar sales literature, that "galvanized steel and zinc-rich body primers would keep corrosion at bay for many years," they probably never dreamed of Robert Dean.

Dean is one Cougar owner, at least, who kept corrosion at bay for 16 years. Dean, who hails from Columbus, Ohio, is the original owner of a '67 XR-7. One of the Cougar's loyal coterie, Dean has treated his Inverness Green coupe to a life of leisure. Its gold leather upholstery still smells new, and the odometer looked back at us with 56,000 miles on it.

Our driveReport mission, which we accomplished with the ease of power steering and automatic transmission, was a pure joy in Mercury's clean, snug and neatly fitted together ponycar. We sailed handily along the six-lane Interstate 270 outside Columbus at 60 mph, and remained unrattled by the potholes on the access road to the zoo, where we shot our photos.

Since the Cougar has always coddled its driver in a comfort not matched by any Camaro or Mustang, it always comes as a shock to find it a taut handler. Until we tested the Cougar's mettle over a few bumps, we would have predicted loss of control. It's the big-car-luxury feel that does it. I mean, if Mercury put all this effort into comfort, you wonder, did anyone remember the shocks and steering linkage?

Of course, they did. This Cougar's power steering, while no match for a quick-ratio sports car, didn't possess the slow understeer of a bulky sedan, either. And all the rubber insulation Mercury packed into the Cougar's sus-

Trunk room is about what you'd expect in a sporty coupe, adequate but hardly gigantic.

pension, in search of a smooth ride, wasn't wasted. Body roll, too, was minimal, though we never took any corners at more than 30 mph.

Acceleration was peppy, even with the base 200 horsepower 289 housed in Dean's Cougar. And had we wanted to go twice the legal speed limit, there were 120 miles-per-hour top speed at our disposal.

Optional in Dean's Cougar is a sport console which, in addition to the clock, houses his optional radio. The console overhead—part of the XR-7 package—contains a map light and warning lights for door ajar, seatbelts and fuel-level which, it seems, wouldn't take a kindergartner at ten paces to notice.

We found the Cougar's brakes, the same drums and shoes standard on the '67 Mustang, adequate. No excessive effort or yardage was required, though we seldom stopped at speed. Power-assist disc front brakes were optional and, no doubt, vital with any of the optional extra-weight engines.

Road feel was surprisingly good for a car as plush as the Cougar, but it lacks the hard-edge that keeps you awake in cars like the Trans Am and Z/28.

I'm not a glove compartment user, so if Detroit did away with them I wouldn't mind, but anything larger than a mouse's breakfast wouldn't fit in the Cougar's. Head room is not generous in the Cougar either, but there's lots of room in the back seat and the trunk is a bit larger than most ponycars'.

At 16 years old, the '67 Cougar is still one of the best friends a special interest auto collector could ever hope to have. ଐ

Acknowledgments and Bibliography
Gary Witzenburg, Mustang—The Complete History of America's Pioneer Ponycar, *Princeton Publishing Inc., 1979; Phil Hall*, Fearsome Fords 1959-73, *Motorbooks International, 1982; George Dammann*, Illustrated History of Ford, *Crestline Publishing Co., 1970; Richard M. Langworth*, Encyclopedia of American Cars 1940-1970, *Publications International Ltd., 1980; John Gunnell*, Standard Catalog of American Cars 1946-1975, *Krause Publications, 1982;* Chilton's Auto Repair Manual for American Cars 1966-1973, *Chilton Book Company, 1972; T. Feaheny and B. Andren, Ford Motor Co.,* The Mercury Cougar—Why and How, *SAE Paper. January 13, 1967;* Car and Driver, *October 1966, January 1969;* Motor Trend, *August 1966, October 1966, November 1966, January 1967, February 1967, November 1967, January 1968, August 1972, August 1973, March 1975, September 1976, January 1978;* Mechanix Illustrated, *July 1974;* Popular Mechanics, *September 1974; press releases and sales brochures from Lincoln-Mercury Division of Ford Motor Company.*

Thanks to Bill Day, Jim Olsen. Dick Judy, Paul Preuss, Bonnie Daws, Lincoln-Mercury Division, Ford Motor Company; Tom Jacobellis, Jeff Kent, Cougar Club of America; Margaret Butzu, Detroit Public Library. Special thanks to Robert Dean for the use of his 1967 Cougar XR-7 and Lindsay Wall of the Columbus Zoological Gardens for the use of her cougar cub.

Mercury Model Year Production, 1939-1975

Year	Production		Year	Production
1939	69,135		1960	271,331
1940	81,128		1961	317,351
1941	82,391		1962	341,366
1942	22,816		1963	301,581
1946	86,608		1964	298,609
1947	85,383		1965	346,751
1948	50,268		1966	343,149
1949	301,309		1967	354,923
1950	293,659		1968	264,853
1951	310,387		1969	398,262
1952	172,087		1970	324,716
1953	305,863		1971	383,561
1954	259,305		1972	460,588
1955	329,808		**1973**	**513,463***
1956	327,943		1974	301,923
1957	286,163		1975	366,335
1958	153,271			
1959	149,987			

* Mercury's biggest production year

Mercury Engines, 1939-1975

Year	Cylinders	Displacement	Bore x Stroke	Output (Gross HP)	Year	Cylinders	Displacement	Bore x Stroke	Output (Gross HP)
					1960	I-6	144.3	3.5 x 2.5	90
1939	V-8	239.4	3.19 x 3.75	95	1960	V-8	312	3.8 x 3.44	205
					1960	V-8	383	4.29 x 3.29	280
1940	V-8	239.4	3.19 x 3.75	95	1960	V-8	430	4.29 x 3.70	310
1941	V-8	239.4	3.19 x 3.75	95	1961	I-6	144.3	3.5 x 2.5	85
1942	V-8	239.4	3.19 x 3.75	100	1961	I-6	170	3.5 x 2.94	101
1946	V-8	239.4	3.19 x 3.75	100	1961	I-6	223	3.62 x 3.60	135
1947	V-8	239.4	3.19 x 3.75	100	1961	V-8	292	3.75 x 3.30	175
1948	V-8	239.4	3.19 x 3.75	100	1961	V-8	352	4.00 x 3.50	220
1949	V-8	255.4	3.19 x 4.00	110	1961	V-8	390	4.05 x 3.75	300, 330
					1962	I-6	144.3	3.5 x 2.5	85
1950	V-8	255.4	3.19 x 4.00	110	1962	I-6	170	3.5 x 2.94	101
1951	V-8	255.4	3.19 x 4.00	112	1962	I-6	223	3.62 x 3.60	138
1952	V-8	255.4	3.19 x 4.00	125	1962	V-8	221	3.50 x 2.87	145
1953	V-8	255.4	3.19 x 4.00	125	1962	V-8	292	3.75 x 3.30	170
1954	V-8	256	3.62 x 3.10	162	1962	V-8	352	4.00 x 3.50	220
1955	V-8	292	3.75 x 3.30	188, 198	1962	V-8	390	4.05 x 3.75	300, 330
1956	V-8	312	3.80 x 3.44	210, 215, 225, 235	1962	V-8	406	4.05 x 3.75	385, 405
					1963	I-6	144.3	3.50 x 2.50	85
1957	V-8	312	3.80 x 3.44	255	1963	I-6	170	3.50 x 2.94	101
1957	V-8	368	4.00 x 3.65	290, 335	1963	V-8	221	3.50 x 2.87	145
1958	V-8	312	3.80 x 3.44	235	1963	V-8	260	3.80 x 2.87	164
1958	V-8	383	4.29 x 3.29	312, 330	1963	V-8	390	4.05 x 3.75	250, 300, 330
1958	V-8	430	4.29 x 3.70	360, 400					
1959	V-8	312	3.8 x 3.44	210	1963	V-8	406	4.05 x 3.75	385, 405
1959	V-8	383	4.29 x 3.29	280, 322	1964	I-6	170	3.50 x 2.94	101
1959	V-8	430	4.29 x 3.70	345	1964	I-6	200	3.68 x 3.12	116

Year	Cylinders	Displacement	Bore x Stroke	Output (Gross HP)
1963	V-8	221	3.50 x 2.87	145
1964	V-8	260	3.80 x 2.87	164
1964	V-8	289	4.00 x 2.87	210, 271
1964	V-8	390	4.05 x 3.75	250, 266, 300, 330
1964	V-8	427	4.23 x 3.78	410, 425
1965	I-6	200	3.68 x 3.12	116
1965	V-8	289	4.00 x 2.87	200, 225, 271
1965	V-8	390	4.05 x 3.75	265, 275, 300, 330
1965	V-8	427	4.23 x 3.78	410, 425
1966	I-6	200	3.68 x 3.12	120
1966	V-8	289	4.00 x 2.87	200
1966	V-8	390	4.05 x 3.75	265, 275, 335
1966	V-8	410	4.05 x 3.98	330
1966	V-8	427	4.23 x 3.78	410, 425
1966	V-8	428	4.13 x 3.98	345, 360
1967	I-6	200	3.68 x 3.12	120
1967	V-8	289	4.00 x 2.87	200, 225
1967	V-8	390	4.05 x 3.75	265, 275, 335
1967	V-8	410	4.05 x 3.98	330
1967	V-8	427	4.23 x 3.78	410, 425
1967	V-8	428	4.13 x 3.98	345, 360
1968	I-6	200	3.68 x 3.12	115
1968	V-8	302	4.00 x 3.00	210, 230
1968	V-8	390	4.05 x 3.75	270, 280, 315, 335
1968	V-8	427	4.23 x 3.78	390
1968	V-8	428	4.13 x 3.98	335, 345, 360
1969	I-6	250	3.68 x 3.91	155
1969	V-8	302	4.00 x 3.00	210, 290
1969	V-8	351	4.00 x 3.505	250, 290
1968	V-8	390	4.05 x 3.75	270, 280, 320
1969	V-8	428	4.13 x 3.98	335, 360
1969	V-8	429	4.36 x 3.59	320, 360
1970	I-6	250	3.68 x 3.91	155
1970	V-8	302	4.00 x 3.00	210, 290
1970	V-8	351	4.00 x 3.505	250, 300
1970	V-8	390	4.05 x 3.75	270
1970	V-8	428	4.13 x 3.98	335, 360
1970	V-8	429	4.36 x 3.59	320, 360, 370
1971	I-6	170	3.50 x 2.94	100
1971	I-6	200	3.68 x 3.13	115
1971	I-6	250	3.68 x 3.91	145
1971	V-8	302	4.00 x 3.00	210, 290
1971	V-8	351	4.00 x 3.505	240, 285
1971	V-8	400	4.00 x 4.00	260
1971	V-8	429	4.36 x 3.59	320, 360, 370, 375

Year	Cylinders	Displacement	Bore x Stroke	Output (Net HP)
				Starting in 1972, horsepower figures are in "Net" ratings
1972	I-6	170	3.50 x 2.94	82
1972	I-6	200	3.68 x 3.13	91
1972	I-6	250	3.68 x 3.91	95, 98
1972	V-8	302	4.00 x 3.00	138, 140
1972	V-8	351	4.00 x 3.505	161, 163, 248, 262, 266
1972	V-8	400	4.00 x 4.00	168, 172
1972	V-8	429	4.36 x 3.59	201, 208
1972	V-8	460	4.36 x 3.85	224
1973	I-6	200	3.68 x 3.13	94
1973	I-6	250	3.68 x 3.91	98
1973	V-8	302	4.00 x 3.00	137, 138
1973	V-8	351	4.00 x 3.505	159, 161, 168, 248, 264
1973	V-8	400	4.00 x 4.00	168, 171
1973	V-8	429	4.36 x 3.59	201, 198
1973	V-8	460	4.36 x 3.85	267
1974	I-6	200	3.68 x 3.13	84
1974	I-6	250	3.68 x 3.91	91
1974	V-8	302	4.00 x 3.00	140
1974	V-8	351	4.00 x 3.505	162, 168, 248, 264
1974	V-8	400	4.00 x 4.00	168, 170
1974	V-8	429	4.36 x 3.59	201, 198
1974	V-8	460	4.36 x 3.85	195, 220, 244
1975	I-4	140	3.78 x 3.13	83
1975	I-6	170	3.66 x 2.70	97
1975	I-6	200	3.68 x 3.13	75
1975	I-6	250	3.68 x 3.91	72, 91
1975	V-8	302	4.00 x 3.00	129, 140
1975	V-8	351	4.00 x 3.505	148, 154
1975	V-8	400	4.00 x 4.00	158
1975	V-8	460	4.36 x 3.85	216, 218

1955-1971 checked by Gary Richards from the International Mercury Owner's Association.

Mercury Clubs & Specialists

For a complete list of all regional Mercury clubs and national clubs' chapters, visit **Car Club Central** at **www.hemmings.com**. With nearly 10,000 car clubs listed, it's the largest car club site in the world! Not wired? For the most up-to-date information, consult the latest issue of *Hemmings Motor News* and/or *Hemmings Collector Car Almanac*. Call toll free, **1-800-CAR-HERE, Ext. 550**.

MERCURY CLUBS

Cougar Club of America
1637 Skyline Dr.
Norfolk, VA 23518
757-587-5498
Dues: $25/year;
Membership 1,200

Ford Mercury Restorers Club of America
P.O. Box 2938
Dearborn, MI 48123
734-525-6249
Dues: $30/year; Membership 360

Mercury Cyclone/Montego/Torino Registry
19 Glyn Drive
Newark, DE 19713-4016
302-737-4252
Dues: $5/year; Membership: 160

International Mercury Owners Association
6645 West Grand Avenue
Chicago, Illinois 60707-3410
773-622-6445
Dues: $35/year;
Membership: 1,200

MERCURY SPECIALISTS AND RESTORERS

Horton Vacuum Headlight Repair
5804 Jones Valley Drive
Huntsville, AL 35802
256-881-6894
Vacuum headlight repair

John's Classic Cougars
P.O. Box 5380
Edmonton, OK 73083
405-340-1636
NOS and used Cougar parts

Mac's Antique Auto Parts
1051 Lincoln Avenue
Lockport, NY 14094
800-777-0948
New, used and reproduction parts

Mark's 1941-1948 Mercury Parts
97 Hoodlum Hill Road
Binghamton, NY 13905
607-729-1693
Used and reproduction parts

Mercury & Ford Molded Rubber
12 Plymouth Avenue
Wilmington, MA 01887
978-658-8394
Weatherstripping and rubber trim parts

Mercury Research Co.
639 Glanker Street
Memphis, TN 38112
901-323-2195
New and used mechanical parts

Mercury Restorations
309 Seashore Drive
Swansboro, North Carolina 28584
910-326-5852
1941-48 Mercury dash restoration

Rocky Mountain V-8 Parts
1124 Clark Circle
Colorado Springs, CO 80915
719-597-8375
Ford and Mercury Flathead engine parts

Wesley Obsolete Parts
116 Memory Ln.
Liberty, KY42539
606-787-5293
Hard to find body and interior parts